TRAVEL + LEISURE'S
unexpected ITALY

The honey-colored hills of Italy's
Le Marche region. (Overleaf:
Piazza San Marco, in Venice.)

TRAVEL + LEISURE'S
unexpected ITALY

Introduction by Nancy Novogrod
Editor-in-Chief

DK

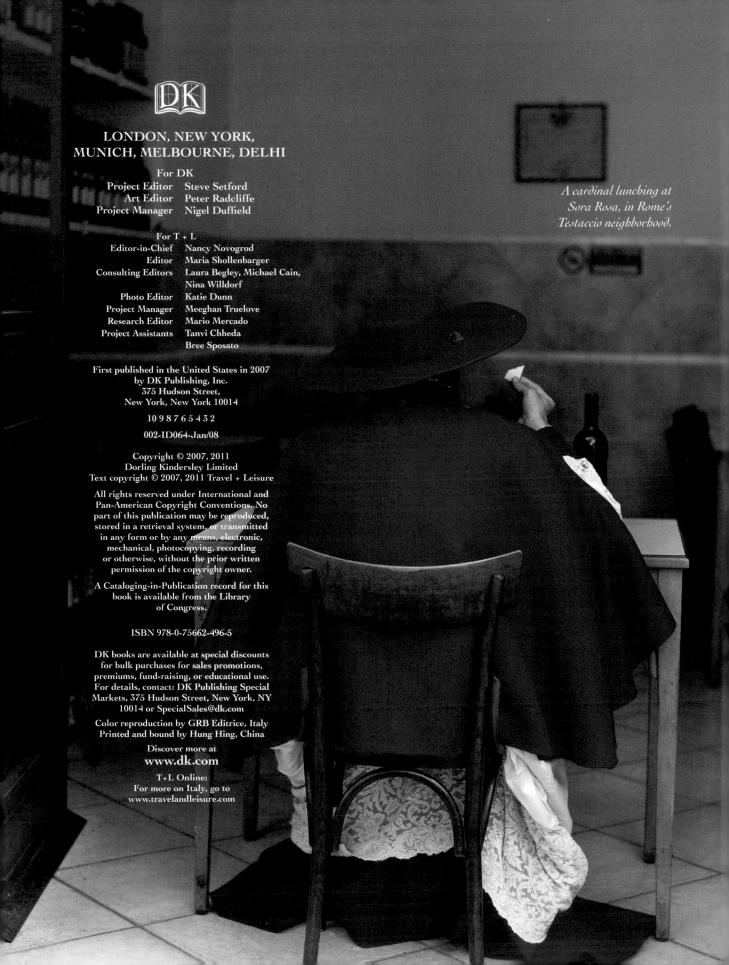

DK

**LONDON, NEW YORK,
MUNICH, MELBOURNE, DELHI**

For DK
Project Editor   Steve Setford
Art Editor   Peter Radcliffe
Project Manager   Nigel Duffield

For T + L
Editor-in-Chief   Nancy Novogrod
Editor   Maria Shollenbarger
Consulting Editors   Laura Begley, Michael Cain,
Nina Willdorf
Photo Editor   Katie Dunn
Project Manager   Meeghan Truelove
Research Editor   Mario Mercado
Project Assistants   Tanvi Chheda
Bree Sposato

First published in the United States in 2007
by DK Publishing, Inc.
375 Hudson Street,
New York, New York 10014

10 9 8 7 6 5 4 3 2

002-ID064-Jan/08

A Cataloging-in-Publication record for this
book is available from the Library
of Congress.

ISBN 978-0-75662-496-5

DK books are available at special discounts
for bulk purchases for sales promotions,
premiums, fund-raising, or educational use.
For details, contact: DK Publishing Special
Markets, 375 Hudson Street, New York, NY
10014 or SpecialSales@dk.com

Color reproduction by GRB Editrice, Italy
Printed and bound by Hung Hing, China

Discover more at
www.dk.com

T+L Online:
For more on Italy, go to
www.travelandleisure.com

*A cardinal lunching at
Sora Rosa, in Rome's
Testaccio neighborhood.*

CONTENTS

Introduction

ITALY IS AN EASY COUNTRY TO LOVE. THERE'S THE RICHNESS AND BEAUTY OF THE LAND—THE ROLLING HILLS TOPPED WITH TOWERING CYPRESSES AND PLANE TREES, THE SOIL that produces some of the world's most prized red wines, most fragrant and delicious fruits and vegetables, and those precious autumn jewels, white truffles. There's the abundant wealth of Italy's cultural heritage, from Etruscan and Roman ruins through masterpieces of Renaissance art and architecture, and music and opera. And then there are the Italians themselves, whose enthusiastic embrace of life informs their instinctive ways with food, fashion, art, and design.

And yet filling the pages of a book called *Unexpected Italy* presents some challenges. If there's anything travelers take along with them on a trip to Italy, it's expectations— along with a reasonable degree of familiarity with what they are likely to find. Those "this is what we come to Europe for" moments Christopher Petkanas describes in his account of the Veneto's villa hotels can be few and far between. That's where *Travel + Leisure* comes in: uncovering the secret places and making them accessible to our readers is a key mission of the magazine. With the assistance of our global network of writers, correspondents, and photographers, we pursue hidden delights and pristine treasures in every corner of the world.

Although some of the more obvious but rewarding pleasures—pizza in Naples, five-star luxury in Florence, La Scala in Milan—have not been overlooked, the articles handpicked from the recent annals of *Travel + Leisure* and collected here trace the less traveled byways. In these pages you will find a route that meanders from the uncrowded Adriatic beaches to the picture-book perfect hill towns of Le Marche; a restaurant hop through two lively, little-known neighborhoods in Rome; and a guide to converted centuries-old farmhouse hotels in Puglia. We turn up the best artisanal producers of *salumi*, cheeses, and olive oils in Tuscany, and in Piedmont, birthplace of the Slow Food movement, we scout out the local spots that offer the most authentic culinary preparations and flavors, and lead you to the best growers of Barolos and Barbarescos in Le Langhe's verdant hills. In pursuit of culture, we track down Piero della Francesca's frescoes in the churches of Arezzo, enroll in a drawing class in Florence, and attend a music festival in Umbria. To facilitate your travel, a map and a resource guide accompany each piece.

The spirit of Italy is generous and vibrantly alive. *Unexpected Italy* is intended to provide the inspiration and the information to uncover those special, intimate experiences that are what you "come to Europe for." *Buon viaggio* in Italia.

Nancy Novogrod

Ripe nebbiolo grapes at the Starderi vineyard, in Barbaresco.

Symbols for maps

✈	International airport	🛈	Tourist information
FS	Railway station	✝	Church
🚌	Bus terminus	P	Parking
🚊	Tram terminus		Building or area of historical interest
M	Metro station		Major church, cathedral, chapel
	Ferry boarding point	🏛	Must-see museum, gallery
	Vaporetto boarding point	∩	Significant archaeological site
	Traghetto boarding point		Impressive castle, fortress,
	Gondola mooring		Area of natural beauty/interest
	Good sailing club or center	🍁	Attractive park/garden
	Interesting market		Major wildlife preserve/zoo

Key to regional maps

▬▬	Motorway	▬▬	Main railway
▬▬	Major road	——	Minor railway
——	Secondary road	▬▬	International border
==	Minor road	——	Regional border
——	Scenic route	△	Summit

Key to pricing icons

Restaurants
Price categories give a range for three courses, not including beverages, sales tax, and tip.

Dining
$ Under $25
$ $ $25 to $74
$ $ $ $75 to $149
$ $ $ $ $150 to $299
$ $ $ $ $ $300 and above

Hotels
Price categories for a standard double room per night.

Hotels
$ Under $150
$ $ $150 to $300
$ $ $ $300 to $500
$ $ $ $ $500 to $700
$ $ $ $ $ $700 and above

The Colosseum in Rome, at dusk.

PART ONE
Destinations

Undiscovered Islands

OFF THE COAST OF TUSCANY AND SOUTH OF SICILY LIE RUSTIC ESCAPES WHERE ENGLISH IS A RARITY AND UNFETTERED AUTHENTICITY A WAY OF LIFE. BY MICHAEL GROSS

GIGLIO
PONZA
LAMPEDUSA

A decade ago, my wife, Barbara, and I spent a week on Italy's Sorrento Peninsula, mostly driving at a snail's pace behind smoke-belching buses on twisting two-lane coastal roads, with the sea just out of reach. A couple of days before we were due to fly home, a restaurant owner overheard me griping about the mean, crowded pebble beaches of the Amalfi Coast and demanded to know why we had not been on the water. The next day, his uncle Yé Yé took us to Capri on his wooden *gozzo* (or belly boat, named for its characteristic shape).

We thought we were quite the cognoscenti. Staggered by Capri's beauty, we returned year after year, but eventually, we had to admit the island was congested, there was too much English spoken at the *spiagge*, too many cigar-waving Americans outside the Grand Hotel Quisisana. Then, a few years ago, Roman friends invited us to join them on a jaunt to their favorite secret getaway: the Tuscan Archipelago, which lies between the Ligurian coast and Corsica, about 300 miles north of Capri. We visited a comma-shaped speck in the

Tyrrhenian Sea called Giannutri, where we snorkeled in crystal waters and swam carefully through a vast colony of sea urchins. Later, we sailed around granite-edged Giglio and lunched on *scampi crudi* at a family-run restaurant in the tiny port. No one there spoke a word of English. We were the only foreigners in the room.

The bustling harbor of Ponza in the Pontine Islands, south of Rome.

The waters off Italy are full of islands, but many of these places are overexposed and overrun. The super-yachts that crowd the small harbors obscure what drew their owners into dock in the first place. Charming little restaurants quickly lose their charm when you can't get a reservation. Only a few spots remain undiscovered—and for good reason. They are difficult to reach, unattractive, unfriendly, or lacking in basic amenities. Giglio was something else: an easily accessible aquatic paradise with some trappings of civilization. We vowed to return soon—and started investigating to see if we could find other, similar Italian islands.

It wasn't easy. The people who know of such hideaways aren't entirely convinced that getting the word out is a good thing. These places have no

Photographs by Alistair Taylor-Young 11

"This is not Portofino or Capri," says Silvana Merlo, a longtime Lampedusian. "It's for people who love the true sea. Everything is stronger here — love, jealousy, the sun, the salt"

advertising, publicists, or fancy Web sites boasting of their attractions in six languages. Our attempt to contact hotels by e-mail and fax elicited little response. Finally, though, we found out about two other clusters that are unknown to most non-Italians: the Pontine Islands, an hour south of Rome, and the Pelagi Islands, 160 miles from Sicily and 80 miles from Tunisia.

These island groups are not for everyone. The food is native and unembellished. Forget designer boutiques — there are none. Even where there are hotels, the accommodations are not luxurious. If your idea of a perfect morning is drinking an espresso while reading the *International Herald Tribune* or watching CNN in your room, you would be well advised to look elsewhere. And if your prerequisites for a happy journey include the regular use of the English language, you may want to skip this chapter.

But despite their inconveniences, these discoveries satisfied our craving for what has become the greatest novelty of all: authenticity.

One of the many grottoes lining Lampedusa's southern coast.

PELAGI ISLANDS

"It is Africa!" announces Renato Righi, owner of El Mosaico del Sol hotel, as he greets us at the airport just outside Lampedusa's single, sunbaked town. And indeed, the island — long, flat, scrubby, subtropical, and distinguished by ancient, endless vistas, a desert palette, and Arabic architecture — feels more like Morocco than Italy.

The other Pelagi include tiny, unpopulated Lampione and Linosa, a strikingly black volcanic rock with a small village, one hotel, and a couple of restaurants. Lampedusa is the largest and the most welcoming, but on first glance not easy to love. Deforested in the 19th century, it was later flattened by Allied bombs at the end of World War II. The peanut-colored terrain remains mostly dusty and barren. In 1986, Lampedusa's U.S. Navy base was the target of a mouse-that-roared bombing raid by Libya's Muammar al-Qaddafi. He missed. The boatloads of refugees from Libya and Egypt are more accurate, landing here regularly — only to be shipped home.

Tourists get a kinder reception. Most of Lampedusa's better hotels throw in a free rental car, all meals, and daily yacht trips. There's Il Gattopardo, a compound on the bay of Cala Creta with thick stone walls and domed roofs inspired by the naturally cooled local dwellings called *dammusi*. La Calandra, a cliffside hotel right next door, is almost as attractive, as is Cala Madonna Club, a former private house on the other side of the island. But all of these require a week's stay. We settled on El Mosaico del Sol, which rents rustic-modern rooms with kitchenettes by the night and has a swimming pool, one of the few on the island.

Although it is the southernmost point in Italy, Lampedusa is easier to reach than Capri or even the more popular Aeolian Islands off Sicily: the airport receives direct flights from all over Italy. Outside of town, however, it is mostly undeveloped, with only two roads. One of these runs along the northern coast, with its sheer cliffs, moonscapes, and an abandoned military installation, before meeting the other, which veers to the south. We spend our first afternoon driving around. Here and there, we spot the signposts of Lampedusa's future: new villas, built by Milanese millionaires. We stop briefly atop the

A promontory overlooking Lampedusa's Cala Creta bay.

cliff that overhangs Spiaggia dei Conigli (Rabbit Beach), a broad, sandy spot popular with both breeding turtles and sunbathers. Still jet-lagged, we decide against parking in the helter-skelter of cars, motorcycles, and scooters and hiking down the long, winding path to the beach.

Instead, we return to town for a stroll and a dip at a neighboring beach, then happily retire to our room to nap. We wake just in time for the cocktail party that owner Righi gives every night. Over local wines and *bottarga* (mullet roe) on crackers, we meet our fellow guests—all Italian—and try to coax a few words from the shy African waiter. We dine in a nearby restaurant, where our use of English makes us so conspicuous that a wide-eyed child spends her own dinnertime watching us intently from behind a pillar next to our table.

Lampedusa's magic and austere glamour are best appreciated on the water. So, the next day, we take a trip aboard the *Balú*, Il Gattopardo's 50-year-old vessel, as it plies the waters off the southern coast. We first take a swim at Cala Madonna, where a tiny white chapel clings to the rocks, then La Tabaccara, a turquoise bay where striated cliffs funnel down into caves. Around the island's western point is Scoglio Sacramento, a Dover-like white cliff. Some guests stay aboard for nonstop sunning;

Lunchtime on the Balú, *a boat from Lampedusa.*

others are in and out of their snorkeling gear, diving at every opportunity.

After a lunch of eggplant, fish, octopus salad, and fried bread, cooked by the *Balú's* captain and accompanied by Sicilian wine, we stop at Spiaggia dei Conigli. Rabbit Island, a little sugarloaf, is connected to the shore by a sandbar; the shallow iridescent water between them is a natural swimming pool. Just off Rabbit Island, we make our last stop, at the Madonna *sott'acqua*, a statue set in a stone arch 49 feet below the surface. We dive down to the ghostly yet benevolent Virgin, who is gazing up from her silent blue sanctuary.

The statue was placed there by Roberto Merlo, the late underwater photographer who founded Il Gattopardo with his wife, Silvana. After 25 years, Silvana can still count her American clients on the fingers of one hand. She says she's never even had a German. That, of course, is what attracted us. "This is not Portofino or Capri," Silvana tells us as we motor back to the port. "It's for people who love the true sea. Everything is stronger here—love, jealousy, the sun, the salt. You find a flower, and even its perfume is stronger. It's all excessive. And when bad weather arrives, it's dangerous. So you must love this place. If not, don't come." She smiles meaningfully and adds, "It's nice that not everyone can love it."

Fishing tackle on the dock in Giglio harbor.

PONTINE ISLANDS

After a quick flight back to Rome, we drive an hour south to Anzio, one of four towns where ferries leave for Ponza, eponym of the Pontines and the archipelago's main destination. Compared to the bustling ferry docks in Naples that service Capri, Anzio's is tiny and refined, attended to by valets in orange shirts. The seven Pontine Islands were a regular stomping ground for Roman emperors beginning with Augustus. These days, they are a haven for sailors, like our Italian friend Marsillio, who calls the area the most beautiful place he has ever visited. En route to Ponza on the 70-minute ferry ride, we spot Zannone, once a private hunting forest and now a plant and wildlife refuge; Ventotene, with its old Roman port, Neapolitan-style town, and ruined imperial villa; and Santo Stefano, dominated by the crumbling remains of an 18th-century prison designed like the circles of Dante's *Inferno*.

Finally, we reach Ponza, a volcanic island shaped like a lizard and made up of sheer cliffs, craggy coastal nooks, grottoes, and ancient ruins. We disembark in the 18th-century Bourbon port, where a sun-bleached amphitheater of colorful houses looks down on the busy stage of the harbor, which is connected by stairs and passages to the cobblestoned pedestrian high street. As we make our way slowly through the friendly chaos of people, scooters, and cars, I can't help but wonder how Ponza has remained unknown to foreigners.

One of the first ladies of Italian fashion, Anna Fendi, who has been coming to Ponza for three decades, explains: "The people here don't want outsiders unless they live the island style of life. They hate rich people with yachts. They don't want to change for them. What they offer is enough. It's the only place in the last thirty years that has stayed the same."

Indeed, this low-key weekend retreat has a delicious simplicity that's been honed over centuries. And fortunately, the advantages of its resistance to change outweigh the drawbacks—some of which were on immediate display when we checked into the Grand Hotel Santa Domitilla, supposedly the best hotel on the island. Our room might be charitably described as adequate, and virtually no one behind the front desk speaks English, even though the property has an elaborate English-language Web site.

In fact, English is so rare on Ponza that two local taxi drivers are famous for speaking it. One, Dominick, actually speaks it well; he grew up in the Bronx. The other, Joe the American, is apparently so called because, as his business cards boast, he "speaks perficty English." Part of the island's allure is how near it is to the familiar, and yet how perficty remote.

Yet some change is in the air even here. In 2002, Fendi and a partner opened La Limonaia a Mare, a luscious B&B set in an old yellow house perched on the rocks. With its broad terrace, roof garden overlooking the port, and five simply decorated rooms, it is restrained enough to seem as if it belongs here, yet stylish enough to appeal to the international jet set.

The restaurants above the port are the only part of Ponza that feel generic: they could be on any island. Acqua Pazza, with tables on a tree-lined piazza, is the best spot in town, with a world-class wine list that has made it beloved by notable visitors like Princess Caroline of Monaco. Oréstorante, tucked into a hillside behind the town's church, has extraordinary views and is a local favorite.

The refreshing lack of pretension that marks Ponza always triumphs. The owner of the restaurant L'Aragosta, next door to Acqua Pazza, once famously turned away the late Fiat mogul Gianni Agnelli when he arrived from his yacht with a party of 12 people but no reservation.

Hand-embroidered Italian linens in one of the five simple rooms at La Limonaia, on Ponza.

Fishing boats in the harbor at Ponza.

Next stop is the beach at Chiaia di Luna, dominated by cliffs that glow like the moon. Just beyond, at Capo Bianco, the light plays more tricks, sun and wind changing the color of the cliffs from gray to yellow to green. A bit farther on are the Faraglioni di Lucia Rosa, named for a legendary beauty who sometime in the misty past flung herself to her death there after she was forbidden to marry. We stop in the busy bay of Cala Feola, where children play in shallow natural pools, and have lunch at a restaurant called Ristorante La Marina. With tables on a terrace over the water, a bar carved into the rocks, cracked-tile-shard décor, and a menu that changes daily, it is, says Silverio, who serves us, "the real Italy."

After lunch, we still have time for a swim at Cala Felice, where a yellow wall of sulfur climbs up from the beach. We scrub ourselves with this natural exfoliant, then wash off in tidal pools swarming with baby shrimp. With an islet called Gavi, shaped like a baked alaska, the wonders continue, then culminate in the Grotta del Bue Marino, where your body takes on the azure shade of the water.

The following day, we head over to Palmarola, six miles away, the nearest and second-largest of the Pontines and considered by many the most glittering jewel of the Mediterranean, studded with palms and surrounded by jagged outcroppings of volcanic rock — and by tuna and dolphin and swordfish. We circle the island for hours, dropping anchor to swim among the *faraglioni*, snorkel through underwater tunnels, or laze on deck beneath La Cattedrale, a rock cliff eroded over the centuries into spires that resemble Milan's Gothic duomo. Palmarola is a day trip: the only accommodations are on the bay of Il Porto, which has a beach with a couple of rudimentary restaurants and a sort of Hotel Flintstone, troglodyte caves for rent. Palmarola appeals to backpackers who want to rough it and Italians rich enough to fly in with their own helicopters.

TUSCAN ARCHIPELAGO

Since visiting Giglio (and its little sister, Giannutri) on a day trip, we'd been curious about what it would be like to stay there. Ironically, the island that inspired our present journey is the one we end up liking the least. There are three settlements on Giglio—a fishing village, a hill town, and the port, all of them connected by a single road. Most of the hotels look as inviting as airport motels—except Pardini's Hermitage, a haute-bohemian establishment

"Don't you know who that is?" the proprietor was asked.

"I don't care about sheep," he replied, confusing Agnelli's last name with *agnello*, Italian for "lamb." "I have no tables." Who needs celebrities when your island is the star of the show?

Here, as on Lampedusa, our own focus is on the sea. There are two beaches right near town: Chiaia di Luna, which can be reached via a 656-foot Roman tunnel running through a mountain, and Frontone, with a bar and restaurant, minutes away by water or land taxi. But there are myriad beaches around the island, and visitors from across Italy zip in and out of them in all kinds of conveyances: grand sailboats, catamarans, cabin cruisers, wooden *gozzos*, large excursion craft, rubber dinghies, kayaks.

We head out on the water in a motorboat. Circling the island, we marvel as the coast unreels like a movie, each cove a fresh revelation, another invitation to anchor and dive in. Just out of the port are grottoes, and the slightly creepy caves where legend has it Pontius Pilate farmed moray eels. Beyond, the sea is pierced by *faraglioni*, rocks as sharp as sharks' teeth. As we swing around Faro della Guardia, the island's southernmost point, Monte Guardia, its highest peak, looms above, then gives way to terraced slopes, where grapes for the local wine, *vino del Fieno*, are grown.

near the island's southern tip, reachable by a short boat ride or, when the seas are rough, a slow trek over a mule track. We don't realize how remote it is until we arrive.

When the hotel skiff meets us at the ferry dock in Giglio Porto, the captain's expression makes it clear that he doesn't approve of people who travel with more than one suitcase. A wordless 20 minutes later, we realize why, when we disembark in the cove below the hotel. Sitting high above, in splendid isolation, is the Hermitage. Our bags are loaded onto a motorized luggage railway, and we ascend the stairways and paths that crisscross the hillside grounds to the entrance.

We quickly discover that the hotel's name is an accurate description: its insularity is its attraction. Going anywhere entails summoning a launch from the port. "You are a prisoner here, but why would you leave?" a fellow guest says to me shortly after we arrive. "It is refined, simple, and insane." Looking around, I begin to understand what she means.

The insanity reveals itself in the chaos of the main house, where books, musical instruments, games, and telescopes are scattered everywhere. Other buildings house studios for pottery and painting. Strewn about the grounds are eccentric sculptures, archery equipment, Ping-Pong and foosball tables, a boccie court, a thalassotherapy jacuzzi inside a plastic tepee (go figure), and a gym. There are several large terraces: one for sunbathing, another for outdoor buffet lunches and barbecues, and a third with an outdoor oven where Ghigo Pardini—who grew up here—sometimes makes pizza. The Hermitage also has a working farm, with sheep, pigs, donkeys for riding, and goats that produce cheese for the restaurant. Aside from an easy way out, the hotel seems to have everything.

Unfortunately, the Hermitage has some drawbacks. Our room is full of mosquitoes and lacks screens or nets. And after eating exquisite seafood on Lampedusa and Ponza, we find the fare here disappointing. Meals are announced by the ringing of a bell and served communally and without choices in a stuffy, nondescript dining room. Though it is possible to dine in the port, leaving to do so would be difficult and expensive, and lunching out would eat up a large chunk of time.

By the end of the first afternoon, we decide that those three coves will be our world on Giglio. By the end of our second, we've concluded that we much prefer this island as a day-trip destination from the mainland. Even if you can't afford chartering your own boat to get here, there is regular ferry service from nearby Porto Santo Stefano to Giglio and Giannutri. And Giglio is so small, a rented dinghy can circle it in half a day, with plenty of time to stop and snorkel or dive.

Giannutri, which has no hotels—only rental apartments—attracts even fewer suitors. But on the bright side: both islands serve up the sights, sounds, and smells of Tuscany by the sea. Their coasts are dotted with sandy beaches, their waters are filled with coral, sponges, and schools of fish, and their steep slopes are covered with wildflowers and maritime pines and are alive with wild rabbits, goats, buzzards, and falcons. There is nothing sophisticated about any of it. Which should ensure that its secrets stay safe for a long time to come.

A lighthouse on the end of a jetty in Giglio's port.

Traveler's Guide to Italy's Islands

GETTING THERE

Since hotels and restaurants close in the off-season, the Pelagi, Pontine, and Tuscan islands are best visited during the summer. The islands are easy to reach from mainland Italy. Alitalia and Lufthansa offer direct flights to Lampedusa from major Italian cities. For Ponza, hydrofoils and ferries (vetor.it) leave from Anzio. Giglio's ferries depart from Porto Santo Stefano. Although cars are allowed on the island, it's easier to park on the mainland. Two ferry lines operate from Porto Santo Stefano: Maregiglio (39-0564/812-920) and Toremar (39-0564/810-803). Purchase tickets at the dock.

LAMPEDUSA

The entrance to a private house in Giglio's harbor.

WHERE TO STAY

LAMPEDUSA

Cala Madonna Club
28 Contrada Madonna;
39-0922/975-401;
calamadonnaclub.it;
doubles from $$$ per night,
all-inclusive.

El Mosaico del Sol
Cala Palme;
39-0922/973-074;
elmosaicodelsol.it;
doubles from $$$$, 7-night
stay, all-inclusive.

Il Gattopardo
Cala Creta;
39-0922/970-051;
equinoxe.it;
doubles from $$$$, 7-night
stay, all-inclusive.

La Calandra
Contrada Cala Creta;
39-0922/971-098;
lacalandralampedusa.it;
doubles from $$$$, 7-night
stay, all-inclusive.

PONZA
Grand Hotel Santa Domitilla
Via Panoramica;
39-0771/809-951;
santadomitilla.com;
doubles from $ $ $.

La Limonaia a Mare
Via Dragonara;
39-0771/809-886;
ponza.com;
doubles from $ $ $.

Villa Laetitia
10 Via Scotti;
39-0771/809-886;
villalaetitia.it;
doubles from $ $ $.

GIGLIO
Il Pellicano
If you decide to base yourself on the mainland, this hotel near the Porto Santo Stefano ferry dock is worth a visit.
Località Sbarcatello;
39-0564/858-111
pellicanohotel.com;
doubles from $ $ $ $ $.

Pardini's Hermitage
Cala Degli Alberi;
39-0564/809-034;
hermit.it;
doubles from $ $ $ $.

Il Gattopardo's Balú, *which sails the Pelagi Islands.*

The jagged shoreline of Ponza.

WHERE TO EAT
LAMPEDUSA
Gemelli
Niçoise–North African fusion.
2 Via Cala Pisana;
39-0922/970-699;
dinner for two $ $ $.

Lipadusa
Seafood, straight from the docks.
6 Via Bonfigilo;
39-0922/970-267;
dinner for two $ $ $.

PONZA
Acqua Pazza
Piazza Carlo Pisacane;
39-0771/80643;
dinner for two $ $ $ $.

Cala Frontone
Island specialties and homemade wine.
Via Frontone;
39-0771/80009;
dinner for two $ $.

Cosí Com'era
Dine outside under the bamboo awning.
5 Via Salita Cristo;
39-0771/808-683;
dinner for two $ $ $.

Gennarino a Mare
One of Ponza's oldest restaurants.
64 Via Dante;

39-0771/80071;
dinner for two $ $ $.

L'Aragosta
Piazza Carlo Pisacane;
39-0771/80102;
dinner for two $ $ $.

Da Masaniello
A local favorite.
Corso Carlo Pisacane;
39-338/363-9910;
dinner for two $ $.

Oréstorante
4 Via Dietro la Chiesa;
39-0771/80338;
dinner for two $ $ $.

Pasticceria Gildo
The best espresso-and-pastry bar in town.
13 Corso Carlo Pisacane
39-0771/80647;
pastry and coffee for two $.

GIGLIO
La Margherita
A family-run restaurant with freshly caught seafood and a terrace.
5 Via T. de Revel;
39-0564/809-237;
dinner for two $ $ $.

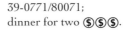

Sempre Napoli

NAPLES IS PRESERVING ITS GILDED PAST WHILE FORGING A NEW IDENTITY AS ONE OF ITALY'S MOST VIBRANT (AND UNDISCOVERED) CITIES. BY GUY TREBAY

There was a butter-curl moon hanging over the Castel dell'Ovo, where the Lungomare juts into the inky Bay of Naples. From where I sat, the scene looked like a postcard pun staged for my amusement: butter moon, castle inexplicably named for an egg. Tires hissing on the pavement below the rooftop terrace of my hotel were the only disturbance on a still, cool evening. *How could this be Naples?* I asked myself. *Where were the police sirens? Where was the chaos and the din?*

I had just arrived from Paris, where my hotel room happened to be located above the service door where Princess Diana and Dodi Al-Fayed made their fateful final exit. Automobile racket on normally sleepy Rue Cambon was so loud that I was forced to shut the windows tight. I had felt jailed in my peach-colored room, with its peach walls, peach upholstery, and mirrored vanity table— a penitentiary as imagined by Barbara Cartland.

Here I had the sudden sense that the two cities had miraculously exchanged personalities, somber Paris traded for Naples's hubbub, Naples's sidewalk carnival rolled up to present an aspect that is unexpectedly prim and sedate. Is there really a contradiction in this, I wonder? Or is it that the best way to meet this gorgeous and filthy and ancient city is to find that place in consciousness Fitzgerald once wrote about, where opposed thoughts can be entertained simultaneously in one's head?

Hadn't I just driven through slick streets to dine on what must be one of the finest simple meals I have ever enjoyed, translucent slivers of *prosciutto di Parma* draped over pungent melon, a *linguine alle vongole* served definitively al dente and studded with minute briny clams? Not the least of the pleasures of dinner at Ristorante da Dora was a bottle of frank, crisp Falanghina and the fact, ordinarily unwelcome to me, that the owner sang.

A hole in the wall on a street too narrow for automobile traffic, Dora was as brightly lit as a surgical theater. The television, when I arrived, was broadcasting images of a bloodbath perpetrated by the Camorra, the Neapolitan Mafia everyone insists does not exist. For some reason I took delight in the take-it-or-leave-it atmospherics, and also in that moment when the owner set down the plate of lobster she was serving and, in a fine, strong alto, let rip.

What was she crooning in that Neapolitan dialect that seems to draw out vowels and round consonants until words are all shoulders, soft and sloping? I have no idea. But the overall effect conspired to make me quite happy; it probably did not hurt that I was a little bit drunk.

Naples struck me immediately as among the few cities left in Europe that retain the power to intoxicate; a grand port that operates as though the earth were yet a sphere of wonders and itself the magnetic center of that sphere. A novelist once noted of the city that it induced a hallucinatory sense of looking through a veil of time, at things occurring before your eyes just as they might have hundreds of years before.

In a way, one is always on that trip in Naples. It is not just that the streets slashing through the Centro Storico or the lanes ramping down sticky, cobbled hillsides were built in Roman times. It is the

The view of Naples from Certosa-Museo di San Martino.

On the Via dei Tribunali.

Naples struck me immediately as among the few cities left in Europe with the power to intoxicate—a grand port that operates as though the earth were yet a sphere of wonders and itself the magnetic center

sense that Neapolitans' intrinsic character derives from these hills honeycombed with caves and catacombs, from claustrophobic lanes fanning from the spine of major avenues as if they were leaves in an ancient tome that is maddeningly hard to crack.

The view is not necessarily easy to reconcile with the city's disheveled nature, its petty crime, its labyrinthine plan and customs, its conceitedness and sluggish pace. Italians in other regions speak of Naples as though it were not part of modern Italy. And that, too, may be behind its appeal. As luxury brands advance on the rest of Italy, Naples revels in its isolation. True, there is a Prada boutique, and a Gucci, and a Vuitton. But these are generally viewed as outlanders, vendors of superficially appealing offerings that cannot hold a candle to local stuff.

I am referring here mainly to *sartoria napoletana*, the tradition of male dandyism for which Naples is justly renowned. Milan remains the capital of Italian fashion, of course, but as the designer Kean Etro once told me, no Italian is in any doubt about where the finest custom tailors, or *sartorie*, are to be found.

The principal Neapolitan names are well known even outside the city: Kiton and Attolini and Rubinacci for suits; Borrelli for shirts; Marinella for ties. But the town is filled with ateliers catering to the supreme stylishness of the local male population and a vanity born of the sense that, as the writer Raffaele La Capria once said, "...in Naples appearing is fundamental, while substance is negligible."

In a brief memoir of his boyhood, La Capria recounted a time when Neapolitans would walk along the Via dei Mille on Sunday, the men appraising each other's suits, the cut and the way the shoulder seams and sleeves were set, the tapering of the trouser waists, the crease of the pants, the width of the lapels.

Anyone skeptical of that tradition's vitality would do well to observe the waiters at sidewalk restaurants along the waterfront, like Gusto & Gusto, where the staff wears smart orange aprons,

Evening falls on the Via Donnalbina.

In the showroom of Rubinacci, famous for its men's suits. 23

The Certosa-Museo di San Martino, a 14th-century former Carthusian monastery on the Vomero hill above Naples.

crisply ironed and nipped to improve the fit. Sitting there one afternoon over lunch, I got the impression I had wandered right out of contemporary Europe and into another era.

My sense that the scene could not have been much different in the 1940's was fortified when an old crone out of a neorealist film shuffled by. Moving along the perimeter of the sidewalk tables in slippers and a housecoat, the woman dipped into her string bag and pulled out a pack of Marlboros. "*Sigarette americane*," she murmured softly: American cigarettes for sale.

From my sidewalk perch that day I also had a front-row seat on the theater of Naples's infamous traffic—that first mild evening had clearly been an aberration—which is ruled, one might say maniacally, by the motor scooter.

To cross a street in Naples is to be terrified, humbled, catapulted back to a moment in childhood when traffic is a wild and treacherous torrent. Cars and trucks and motorcycles race along constantly, erratically, apparently heedless of such an insignificance as pedestrians. "Ya almost went to join my late aunt Minnie, baby," a GI shouts to a Red Cross nurse narrowly saved from a hit-and-run during wartime Naples in John Horne Burns's classic novel *The Gallery*.

A day never passed in Naples when Aunt Minnie was far from mind.

Even cocooned in a taxi I was made aware of how potential death is always two seconds away in an automobile. Driving to the Kiton factory in an industrial suburb one afternoon, I passed four crashes on the autostrada. This was hardly surprising, given the tendency to pass on the right and tailgate with a passion I associate with another Neapolitan quirk, the need for physical connection. Perhaps it is a stretch, but this tactile compulsion might account for certain of the virtues of *sartoria napoletana*. Although the earnings of most local tailoring companies are relatively small, their influence is not. The soft and sensual, almost feminine cuts one associates with Giorgio Armani's classic style are an essentially Neapolitan invention, as is the natural shoulder local tailors grafted onto the Savile Row suits they copied during a 1920's wave of Anglomania.

No one has exported the concept with greater success than Ciro Paone, the tempestuous entrepreneur whose $5,000 Kiton suits are the gold standard of power dressing for American Masters of the Universe. Four hundred tailors are employed at the company, most sewing suits by hand.

With taxi drivers in the Piazza del Gesù Nuovo.

Striding across the work floor that day in a blue double-breasted suit, Paone grasped lapel pieces or chest pads from tailors whose hands seemed in constant motion as they covered garments with thousands of cross-hatched stitches. "Ninety-nine percent of the stitches are invisible," Paone claimed, as he flaunted the suppleness of a shoulder pad, the underside of pocket flap, a breast pocket termed a "little boat" because of the way the fabric resembles a tiny canoe with the corners pinched.

On the way back to town, I mulled over a question Paone had posed: "Did you ever see a shrimp in the sea?" I was forced to admit I had not. "A shrimp goes back to go a step forward," he said. "And we Neapolitans do the same. We consolidate traditions and history helps us. In Naples our surroundings are full of traditions."

To a surprising extent this remains accurate. In Naples one still finds cameo carvers, coral workers, the finest *stuccodores*, and candy makers at the celebrated Gay-Odin factory who toil behind the

Corso Umberto I.

scenes turning out confections called Tears of Love. In a sloping lane where the austere church of San Lorenzo Maggiore meets the Via dei Tribunali, craftsmen like Giuseppe and Marco Ferrigno make the cork-bark crèches for Nativity tableaux and the figures to populate them. Although momentarily tempted to buy an entire Nativity scene, with wise men, drunkards, and a marzipan-pink Baby Jesus, I settled instead for a figure referred to as a soul in purgatory. With his torso and upraised arms engulfed in flames, he now sits on my desk to remind me of that other nebulous sphere known as limbo, a state that every writer knows to exist, regardless of what the Vatican says.

One afternoon I made the half-hour drive to Torre del Greco to meet Basilio Liverino, an octogenarian jeweler who presides over his family's venerable coral business, set in a Brutalist building above a subterranean hillside vault housing what is arguably the largest collection of coral objects in the world.

"I bought my first piece in Florence when I was sixteen," Liverino told me, as we sat in a conference room beneath a print of a Medici cherub with a coral horn slung around his pudgy neck. Today the collection runs to more than a thousand objects—combs and boxes and mirrors and chalices and necklaces and breastplates, many carved from a type of coral called *Sciacca* for a deep trench off the coast of Sicily, where coral washed by prevailing currents accumulated for an aeon before being discovered in the 19th century.

"People think there is no more coral, that it is finished," said Liverino's son, Vincenzo. And it is true that industrial pollution and global warming have destroyed many of the world's great reefs. But coral is still fished in the deep waters off Sardinia and elsewhere in the Mediterranean, and it is that coral Liverino uses for objects the company crafts for Pomellato and Cartier. "We never treat, we never color," said Vincenzo as he guided me through the museum and workrooms where the dull raw material of this "red gold" is sorted, polished, cut, and then mounted or strung. "We make everything by hand," he added.

Back in Naples, I stopped at a jewelry shop to buy myself a coral-horn keychain, always on the lookout for additions to the list of superstitions I irrationally observe. It was hardly a notable purchase, given the quality of what I had just been shown. Yet it pleased me, this *corno*, and although probably no more effective at warding off the evil eye than other methods, carrying the little phallic amulet in my pocket seemed like an acceptable adaptation to the local male habit of making constant manual reference to one's genitals.

When I mentioned this nearly universal practice to Pasquale Venditti, a guide who has spent four decades herding tourists around Pompeii, he shrugged. "We are not so different from the Romans as we think," he said, and then invited me to the famous brothel in the ruins where each cell is adorned with a graphic fresco advertising the occupant's sexual specialty.

Things do change, of course, in ways depressing as well as good, as I learned one evening at Lucilio, a restaurant tucked behind the Hotel Excelsior. Built in the late 19th century, the tidy place is run by the Di Pinto family, whose forebears were *ostricari*, or oyster sellers. Their stands once lined the Lungomare, crazily decorated with tutti-frutti friezes made from shells.

In those days, *nassaiuoli*, or basket fishers, hauled their catch in woven *nasse*, lining up on the quays alongside mussel vendors, offering mollusks recently plucked from the rocks to be used in a spicy local fish-and-pepper soup called *mpepate* in Neapolitan dialect.

"Then, it was no problem," said Antonio Di Pinto, the restaurant's bookish-looking proprietor, referring to fresh-caught fare. "Now, with the pollution, it is dangerous," he went on. His point was underscored by a menu note disclosing that the octopus served at the restaurant is frozen and shipped in.

Pasta that night was *paccheri*, wide tubes whose name in dialect translates roughly as "big slap." It was followed by swordfish, accompanied by a bottle of Fiano di Avellino, a wine that experts like to call "assertive." Di Pinto brought out a photo book filled with images of a defunct festival called Nzegna, a carnival that reversed the social hierarchies of the Bourbon court and crowned local vegetable sellers king and queen. Processing through the streets, the *verdummari* went down to the port in vegetable-covered barks, there to be ceremonially tossed into the bay.

What astounded me was not so much the costumes or the rituals but the faces in the photographs, so heavy, ripe, and seemingly particular to this place. It is too little remarked how much pleasure in travel derives from the simple act of staring at others. Although it is not considered politically correct to revel in human difference, to an inveterate gawker and generalizer it is hard to ignore how Milanese men tend to carry themselves with prim Teutonic

At Europeo Mattozzi.

self-importance, while in Rome a nose is hardly worth thinking about if it lacks a fleshy tip or an aristocratic bump. In Naples, a certain kind of big-eared skinny guy, of a sort I call the Sinatra, is much to be seen, as is his sleepy-eyed counterpart, a guy who calls Dean Martin to mind.

Whether the Sinatras and Martins (Crocettis, originally) came from Naples, I don't know. But that these faces seem so recognizable to me cannot be unrelated to the huge migration of Neapolitans to the United States in the early part of the 20th century. The exodus, prompted by years of famine and rural unemployment, probably helped set in play the city's decline, a loss of vitality so acute that a quarter century ago, as the writer Nicola Spinosa observed, Naples was sliding down a slippery slope of what he described as degradation and marginalization. It was no help that the city was devastated by one of its periodic earthquakes in 1980.

Shabby still, but substantially rebuilt, Naples now has an energetic mayor who has initiated projects that include the promotion of contemporary art. "That is a very Neapolitan thing," said Alba Clemente, whose husband is the Naples-born painter Francesco Clemente. "Absorb and continue. It's a survival policy." As in other port cities, Neapolitans tend to hold fast to their customs while also quietly incorporating whatever aspects of the new may suit their immediate needs. "It doesn't work some of the time," Ms. Clemente said. "But most of the time, it does."

It's culture by accretion, and what has accumulated over time is enough to keep a visitor occupied for three lifetimes and not the three days guidebooks claim are enough to knock the city off. Even without dipping into the contemporary art scene, or the famous opera house, I was kept in constant motion and a heady state of excitement at the art-historical mother lode for most of a week.

At random, one might call out the famous National Archaeological Museum, with its justly renowned Roman bust of the emperor Caracalla, vain and sexy with his cruel gaze and deeply cleft chin; or Caravaggio's profoundly psychological *Seven Acts of Mercy* in the 17th-century Pio Monte della Misericordia; or the strikingly fresh ancient mosaics in the baptistery of the Duomo.

But there is also the Capodimonte, a huge palazzo whose rooms are arranged in a telescoping enfilade, so that one moves easily from a Masaccio *Crucifixion*, with its perverse perspectives, to a kooky 1425 *Assumption* by Tommaso di Cristoforo Fini,

with dozens of tiny angels swarming like bats, only to pull up in front of Bellini's highly graphic circumcision of Christ, both mother and child looking distinctly ill at ease.

Few things build an appetite for lunch like a morning of Depositions, Annunciations, Adorations, Crucifixions, and Flagellations. From the hilltop where the Capodimonte is situated, I hiked back toward the city center to the celebrated restaurant Europeo Mattozzi, where I was shown to a table in a windowless back room and then upgraded when I dropped Ciro Paone's name.

Swept to a table in the front, I had a fine view of the kitchen where the resident *pizzaiolo* was flipping dough. After trying all the pizzas in the city of that fast food's invention, the American food writer Ed Levine declared the pizza at Europeo "a slice of heaven." And that may be. But most pizzas in Naples are prepared in more or less the same sort of oven, at the same temperature (700 degrees), with the same two-inch "lip," and using the same mozzarella and industrial tomato sauce—and so, to my mind, most of them amount to the same boring cartwheel of baked dough.

The rest of the fare at Europeo, a place owned for the past century by the Mattozzi family and operated now by the genial Alfonso Mattozzi and his daughter Fabiana, was seductive, even to one who deplores gastroporn. For starters, there was a huge globe of buffalo mozzarella and accompanying antipasti of marinated octopus, fried zucchini flowers, and *fragaglie*, tiny fish that are deep-fried and startlingly good. Pasta with chickpeas and parsley was followed by grilled swordfish and accompanied by a 2003 Perella made from grapes grown on the cindery hills of ancient Paestum. When an agitated woman at the next table had finished haranguing someone on her cell phone ("Yes, I have his number! What are you talking about, 'Coordinate'? Stop being a pain in the ass. Good-bye."), I thought it was probably wise to offer her a glass.

Afterward, I caught a taxi to another of the city's wonders, the deconsecrated hillside abbey that is now the Certosa-Museo di San Martino, where, among treasures nearly impossible to catalog here, I was struck in particular by a quincuncial garden and graveyard fenced by a marble balustrade adorned with marble skulls of long-dead monks. Each *memento mori* was a distinctly rendered, albeit mortified, portrait. Each in its own unlikely fashion served as a merry reminder, somewhat redundant in Naples, I thought, to seize the day.

Travelers' Guide to Naples

WHEN TO GO

Visit Naples in the spring and fall when temperatures are warm, flowers are in bloom, and clear skies make for ideal views of Vesuvius. Avoid the hot summer—August in particular—when most businesses are closed for vacation.

GETTING THERE

There are easy connections to Naples from many European cities; from mid-May through mid-November, Eurofly (eurofly.it) operates direct flights from New York.

EXPLORING CAMPANIA

Naples is an ideal base from which to explore Campania. To the north, verdant plains sweep down to Santa Maria Capua Vetere. To the east is the mountainous province of Benevento. Tragic, earthquake-ravaged Avelino and its province lurk on a plain beyond Vesuvius. The northern coastline is not as enticing as the Roman ruins lining it at such places as Cuna. The Amalfi Coast, south of Naples, is stunning. Beyond the tip of the Sorrentine Peninsula and along the Cilento coast there is good swimming, as on Capri, Ischia, and Procida in the gulf of Naples.

While in Campania...

Amalfi Coast ❻
Benevento ❺
Capri ❾
Caserta ❹
Ischia and Procida ❿
Naples (Napoli) ❶
Paestum ❽
Pompeii ❷
Ravello ⓫
Salerno ❼
Santa Maria Capua Vetere ❸

0 kilometers 25
0 miles 20
For map key see p.7

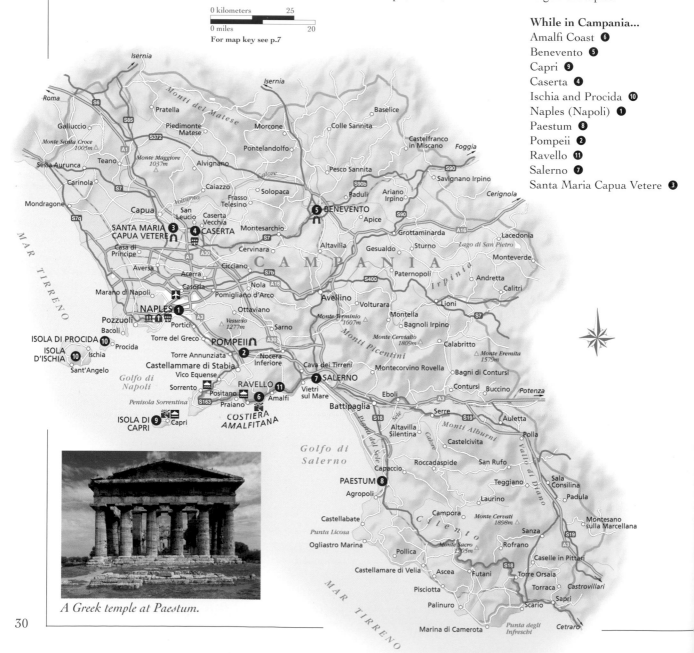

A Greek temple at Paestum.

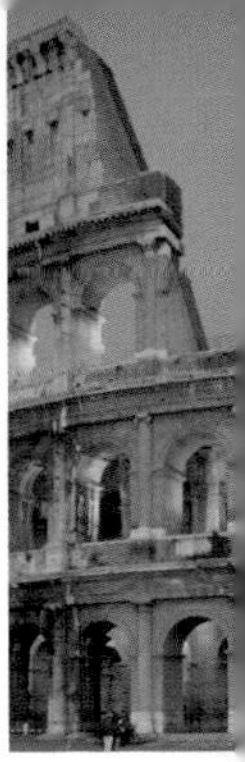

WHERE TO STAY

Chiaja Hotel de Charme
Small, friendly, well-priced hotel in a convenient location.
216 Via Chiaia;
39-081/415-555;
hotelchiaia.it;
doubles from $$.

Hotel Excelsior
One of the city's most luxurious properties, on the water.
48 Via Partenope;
39-081/248-1306;
starwood.com;
doubles from $$$.

Palazzo Alabardieri
Comfortable and small, near the Piazza dei Martiri.
38 Via Alabardieri;
39-081/415-278;
palazzoalabardieri.it;
doubles from $$$.

WHERE TO EAT

Ciro a Mergellina
For platters of freshly caught fish.
17 Via Mergellina;
39-081/681-780;
dinner for two $$.

Da Michele
Famous pizza place serving two kinds: with cheese and without.
1/3 Via C. Sersale;
39-081/553-9204;
lunch for two $.

Di Matteo
Sit downstairs to watch the pizzaioli, *and try a* pizza fritta, *stuffed with* provola *(a ricotta-like smoked cheese) and pork.*
94 Via dei Tribunali;
39-081/455-262;
lunch for two $.

Europeo Mattozzi
One of the city's best (and best-loved) restaurants.
4 Via Campodisola Marchese;
39-081/552-1323;
dinner for two $$$.

Gelateria Otranto
An astonishing selection of gelato and sorbet.
78 Via Scarlatti;
39-081/558-7498;
gelato for two $.

Hosteria Toledo
Small, traditional restaurant; try the sfizietto Toledo *(a kind of fritto misto) and the* paccheri ai frutti di mare.
78/A Vico Giardinetto a Toledo;
39-081/421-257;
dinner for two $$.

La Caffettiera
Excellent drinks and snacks served to a genteel Neapolitan crowd; grab a seat on the outdoor terrace.
30 Piazza dei Martiri;
39-081/764-4243;
drinks for two $.

Lucilio
Try this family-owned restaurant for great seafood.
11 Via Lucilio;
39-081/764-6882;
dinner for two $$$.

L.U.I.S.E.
A perfect example of the Neapolitan tavola calda, *a type of lunch counter with hot and cold dishes.*
Multiple locations, including Via Santa Caterina, at the Piazza dei Martiri; 39-081/417-735;
lunch for two $$.

Osteria da Tonino
A favorite local lunch place serving simple food.
47 Via Santa Teresa a Chiaia;
39-081/421-533;
lunch for two $$.

Ristorante da Dora
This charming small restaurant is known for its fish.
30 Via Ferdinando Palasciano;
39-081/680-519;
dinner for two $$$$.

Rosiello
Elegant and with a truly unbeatable view.
10 Via Santo Strato;
39-081/769-1288;
dinner for two $$$.

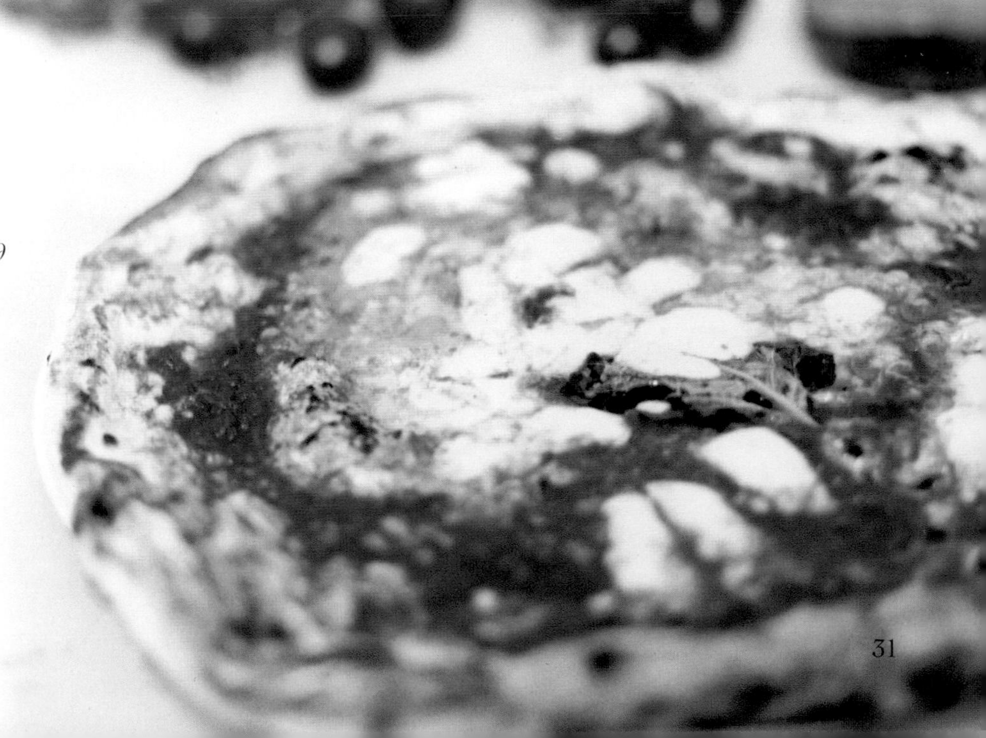

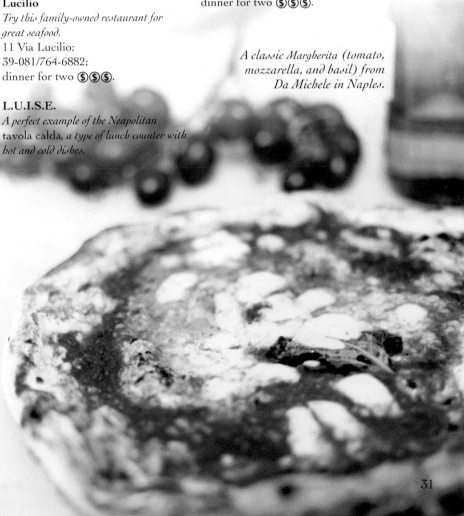

A classic Margherita (tomato, mozzarella, and basil) from Da Michele in Naples.

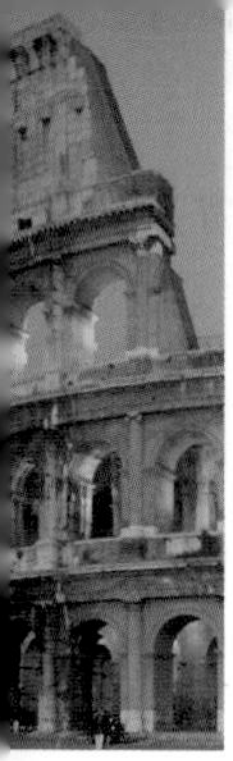

TOP HISTORIC SIGHTS IN NAPLES

Capodimonte ⑫
What began in 1738 as a hunting lodge soon grew to become a vast, Neoclassical royal palace. It is now a museum housing fine and decorative Dutch, Spanish, and Italian art.

Cappella Sansevero ⑤
Remarkable 18th-century sculpture fills this small family chapel. Of particular note are Antonio Corradini's *Modesty*, and Giuseppe Sammartino's *The Dead Christ*.

Castel Capuano & Porta Capuana ③
Begun by Norman king William I and completed by Frederick II, Castel Capuano was a royal palace until 1540, when it became the Court of Justice. The nearby Porta Capuana (completed 1490) is a fine Renaissance gateway.

Castel dell'Ovo ⑩
The Normans built the first castle on this Santa Lucia waterfront site in 1154. It achieved its present form in the 16th century.

Castel Nuovo ⑦
This Renaissance castle's bulky towers of volcanic stone are offset by one of the most graceful archways of the period, delicately carved in white marble.

Certosa di San Martino ⑪
Housed in a former monastery, this museum captures the spirit of Naples. Come for superb views from the gardens, for Neapolitan Baroque masterpieces, and for the world's finest collection of nativity figures.

Duomo ④
In effect, Naples' cathedral is at least three churches in one, including a treasure-laden Paleo-Christian basilica from the 4th century. The large and resplendent side chapel is dedicated to the city's patron saint, San Gennaro.

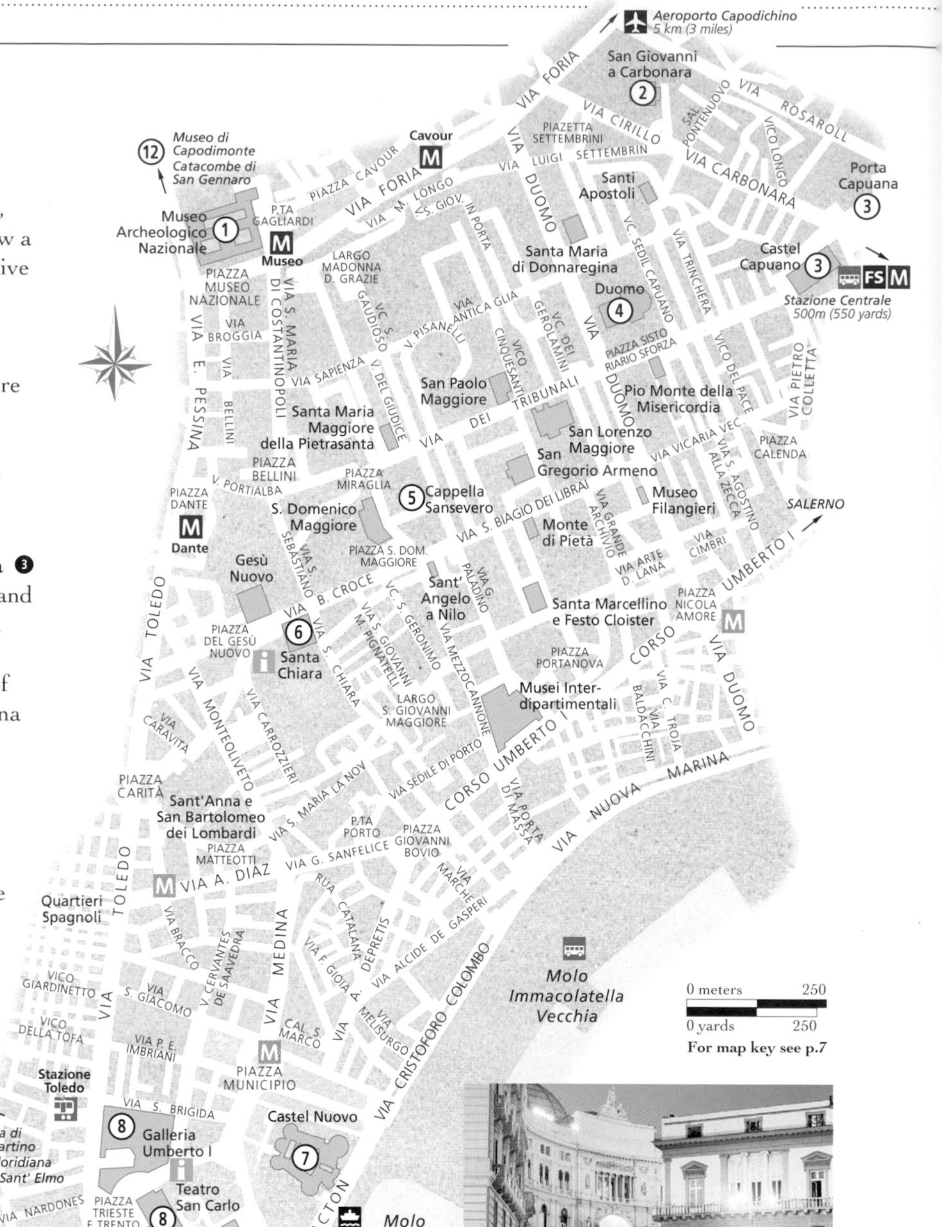

Galleria Umberto I & Teatro San Carlo ⑧
The handsome arcades of the Galleria Umberto I were built in 1887, and rebuilt after World War II. They face

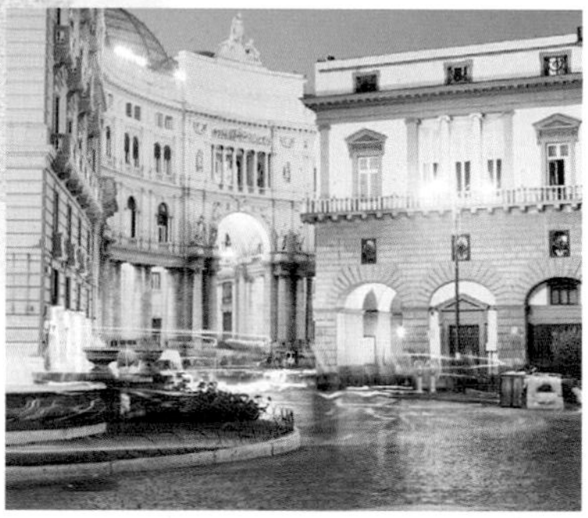

Piazza Trieste e Trento in Naples.

the Teatro San Carlo, Italy's oldest and largest opera house. Built in 1737, the theater's fine auditorium was once the envy of Europe.

Museo Archeologico Nazionale ①
A repository of ancient art unearthed from Pompeii and other archaeological

digs around Vesuvius. The amazing finds evoke a Classical civilization of impressive refinement and grandeur.

Palazzo Reale ❾
With its commanding position near the bay, the Royal Palace dominates the grandest part of the city.

San Giovanni a Carbonara ❷
Inside this 14th-century church are glorious medieval and Renaissance monuments, including Marco and Andrea da Firenze's masterpiece, the Tomb of Ladislas.

Santa Chiara ❻
The façade of this church, rebuilt after bomb-damage in World War II, is like a huge cliff of buff-colored tufa, relieved only by its portico and giant rose window. The interior decor has been returned to its Gothic origins.

WHERE TO SHOP
Naples is an excellent source for inexpensive, impeccably tailored clothes, especially for men, and alterations are usually free of charge. The best stores are concentrated in the Chiaia district. Whether or not you buy anything, don't miss a stroll down Via San Gregorio Armeno in Spaccanapoli, where shops sell the city's famed Nativities. Naples does not have much of a browsing culture; service in shops tends to be solicitous, sometimes overly so.

Borrelli
Justifiably famous (and expensive) men's wear.
68 Via Filangieri;
39-081/423-8273.

Eddy Monetti
Men's and women's clothes typical of the Neapolitan style.
45 Via dei Mille;
39-081/404-707.

Gay-Odin
The city's best cioccolateria.
Multiple locations, including Alt. 37 Via Cervantes;
39-081/551-9026.

Magnifique
Custom-made and ready-to-wear men's shirts and shoes.
37C Via Filangieri;
39-081/421-940.

Marinella
The city's most revered source for ties.
287A Riviera di Chiaia;
39-081/764-4214.

Milord
Men's wear for the hipper Neapolitan.
53 Vico Cavallerizza;
39-081/422-982.

Nino di Nicola
Affordably priced and well-made men's suits and shirts.
69 Via Santa Caterina;
39-081/404-349.

Fratelli Tramontano
Beautiful leather goods.
142–143 Via Chiaia;
39-081/668-592.

WHAT TO DO
Basilio Liverino
Fascinating coral museum.
61 Via Montedoro, Torre del Greco;
39-081/881-1225.

Paestum
Some of the best preserved Greek temples in the world stand in timeless splendor on this evocative plain south of Naples.

Pompeii & Herculaneum ❻
The world's most famous archaeological site displays a culture suspended in the moment when Vesuvius erupted nearly 2,000 years ago.

WHAT TO READ
The Volcano Lover
By Susan Sontag
A rich historical romance, based on the lives of Sir William Hamilton, the English ambassador to the court of Naples in the late 1700's, his wife, Emma, and Admiral Lord Nelson.

Falling Palace: A Romance of Naples
By Dan Hofstadter
A memoir of falling in love with the city.

A view of the Amalfi Coast from the hilltown of Ravello.

The Other Side of Italy

FAR FROM CAPRI'S CRUSH AND TUSCANY'S THRONGS, THE UNTRAMMELED BEACHES AND PRISTINE HILL TOWNS OF LE MARCHE HARBOR VENERABLE RENAISSANCE TREASURES (AND SUPERB SUNBATHING). BY GINI ALHADEFF

The artist Enzo Cucchi, one of Italy's finest, and a native of Le Marche, has a craggy profile that competes with the craggy cliff of Conero, where he told us to meet him at the Hotel Emilia, or rather, hotel emilia, as it modestly bills itself. Not modesty but frill-lessness, one soon discovers, is what the hotel offers, and when we got there and saw its unadorned white masses, which look like someone's demurely grand villa set into a green plain overlooking a dizzying drop to the sea, I instantly knew my story on Le Marche was on solid ground from the I-don't-care-if-I-never-go-anywhere-else point of view. The spare interiors, punctuated by Achille Castiglioni lights, and the 1970's structures that look like they might have been built by a cousin or disciple of Le

Honey-colored hills,
typical of Le Marche,
34   *near Urbino.*

Corbusier (but were in fact designed by Paola Salmoni, an architect from Ancona) go well with the hotel's guests, who come in various nationalities but share one distinguishing trait: they all speak in low voices. And they are all quite thin—though the food at the Emilia is fabulous, by the pool as in the dining room. You can eat your spaghetti with *cozze* (mussels) while absentmindedly following the movements of a young lissome couple playing Ping-Pong in white bathing suits or a sunbather wearing a triangular black tulle pareu embroidered with tiny mirrors over her thong bikini when not reclining on a chaise covered by the hotel's signature lilac towel.

Cucchi likes to walk down to the beach of Portonovo below (no doubt in his biscuit-colored moccasins) and take a cab back up, since it's quite a climb. The Emilia provides a shuttle to and from the beach, which has white and black pebbles and is, according to Cucchi, the most beautiful on the entire Adriatic coast.

At six that day, I followed Cucchi's speeding BMW down the winding narrow road to the straight coastline of Senigallia. We parked and went to sit on the terrace of a café called Mascalzone, "the Lout." There I had an orange-colored Crodino, a bittersweet nonalcoholic drink of mysterious

Hotel Emilia, above the Adriatic.

Changing rooms at the public beach in Senigallia.

from all over Europe to places like Senigallia, whose medieval center not all visitors notice and where a few hundred cafés and *bagni* are packed from late morning until sunset.

Le Marche is a lesser known part of Italy, with a 111-mile-long coastline—a protruding left hip on the Adriatic Sea—and stretches of unspoiled countryside extending into Umbria. The hills are the real monument here, and the way to see them is by accumulating hours driving through them or observing them from a window in a house on top of such a hill, like the one where my friends Remo Guidieri and Danielle Van de Velde live and write when they are not in Paris, in a town called Moresco. From most of the windows of their house, you can see snowcapped mountains on one side and the Adriatic Sea on the other. In between are the hills.

Le Marche was so named in 1105 when three marches, or border regions, between papal and imperial lands were joined by the Holy Roman Emperor Henry IV. One can go practically anywhere in Le Marche, taking the highway along the coast when necessary for speed, and be back by nightfall.

composition, and Cucchi had a glass of Verdicchio, a dry white wine that was one of the first to be exported to America. The drinks and green olives were brought to us by a sultry pirate in a black stretch hair band, low-slung black harem pants, and a black tank top, with pink bra straps peeping through. The terrace faces the street, but I sat with my back to it so I could see the beach and a volleyball court with an ongoing game. Everyone played in bathing suits; the women reminded me of the mosaics at the ancient Roman Villa Casale in Sicily's Piazza Armerina, which show women playing ball in bandeau tops and briefs—an early version of the bikini. The popes may have stuck their golden staffs and built their churches and monasteries all over the hills, but here the way of indulgence has won over that of penance.

A schizophrenic existence is possible in Le Marche, as one shuttles back and forth between the austere hill towns and the sybaritic resorts and bathing establishments along the Adriatic, where for four to five months of the year raked sands are ornamented by a forest of striped, polka-dotted, and bright-colored umbrellas, and neat rows of deck chairs and sun beds present a world dedicated to rest and recreation, set within a "real" one of small cities, traffic, shops, and bustling life. People come

A kite surfer in Senigallia.

Like the hills that can only be "seen" in increments, through a progression of miles and hours, Le Marche's treasures are scattered all over the region—a few, sometimes one, to every hill town

Every evening of my stay with the Guidieris, after scouring the countryside, I would return to the long refectory table in their dining room and sit on the wooden bench next to Remo or Danielle to plot the following day's itinerary.

Moresco, a fortress with some 600 inhabitants, about 40 miles south of Conero, is the same small town the Guidieris came to about 20 years ago, when Le Marche was the not-Tuscany, not-Umbria of Italy if you'd arrived too late in either of those regions to buy or rent anything. A heptagonal Moorish tower dominates a triangular settlement built mostly of stone. On a Sunday morning, the streets and square look as they must have centuries ago: deserted and quiet till the doors of the church open and the parishioners all spill out, chattering among themselves.

One Sunday Remo came as my guide, and a few hours expanded to what seemed like days as we

drove around the more hidden Marche that he seemed to know intimately. Like the hills that can only be "seen" in increments, through a progression of miles and hours, Le Marche's treasures are scattered all over the region—a few, sometimes one, to every hill town.

Near Montecosaro, the bare-brick Romanesque church of Santa Maria a Pié di Chienti, flanked by a smoke-filled café teeming with men playing cards, has veined alabaster windows that look like abstract stained-glass designs and bathe the interior in pale golden light. En route to Fiastra, we passed the Marchigiano designer Diego della Valle's immense new shoe factory. Shoes constitute the chief industry of Le Marche, aside from tourism.

At the abbey of Fiastra it occurred to me that cloisters might have been the draw, or at least the consolation, of a monastic life. Fiastra is one of the most serene, with a shaded portico and an ample courtyard that has a well at the center. The windows of the monks' cells line the story above the arches. Fiastra is surrounded by a large park and a nature preserve of some 4,000 acres; in their private yard by the abbey the monks could be glimpsed tending to the plants and trees.

We went to Monte San Giusto to see Lorenzo Lotto's *Crucifixion*, the altarpiece in a tiny church, Santa Maria in Telusiano. At the top are depicted three crucifixes, Christ and the two thieves; then soldiers on horseback, holding lances poised at all angles; and below, Mary, wrapped in a dark blue veil, collapsing to the ground at the dark heart of the painting, her arms flung out, a man holding her up on one side, a woman on the other, as though she, too, were being crucified. The thieves, their white loincloths flapping in the wind, seem about to fly off their crosses.

In Fermo, we stopped briefly to see the late archbishop, Don Gennaro, who had grown up in the north, by Lake Iseo, and was the neighbor of an old friend of mine. I made a faux pas by inquiring whether Loreto came under his jurisdiction. It doesn't; as one of Italy's most important sanctuaries, along with Assisi, it has its own see. Pilgrims flock

Crucifixion *(1531) by Lorenzo Lotto, the altarpiece of the Church of Santa Maria in Telusiano.*

A view of Urbino's tiled rooftops, from the studiolo *in the Palazzo Ducale.*

RBINI · DVX · MONTISFERETRI · ACDVD

*The courtyard of the
Palazzo Ducale, Urbino.*

PLVRIES · DEPVGNAVIT · SEXIES · SIG

from all parts of the world to worship the Madonna of Loreto, who appears black because the original statue was made of dark wood. She is wrapped tightly in a brocade cone decorated by horizontal crescents, with the baby Jesus swaddled so that his smaller head protrudes next to hers. She looks a bit as if she had materialized from another planet, and her house is reminiscent of a Hindu temple—dark, the bricks blackened by time and candles, and packed with so many faithful you can barely find a place to stand. Legend has it that the Madonna's humble dwelling in Nazareth flew itself, or was carried by angels, all the way to Loreto from the Holy Land. Actually, according to more recent findings, it was built next to a cave, then moved to Italy by ship at the time of the Crusades. The Holy House, one of the most beloved Catholic shrines, was encased in sculpted marble panels by the architect Donato Bramante, as it seems the original construction was thought too "rural." Those are, in turn, contained in a basilica, so it is a shrine within a shrine within a shrine.

The Madonna of Loreto and Saint Joseph of Copertino, whose sanctuary is in Campo Cavallo near Osimo, about 12 miles to the north, are both said to protect fliers, or aeronauts, as they used to be called. Apparently Saint Joseph could float off the ground; the current monks at the saint's former convent say he "took God so seriously he could literally fly." Flying is an appealing prospect from the cliff of Conero or from Recanati's walled ramparts.

Recanati is a pilgrimage site for writers. Its glory is the 19th-century poet Giacomo Leopardi, who railed against his native town and the straitlaced atmosphere of Le Marche. His only distractions were the extraordinary library (which can be visited) assembled by his father, Count Monaldo, the sweeping views, and a hill he immortalized in "The Infinite," Italy's most celebrated sonnet. Now one ventures out to see Lorenzo Lotto's *Annunciation* at the small Colloredo-Mels museum in the historical center of town. It is a thrilling interpretation of the event: a muscular, wild-eyed, blue-winged angel lands bearing a tall white lily, a tabby cat leaps out of the way, arching its spine, and the Virgin Mary —a brunette for a change and apparently no older than 16—throws up her hands and ducks, as though the angel had landed with a crash, taking her by surprise. Lotto, who was born in Venice around 1480 and lived in Le Marche early in his career, moved back there toward the end of his life, becoming a lay brother at the monastery of the Holy House in Loreto. He was poor and, by most accounts, racked

Catia Uliassi in the restaurant Uliassi, which she runs with her brother, Mauro, the chef.

by religious doubt. As for Leopardi, he fled from his chilly parents and his father's library, where in seven years he had taught himself everything from the classics to astronomy, and died of typhoid in Naples, possibly after eating a gelato. Gelati are no longer lethal, and an attack of melancholy in Le Marche can be cured by a two-hour drive to Rome, or a 10-minute one to the sea.

Even in the fall and winter, except perhaps over the Christmas holidays, one can go to a wonderful fish restaurant like Uliassi in Senigallia, run by the chef Mauro Uliassi and his sister, Catia, and on a sunny day have lunch on the terrace and look out onto the sandy beach and a limitless expanse of gray-green Adriatic. There we tasted a *fritto*— assorted fried fish and vegetables—that had the best aspects of tempura and Italian frying combined: tiny tender octopus, sticks of zucchini and eggplant, a zucchini flower splayed out in a fan shape on the wooden tray it all came on. The delicious squid-ink *strigoli*—a tubular pasta—came with clams, octopus, and cherry tomatoes.

The previous evening, Enzo Cucchi had arranged for us to have dinner at La Madonnina del Pescatore, 41

in Senigallia's Marzocca area. There is a statue of the Madonna that fishermen pray to before setting out to sea—hence the name of the restaurant. That's where the quaintness stops, since the place, which opened in 1984, is a minimalist concrete box with a glass façade. The waitresses dress in beige. As soon as we sat down, they brought us Parmesan sorbet in crisp cylindrical wafers. We had eight light-handed courses in all, including raw shrimp marinated in orange sections, fried whitebait (*bianchetti*) as small as paper clips, and a Senigalliese *brodetto*, or fish soup. It was a kind of culinary magic show.

To reach Le Marche from anywhere else in Italy, sooner or later one must scale the Apennines, so it is with eyes washed in snow and dazzled by peaks that one comes to the rolling hills of Le Marche, especially in winter.

Even Urbino, the masterpiece of Renaissance architecture described by Baldassare Castiglione in the opening lines of *The Book of the Courtier* as a city in the form of a palace, would be hard to imagine without the surrounding landscape, which is visible from every balcony and window of the Palazzo Ducale.

Like other Italian "capitals," Urbino is a small town that someone, in this case the Duke of Montefeltro, suddenly envisioned as the center of the universe. The duke, judging from Piero della Francesca's portrait of him, must have had an appetite for the truth, for it is not a flattering picture—his beaklike nose appears broken at the

The café Mascalzone ("the Lout"), Senigallia.

bridge, and he has a wart beneath one ear, dark circles around his hooded turtle eyes, thin lips. But the red hat the duke decided to put on does ennoble the whole and is as brilliant a solution as any he made in the course of transforming Urbino into a Renaissance hub. He was the Lorenzo il Magnifico of this part of Italy. An admirer of Machiavelli, he arranged to have his half-brother killed in a court intrigue, after which the people of Urbino called on him to be their ruler. We may have his guilty conscience to thank for one of the most wondrous commissions inside the exquisitely unusual ducal palace Francesco di Giorgio Martini designed for him: the very moving Cappellina del Perdono, or Chapel of Forgiveness.

The duke's study, the Studiolo del Duca, is a cubicle completely paneled with intricately inlaid wood depicting arches through which you see unlimited landscapes—one shows a squirrel devouring a nut, another a cupboard stacked with books in haphazard piles. In that inspiring cell the duke may have thought up his plan to invite Piero della Francesca to Urbino to paint his *Flagellation of Christ* and portraits of his wife and of himself. (At his court lived another painter whose son, Raffaello Sanzio, became known to the world as Raphael, and whose house is only a few blocks away from the Palazzo Ducale.) One can also visit the immense vaulted spaces of the stables, the kitchens, and the duke's bathing chamber in the basement.

I asked Remo's friend Nello, the pharmacist of Moresco, who still mixes his own remedies and collects Byzantine icons, to characterize the cooking of Le Marche, and he said, "Not chiles." So if not chiles, I pressed him, then what? "Cloves," he replied. A recipe for the most typical local dish, a lasagna called *vincisgrassi*, invented in 1799 in honor of Prince Windisch-Graetz, an Austrian general stationed in Le Marche, also includes cinnamon and nutmeg in a sauce of sweetbreads, calf's brains, prosciutto, porcini mushrooms, and, naturally, béchamel. Driving from Moresco to Ascoli Piceno, home of the Venetian Renaissance painter Carlo Crivelli (and of the stuffed and fried green olives called *ascolane*, which you eat with *creme*, dollops of sweet fried custard), the rhythm of the rippled landscape becomes hypnotic. The first glimpse of Ascoli is of its many bell towers (there were once 200), a surreal gathering one can imagine holding a rarefied philosophical discussion when no one is watching. In the restored Art Nouveau Caffè Meletti, we had a tuna-and-artichoke sandwich on white bread, which seems to be a staple at most cafés in Le Marche.

Between hill towns, we visited Pesaro, a genteel turn-of-the-19th-century beach resort with tree-lined avenues and freestanding Art Nouveau villas, and

A bust of Raphael on view in Raphael's Birth House, in Urbino.

ate at Il Cortegiano, a restaurant set in a neo-Gothic palazzo, where we were given a table with a view of a shaded garden and a wall inset with majolica. This town's reigning spirit is Gioacchino Rossini, who is celebrated every August in a festival exclusively dedicated to the performance of his operas.

On our arrival in Le Marche, we had driven up the highest hill overlooking the Adriatic, to the medieval Cathedral of San Ciriaco. In it, aside from the saint's relics, was a painting of the Virgin said to protect travelers from storms at sea. Then we headed toward Iesi, the hometown of the composer Pergolesi. It started to rain. We wanted to stop for lunch but could barely see the road, and then, on an incline, the engine flooded and we stalled. Suddenly a car appeared, overtook us, then stopped. Using a nylon rope he happened to have with him, the driver hitched us to his car, then hauled us up the hill till our engine started again. We asked for directions to a restaurant, and he said we should follow him, since he was on his way to lunch. He led us through the deluge to the middle of a flat plain and a trattoria that looked nothing like a restaurant: it was hidden, like most treasures of Le Marche, for all to see.

The Studiolo del Duca, in Urbino's Palazzo Ducale, built for the Duke of Montefeltro.

The interior of the Cathedral of San Ciriaco, Ancona.

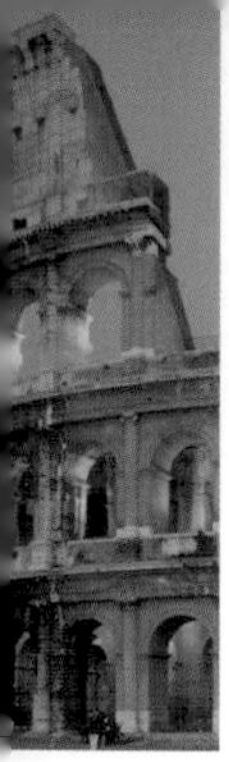

Travelers' Guide to Le Marche

GETTING THERE

You need to be a good driver in Le Marche; the roads are narrow and often steep. Fly to Ancona and rent a car. For speed, take the A14, which connects the entire region along its 111-mile coastline, from Pesaro in the north to Ascoli Piceno in the south. For pleasure, drive the *strade statali* through Le Marche's beautiful landscapes.

EXPLORING LE MARCHE

The medieval towns of Urbino and Ascoli Piceno are the region's highlights, but the rolling hills of the interior have an abundance of smaller towns and all-but-undiscovered villages. San Leo, with its dramatic fortress, is one of the most picturesque. Most of the countryside is a pretty mixture of woods and remote hills, rising in the west to the majestic Monti Sibillini. The Grotte di Frasassi cave network, southwest of Jesi, contains some of Europe's largest publicly accessible caverns. Ancona and Pèsaro are the main attractions on the vast coastline.

While in Le Marche...

- Ancona 9
- Ascoli Piceno 12
- Conero Peninsula 10
- Fano 4
- Grotte di Frasassi 7
- Jesi 8
- Loreto 11
- Pèsaro 3
- San Leo 1
- San Marino 2
- Urbania 6
- Urbino 5

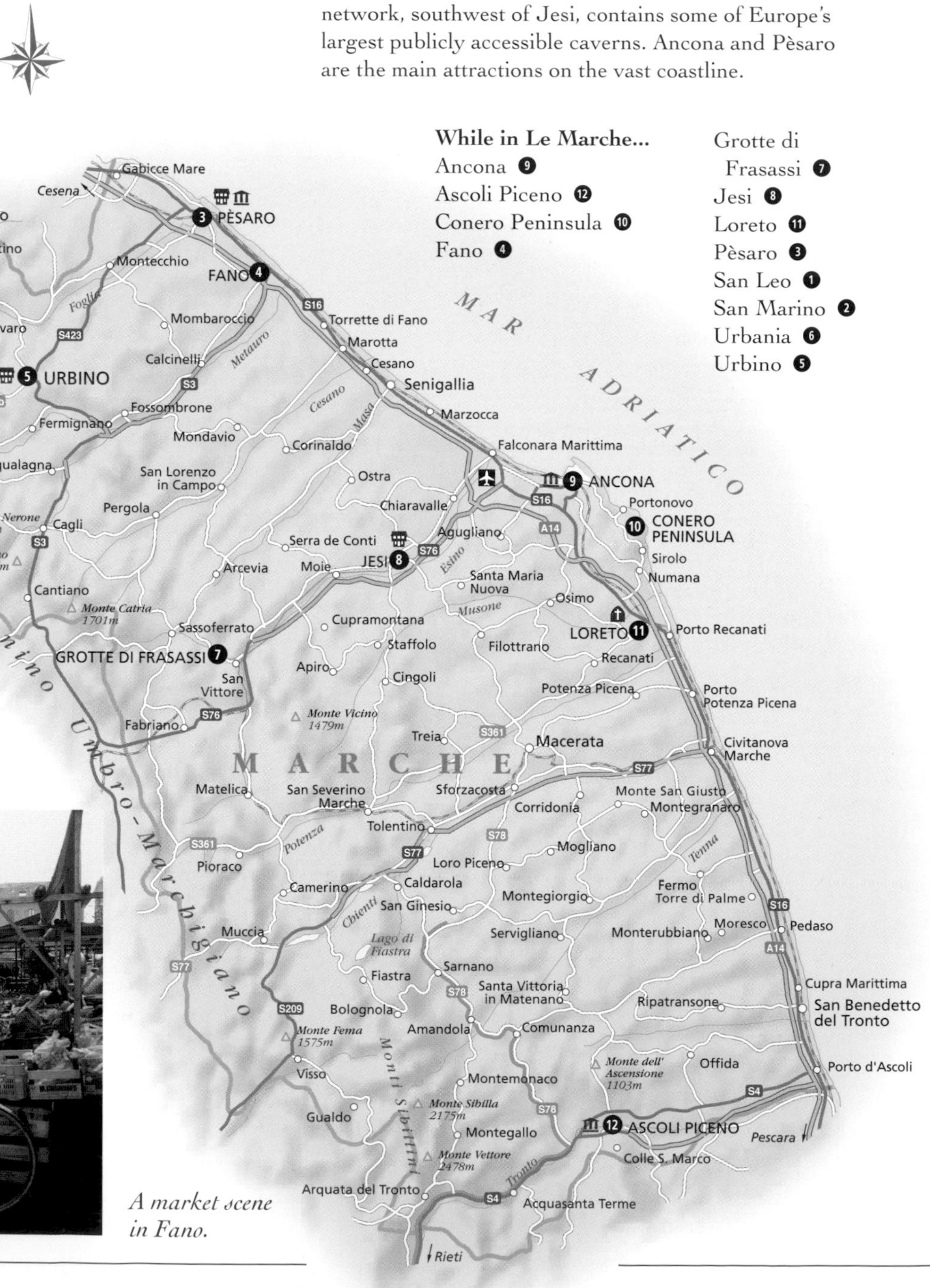

For map key see p.7

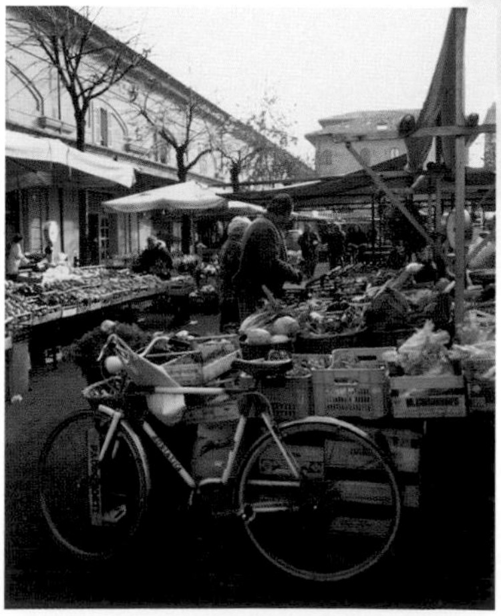

A market scene in Fano.

WHERE TO STAY

Most hotels are along the coast or in the Conero area, near Ancona. For a feel of hill-town life, rent a house. **Le Marche Explorer Rental Properties** (le-marche-explorer.com) represents an extraordinary selection of restored farmhouses, convents, and apartments at rates from ⓢⓢⓢⓢⓢ a week. Or try a room or suite in an *agriturismo* villa or bed-and-breakfast like Palazzo dalla Casapiccola. Hotels without description appear in the story.

Hotel Fortino Napoleonico

A converted fortress, with a swimming pool, a garden, and endless curving beaches in front and on either side.
166 Via Poggio, Portonovo;
39-071/801-450;
hotelfortino.it;
doubles from ⓢⓢⓢ a night, seven-night minimum stay (during the summer months).

Hotel Emilia

Poggio di Portonovo, Ancona;
39-071/801-145;
hotelemilia.com;
doubles from ⓢⓢⓢ.

Albergo San Domenico

Set in a 14th-century monastery and 16th-century convent, facing the ducal palace.

The main entrance to the Palazzo dalla Casapiccola, in Recanati.

3 Piazzale Rinascimento, Urbino;
39-072/22626;
viphotels.it;
doubles from ⓢⓢ.

Palazzo dalla Casapiccola

Ten suites in a 17th-century mansion in the historic center of Recanati, with a beautifully maintained garden.
2 Piazzola Vicenzo Gioberti;
39-338/138-0055;
palazzodallacasapiccola.it;
suites from ⓢⓢ.

WHERE TO EAT

As in the rest of Italy, lunch or dinner in Le Marche is a perfect pretext for a drive.

Da Andreina

Charcoal-grilled game in a brick house on the outskirts of Loreto.

14 Via Buffolareccia;
39-072/164-934;
dinner for two ⓢⓢⓢ.

Il Castiglione

Baked branzino in the elegant dining hall of a 20th-century villa.
148 Viale Trento, Pesaro;
39-072/164-934;
dinner for two ⓢⓢⓢ.

La Madonnina del Pescatore

11 Lungomare Italia, Marzocca di Senigallia;
39-071/698-267;
dinner for two ⓢⓢⓢⓢ.

Migliori

A food shop for ascolane (stuffed olives) and creme (dollops of custard), ready to be fried and eaten together.
2 Piazza Arringo, Piceno;
39-0736/250-042.

The private family chapel in the Palazzo dalla Casapiccola, in Recanati.

47

Ristorante Farfense
Potato dumplings in meat sauce, served in a brick-vaulted dining room in a former monastery, with views of the sea 25 miles away.
41 Corso Matteoti, Santa Vittoria a Matenano (near Ascoli Piceno); 39-0734/780-171; dinner for two $$$.

A table at Uliassi, in Senigallia.

Il Saraghino
On the beach at Numana, mixed fried fish and vegetables and tagliatelle with squid ink.
209 Via Litoranea, Lungomare di Levante, Numana, Marcelli; 39-071/739-1596; lunch for two $$$.

Susci Bar Clandestino
Young chef Moreno Cedroni, who has developed an Italian version of sushi (he spells it susci*), and his wife represent the new face of Le Marche cuisine.*
Baia di Portonovo; 39-071/ 801-422; dinner for two $$$$.

Uliassi
6 Banchina di Levante, Senigallia; 39-071/65463; uliassi.it; dinner for two $$$$$.

Caffé Meletti
Aperitifs and antipasti in an authentic Art Nouveau setting.
Piazza del Popolo, Ascoli Piceno; 39-0736/259-626.

WHAT TO DO
Galleria Nazionale delle Marche
Paintings by Paolo Uccello and Piero della Francesca.
Palazzo Ducale, 3 Piazza Duca Federico, Urbino; 39-072/22760.

Raphael's Birth House
The artist was born and taught to paint by his father here, though none of his paintings are on display.
57 Via Raffaello, Urbino; 39-072/232-0105; accademiaraffaello.it.

Rossini Opera Festival
Performances of works by the native-son composer, every August in Pesaro.
39-072/1380-0294; rossinioperafestival.it.

Pinacoteca e Museo delle Ceramiche
Ceramics from the 1500's to the present, including 1900's majolicas of Pesaro's Ferruccio Mengaroni.
29 Piazza Toschi Mosca, Pesaro; 39-072/138-7541; museicivicipesaro.it.

A view of Ascoli Piceno, one of the region's prettiest towns.

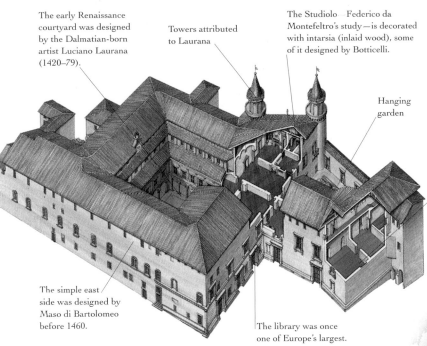

The early Renaissance courtyard was designed by the Dalmatian-born artist Luciano Laurana (1420–79).

Towers attributed to Laurana

The Studiolo — Federico da Montefeltro's study — is decorated with intarsia (inlaid wood), some of it designed by Botticelli.

Hanging garden

Built for Duke Federico da Montefeltro, ruler of Urbino from 1444 to 1482, the Palazzo Ducale is a tribute to courtly life and the intellectual ideals of the Renaissance.

The rooms in this wing are known as the Appartamento della Francesca.

The simple east side was designed by Maso di Bartolomeo before 1460.

The library was once one of Europe's largest.

Villa Imperiale
A fortress plus a Renaissance villa, built in four levels on a hillside, with geometric gardens.
Via dei Cipressi, Pesaro;
39-072/169-341.

Santa Casa and Basilica
The Holy House of the Black Madonna. The surrounding area is full of shops selling fascinating souvenirs.
Palazzo Apostolico, Piazza della Madonna, Loreto;
39-071/970-104.

Museo Villa Colloredo Mels
Via Gregorio XII, Recanati;
39-071/757-0410.

Santa Maria a Pié di Chienti
Montecosaro, Macerata;
39-073/386-5241.

Church of Santa Maria in Telusiano
Monte San Giusto, Macerata.

Abbadia di Chiaravalle Fiastra
Via Abbadia di Fiastra;
39-0733/202-942;
abbadiafiastra.net.

La Basilica di San Nicola di Tolentino
Another glorious cloister, from the 14th century.
Tolentino, Macerata;
39-0733/976-311.

Other Towns Worth Seeing
Camerino, Cupramontana, Fabriano, Fermo, Osimo, San Severino Marche, Senigallia, Torre di Palme.

WHAT TO READ
Leopardi: Selected Poems
Translated by Eamon Grennan. Work by Le Marche's most famous author.

Cucina of Le Marche
By Fabio Trabocchi
A cookbook-memoir tribute to the region's culinary bounty.

The exterior of the Palazzo Ducale, Urbino.

49

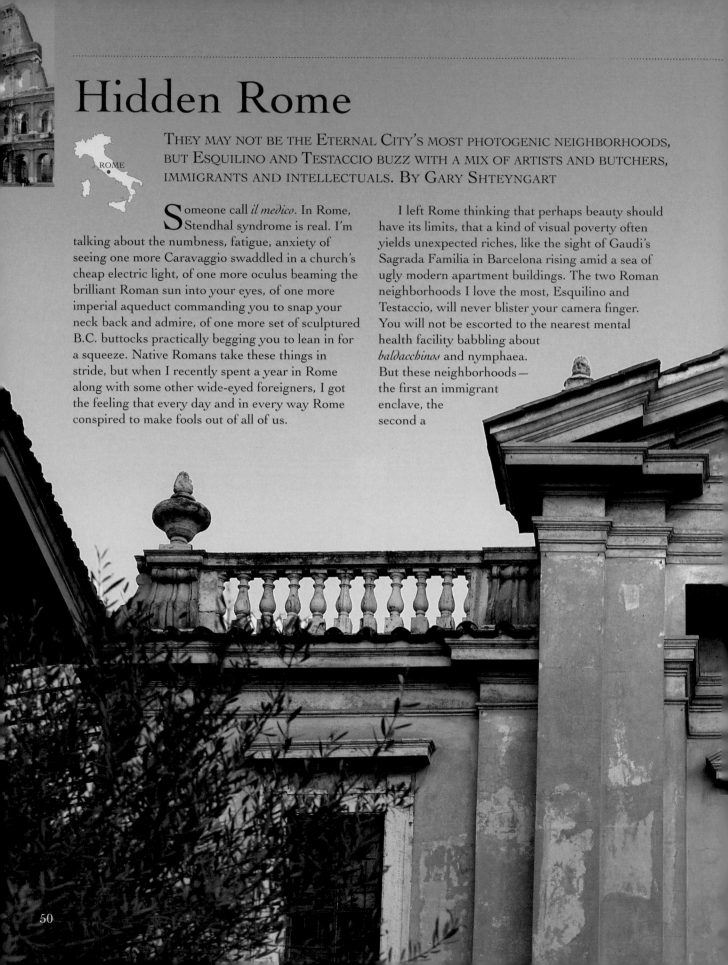

Hidden Rome

THEY MAY NOT BE THE ETERNAL CITY'S MOST PHOTOGENIC NEIGHBORHOODS, BUT ESQUILINO AND TESTACCIO BUZZ WITH A MIX OF ARTISTS AND BUTCHERS, IMMIGRANTS AND INTELLECTUALS. BY GARY SHTEYNGART

ROME

Someone call *il medico*. In Rome, Stendhal syndrome is real. I'm talking about the numbness, fatigue, anxiety of seeing one more Caravaggio swaddled in a church's cheap electric light, of one more oculus beaming the brilliant Roman sun into your eyes, of one more imperial aqueduct commanding you to snap your neck back and admire, of one more set of sculptured B.C. buttocks practically begging you to lean in for a squeeze. Native Romans take these things in stride, but when I recently spent a year in Rome along with some other wide-eyed foreigners, I got the feeling that every day and in every way Rome conspired to make fools out of all of us.

I left Rome thinking that perhaps beauty should have its limits, that a kind of visual poverty often yields unexpected riches, like the sight of Gaudí's Sagrada Família in Barcelona rising amid a sea of ugly modern apartment buildings. The two Roman neighborhoods I love the most, Esquilino and Testaccio, will never blister your camera finger. You will not be escorted to the nearest mental health facility babbling about *baldacchinos* and nymphaea. But these neighborhoods— the first an immigrant enclave, the second a

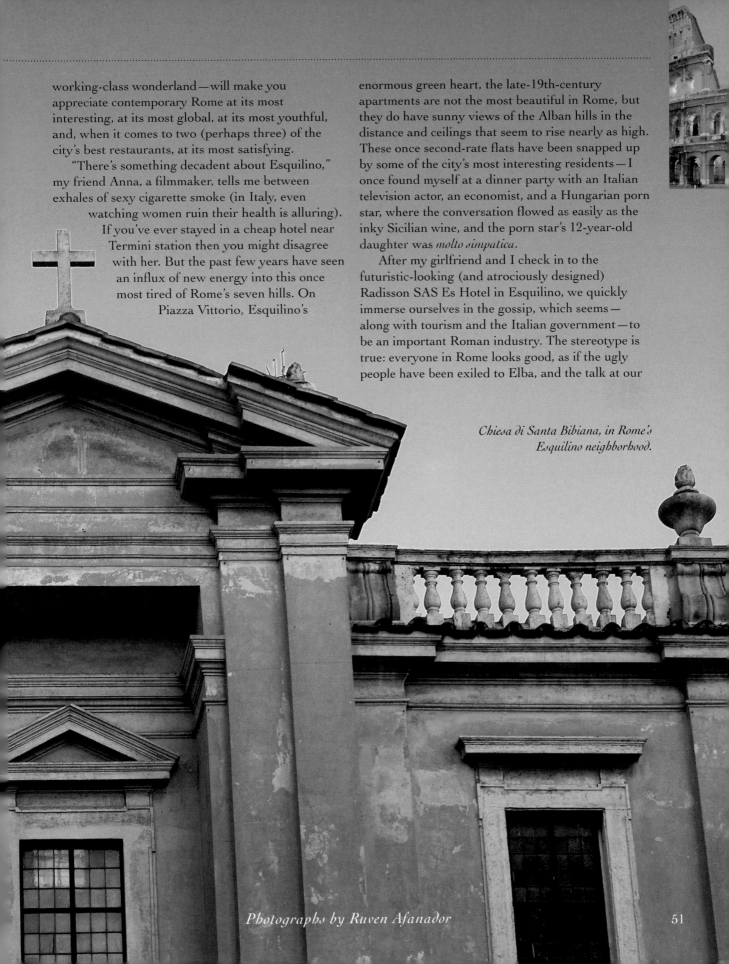

working-class wonderland—will make you appreciate contemporary Rome at its most interesting, at its most global, at its most youthful, and, when it comes to two (perhaps three) of the city's best restaurants, at its most satisfying.

"There's something decadent about Esquilino," my friend Anna, a filmmaker, tells me between exhales of sexy cigarette smoke (in Italy, even watching women ruin their health is alluring). If you've ever stayed in a cheap hotel near Termini station then you might disagree with her. But the past few years have seen an influx of new energy into this once most tired of Rome's seven hills. On Piazza Vittorio, Esquilino's

enormous green heart, the late-19th-century apartments are not the most beautiful in Rome, but they do have sunny views of the Alban hills in the distance and ceilings that seem to rise nearly as high. These once second-rate flats have been snapped up by some of the city's most interesting residents—I once found myself at a dinner party with an Italian television actor, an economist, and a Hungarian porn star, where the conversation flowed as easily as the inky Sicilian wine, and the porn star's 12-year-old daughter was *molto simpatica*.

After my girlfriend and I check in to the futuristic-looking (and atrociously designed) Radisson SAS Es Hotel in Esquilino, we quickly immerse ourselves in the gossip, which seems—along with tourism and the Italian government—to be an important Roman industry. The stereotype is true: everyone in Rome looks good, as if the ugly people have been exiled to Elba, and the talk at our

Chiesa di Santa Bibiana, in Rome's Esquilino neighborhood.

*The past few years have seen an influx of new energy into
this once most tired of Rome's seven hills*

A cardinal lunching at
Testaccio's Sora Rosa.

Osteria degli Artisti, in Esquilino.

first party is about who's doing what to whom, along with tales of unplanned pregnancies, inauthentic-looking breast jobs, and the latest excesses of the hated Silvio Berlusconi ("He looks like an orange ball, no?"). But as much as we love the gossip, we crave food, and Esquilino quickly delivers.

We head past the gate of Porta Maggiore (where an ancient Roman baker built himself a commemorative oven the size of a town house) to Osteria degli Artisti, a restaurant celebrating the cuisine of the southern Campagna Campania? region. The appetizers alone are enough to jolt me out of my antiseptic North American life and into a world of fresh escarole mixed with golden raisins, pine nuts, and capers, all soaked in a deep-yellow pool of olive oil. The grouchy owner slaps his hands, says, "*Allora, signori,*" then launches into the pastas of the day. We decide to take a detour from carbohydrates and go for the tender anchovies, lightly battered, just asking for a pinch of lemon or two, fish with bones so fine they melt away. The freshness of the ingredients and that vaunted Southern Italian simplicity settle my stomach and make me content. That night I dream I have died and been admitted to the farthest reaches of heaven, where Hungarian porn stars and alluringly dressed Cinecittà actresses form an impromptu ladies' choir, and Berlusconi himself humbly serves us Campari and soda, his orange head bobbing above a cheap rented tuxedo. When I lived in Esquilino a few years ago, I ate at Osteria degli Artisti nearly every week, and half my diary was composed of dreams like this.

And yet many Romans have a different, less affectionate view of this part of their city. Even the most Marxist of them will complain about *i cinesi*, the Chinese immigrants who took Esquilino by storm several years ago. "I don't like the Chinese people," one Italian woman tells me. "The Africans I like. They have gestures, expressions, smiles." What the Chinese have, on the other hand, are shops. Small, mysterious little enterprises that spiral in every direction from the Piazza Vittorio, each containing several mannequins forlornly gazing at small piles of unsold clothes. I have never seen a single customer enter or leave any of the establishments, which leads to many angry speculations on the part of the locals—about everything from drugs and prostitution to the warehousing of black-market tigers. But take any of these streets to Piazza Vittorio, the neighborhood's center, and you will see a different spirit prevail.

The piazza, with its endless salmon-hued arcades, was laid out by the Turinese after Italy's unification in the 1870's. Now, at the start of the 21st century, all that rational Northern planning has given way to a melting pot that would make New York's Lower East Side proud.

The palm-studded green piazza—arguably the biggest in Rome and home to a sculpted pair of monstrous dwarfs guarding the procedure of transmuting base metal into gold (I've tried; nothing so far)—has the energy of a Moroccan souk. When the sun shows its face, immigrants from nearly every corner of the globe gather here to kick around footballs, aim their cell phones toward Dhaka, sing about their homelands, and sometimes overdose. Older Italian men sonorously flirt with Ukrainian domestics, while beneath the colorful arcades South Asians sell knock-off baby shoes and weird mechanical squawking animals to each other. The piazza has three other claims to fame. There is the Piazza Vittorio Orchestra, an inspired collection of 16 musicians from almost as many countries who seamlessly integrate instruments from the Arabic oud to the Brazilian cavaquinho. There is the ghetto-fabulous MAS discount superstore, frequented by poor day laborers and savvy Italians alike, where five euros buys you a fine Bill Cosby–style sweater.

And there is Maria Pia, the best fortune-teller in all Rome. Look for her on the corner of Via Carlo Alberto—she's the woman in the black beret next to the drunk. Maria tells me that Egypt is calling me and that my next novel will be an unqualified international triumph. What makes Maria Pia so prescient, according to my artist friend Angela, who lives in a gorgeous sun-filled apartment right above her, is that she regularly talks to aliens.

Terrestrial or not, Rome has always been a place for exiles, and after witnessing the hurly-burly of Piazza Vittorio, I head to Via Palestro, where above the small Russian Orthodox Church I find Princess Elena Wolkonsky, the charming descendant of one of imperial Russia's most powerful families (her grandfather was Pyotr Stolypin, the prominent and controversial prime minister during the reign of Czar Nicholas II). Princess Elena lives in one high-ceilinged pastel room overlooking the balcony where the Russian priest sups with his parishioners after services while some of his five children play soccer in the dusty courtyard below. She talks about Russia, her family, and, in particular, her English governess, Miss Bannister, who also happened to be a governess for the Tolstoy family and helped the Wolkonskys escape the Russian Revolution. I feel as if I've entered a brightly lit Nabokovian repository of memories, but my Roman-born hostess is not exactly an exile. Although she is no longer in the first flush of youth and has some difficulty ambulating, once she gets into her little Renault and starts zipping through city streets shouting *Dai!* ("Come on!") at the younger, slower drivers, I realize that she is gleefully, breathtakingly Italian.

Lunch in the Eternal (or Internal) City often lasts so long that I find myself merely biding my time until the next meal. After lunching with the princess and taking a restorative two-hour nap, my girlfriend and I head to another part of Esquilino to have dinner with Anna in one of my favorite Roman restaurants. Trattoria Monti, just off Piazza Vittorio, is known to some of my friends for its waiters, the brothers Enrico and Daniele, who are the kind of tall, dark, well-browed, and gentle creatures many would like to take home. Whatever your amorous interests, there is no denying that some very serious food is served within this airy-but-intimate barrel-vaulted space. The cuisine of the Marches region, located in the central part of Italy's eastern coast, takes pride of place here. I daydream of its mixed appetizer platter, a testament to the delights of crisp, light frying—stuffed fried olives, fried artichokes, ethereal fried vanilla cream, and *ciauscolo*, a soft,

Dinner at Trattoria Monti, off Piazza Vittorio.

*The Pyramid of Caius
Cestius, in Testaccio.*

Padre Antonio, a priest at Esquilino's Santa Bibiana church.

lardy, spreadable sausage taken from the pig's belly, ribs, and shoulder. We are knocked senseless by a codfish carpaccio with red onions and truffles and a *tagliatelle al ragù marchigiano*, whose intense meatiness we match with a strong, fruity Sardinian Santadi. But my most beloved dish has always been the fried lamb brains with fried zucchini. Here are brains without peer—creamy and soothing—the ultimate comfort food. "My parents fed me this to make me smart," says Anna, who is certifiably brilliant, as she adds a squeeze of lemon. "Mmm, childhood," echoes her fiancé, Serafino. We finish with a fairly pornographic persimmon mousse with toasted almonds and pistachio cream, but Anna makes us order a second dessert. "After making love all night," Anna says with perfect lascivious timing, "you should eat zabaglione cream, because it gives you back your strength."

The next day, after following Anna's advice, we end our Esquilino sojourn at my favorite church. A fitting representation of the neighborhood as a whole, Santa Bibiana is squeezed in between a tunnel and a smokestack, fronted by tram tracks and facing the Cobra adult-video store. The façade was the first architectural work of Baroque wonder boy Bernini, and the interior is a tiny jewel. Even my agnostic friends sometimes attend mass here, and senior lovebirds come to renew their 50-year-old vows. The intimacy of the space contrasts with the gilded overdrive of Rome's more famous churches, and the beatific Bibiana holding the palm leaf of martyrs (she was, um, flogged to death) fills this little church with kindness and calm. I am most pleased to find out that Bibiana is the patron saint of people with seizure disorders and those suffering from hangovers. We'll need her mercy where we're going next.

The ghosts of a million calves float over Testaccio, perhaps the most authentic neighborhood in Rome. The enormous *mattatoio*, the city's main slaughterhouse until it closed in 1975, was the center of Testaccio's economic life for about a century. The sculpture of a winged god punching out an innocent bull atop the building pretty much says it all. The last trendy thing to be built here was the 90-foot-tall Pyramid of Caius Cestius, circa 12 B.C. This seemingly misplaced monument made out of white Carrara marble was commissioned by a self-loving Roman functionary after the Cleopatra–Mark Antony love scandal made the Egyptian style de

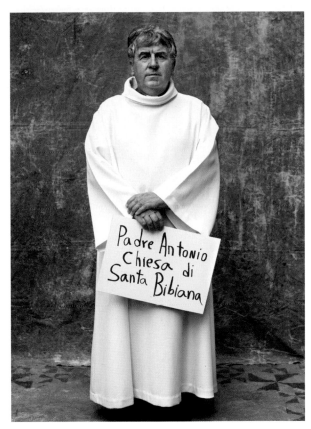

rigueur. For the next 2,000 years Testaccio played the role of a salt-of-the-earth backwater, but today it has become the address of choice for those who want to eat an animal or simply party like one.

Testaccio is located in the southern part of central Rome, across the river from Trastevere, its better-known, more polished rival with a West Village vibe and crowds of carousing American expatriates ("Yo, Deb, check out dis, like, guy"). Testaccio, a neighborhood of undistinguished 19th-century buildings, some of which are shabby enough to be in Naples, isn't quite there yet. Instead it is the home base for the real *cucina romana*, embracing the so-called fifth quarter—the leftover parts of the animal (tripe, nerves, Adam's apple) that used to be part of the slaughterhouse workers' pay—along with Jewish and regional country favorites such as artichokes and anchovies. After dining in a leisurely fashion on a piece of intestine and a glass of cheap red, everyone heads to Monte Testaccio, a bizarre mountain built entirely out of discarded amphorae that is now the scene of half of Rome's youthful couplings.

To show me the real Testaccio, my friend Flavio takes me to the kind of place that used to proliferate throughout Rome—an "old man bar" where a euro-and-a-half will pay for a *mezzo litro* of the most

common Frascati wine. In this much too bright Formica canteen on Via Galileo Ferraris, senior Testaccini with the kind of features that used to inspire foreign painters (one missing an eye, the other a slice of nose) and who speak only the local dialect, play cards and scarf down prosciutto. Like most of Flavio's own family, they are retirees from the slaughterhouse, and one can certainly say these gentlemen are rooted in place. I literally have to climb over a patron, muttering "*Permesso, permesso,*" to get to my seat.

The slaughterhouse is gone, but its spirit lives on in the Testaccio covered market, acknowledged by many to be the best in Rome. The tomato man with the ponytail and corncob teeth will explain which tomatoes go with which kind of pasta. At the Pasta all'Uovo shop there are ravioli and tortellini *di zucca* (with pumpkin), which are like little wrapped gifts you give yourself. The fishmonger at La Boutique del Pesce serenades his tuna, "*Tonno bello, tonno bello,*" while a neighboring stand shows off anchovies with blood-red heads and live eels kicking their last. "How good is my fish?" asks the fishmonger rhetorically. It's not bad at all.

Flavio's uncle Cesare and aunt Delia run a butcher stand in the northwest corner of the market. Chummy, smiling Cesare in his butcher's smock and woolly cap is a huge Beatles fan, and keeps a magnet depicting the group and a picture of himself as a youngster in a Beatles-esque band behind the counter. The family stand has been around since 1918, he tells me over a display of little skinned rabbits and a glossy, beautiful lamb's head. The loose, fatty *salsicce* he sells practically dribble over the tongue. For a helping of vegetables, I head for the nearby stands stacked with perfectly shaped lunar-domed mushrooms and fresh zucchini flowers, which look like giant tulips and taste like paradise after a short bout of frying.

A dedicated aficionado of Roman cuisine would do well to rent an apartment near the market, supplementing the fresh produce with trips to the famed Volpetti deli on Via Marmorata. Inside Volpetti's cramped premises, meats, cheeses, olive oils, and other edibles gather from across Italy to tantalize and overwhelm the casual visitor. On this trip, we assemble a sweet-and-peppery basket of *gorgonzola piccante*, boar sausages no bigger than my thumb, and a spicy *'nduja*, a salami from Calabria that tastes like an angrier, in-your-face cousin of the French andouille.

After gorging is complete, a walk to the pleasant grounds of the Cimitero Acattolico (better known as the Protestant Cemetery) is in order. Built outside the city walls in accordance with Vatican strictures against burying non-Catholics within the city, the cemetery is a peaceful collection of souls of all denominations, a quiet, sun-dappled oasis of palms and cypresses where the diversity of the entombed speaks of Rome's centrality to the world. Here are the graves of prominent Americans, Russian royalty, Rome-besotted Muslims and Jews, and, of course, the daisy-strewn grave of Shelley in the shadow of the outlandish Cestius pyramid. Lovers of Keats can also bid their farewell here, while leftists should, against their better judgment, take the path to the right, where they will find the simple grave of Antonio Gramsci, the father of Italian communism. Wherever you turn, cats glower at you from their tombstone perches, and the sweet rot of flowers and serenity reign. This is the only place that I've ever visited—other than the Garden State Mall in Paramus—that has made the cessation of life seem appealing.

But dinner approaches, and it is time to rejoin the living. This is where the vegetarian reader may want to part company with me for a while.

MAS, a store off Esquilino's Piazza Vittorio.

*Testaccio butcher
Cesare Finanzieri.*

Testaccio's trattorias will not win any awards for ambience and décor, but these noisy, overlit places offer an encounter with an animal that you will find in few places. I spend an entire week eating in almost every restaurant in the neighborhood and grilling, so to speak, the natives on their favorite choices. The talk of the hood is Da Felice, which once looked like a cafeteria with fluorescent lighting but is now a typically Euro-smooth wood-and-brick joint. The owner used to be ridiculously selective, refusing entrance to anyone who didn't look as if he or she had just tussled with an ox or happened to be Roberto Benigni, who lives nearby. Now Da Felice is no longer selective and the food has gone south. Only Roberto Benigni remains, eating quietly with his wife, his trademark goofy face floating above his pasta. The one bright spot is the creamy, voluptuous artichoke. As for the dry veal roll, I almost choke. "Benigni's gonna beat you up if you don't finish," the waiter scolds me. It's a chance I'm willing to take.

Far better is Da Bucatino, an old-school, wood-paneled place on a raucous street corner that pretty much detonated when the A.S. Roma soccer club took the 2001 Italian Cup. The *bucatini all'amatriciana*, as Roman a dish as there is, is divine here, featuring smoky pieces of pig cheek and thick, hollow bucatini you could flog a small child with. Look out for a very garlicky *puntarella* salad, the tangy, bitter chicory roots soaking up the fresh anchovies and vinegar.

But most of the locals, my friend Flavio's butcher uncle included, talk up Augustarello. A spare room; working-class local clientele; a bottle of decent Sangiovese on the table; a fat proprietor who micromanages the daily pasta selections—this is what a Roman trattoria should be like. And unlike many other places, they really do charge only half the price for a *mezza porzione*, allowing you to pick through many delicious options. *Salsicce con fagioli*, for example, are the best franks and beans in the world, highlighted by delicate, succulent chunks of pigskin. An understated *rigatoni alla carbonara* avoids the cardinal sin of *carbonara*—too much egg—leaving just enough yolk to gently coat your fork. And then there are the tender *animelle* (sweetbreads), grilled to perfection, along with a chewy, lightly fried *pajata*, a Roman specialty: a baby lamb's (or calf's) intestines still stuffed with its mother's milk. When I lived in Rome, my American guests would invariably have a moral crisis over this dish, but one taste would set them straight. The Augustarello version—salt, pepper, olive oil, intestine—leaves nothing to chance. Holy or not, this is real communion with an animal.

Those seeking a more refined wine list with their Testaccio meal should head to the old stalwart Checchino dal 1887, located inside a congenial cave bored into Monte Testaccio. After passing the gauntlet of outstanding cheeses by the door, try the *scottadito*, or "finger burners," spit-roasted baby lamb chops that you are allowed to eat with your hands. But the real fun begins in the cavernous wine cellar, which still shows shards of ancient amphorae. Francesco Mariani, the restaurant's burly host, steers us toward a Tenuta Belguarda from Tuscany, a Cabernet Sauvignon–Sangiovese whose notes and structures were so complex I had to go back to our hotel room to think about them.

There is more exceptional wine to be found—not to mention a respite from Testaccio's innards frenzy—at Bottiglieria DOC, on the dead-quiet Via Beniamino Franklin. This recently opened subterranean wonder zeroes in on fresh pastas and seafood. We are served the lightest potato *gnochetti*, followed by grilled tuna and squid topped with olives and capers and bathed in olive oil with lemon and freshly ground pepper. After a crisp, buttery Sicilian wine, I got the pleasant feeling we were leaving old Testaccio behind, bound for warmer, quasi-African climes.

By now you will be fat. The question is what to do with the newly found treasure around your waist. The man-made Monte Testaccio, atop which live pigs were once packed into barrels and rolled downhill during pre-Lenten celebrations, is now a magic mountain of sorts, home to Rome's most interesting selection of dance clubs. The chill, knowledgeable crowd goes to Metaverso, a small, pleasant white cave festooned with some kind of Keith Haring–type graphic art. Reggae, electronica, and drum 'n' bass rule the night here, and there's something oddly inspiring about middle-class Italian boys in dreadlocks trying to drop the Jamaican dance-hall steps, even if they do look like they're digging a hole.

Down the street, at Zoobar, there's an older scene, with good live shows, random bands, and a complete lack of pretension. The woman of your dreams might be wearing a gaudy belt, tight cutoffs, and high boots; the man-child you crave may be sporting Vans, tight pants, and a shag haircut. The music will be eighties and beyond, with a profusion of Talk Talk, Madonna, and maybe a foray into early Daft Punk. If all else fails, there's a new branch of the MACRO modern-art museum, housed inside the old slaughterhouse, open from four in the afternoon to midnight, late enough to accommodate art-minded clubbers. Meat conveyors overhead, cobblestones beneath your feet, stables to the left

CETTA
TESA

RIGATINO
TOSCANO
Poco
Salato 19,06

PANCETTA
AFFUMICATA
€18,08

LOMBO
Fratelli
Rustici
€69,00

CULATELLO
DI ZIBELLO
80,00

Cured meats at Volpetti, a Testaccio deli. 61

A fishmonger in the
Testaccio market.

and right—it's just the venue for group exhibitions with a focus on multimedia.

From calf slaughter to blockbuster art—the presence of MACRO is a sure sign that Testaccio is changing, a transformation some welcome and others bemoan. Directly to the south lies Garbatella, a neighborhood that looks even worse than it sounds but whose decrepit markets will soon be converted into a Rem Koolhaas postmodern extravaganza called the City for Youth, which will feature the usual mix of shops, restaurants, and "cultural" institutions. Rome has clung to its traditions with far more ferocity than any other major Mediterranean city, and this traditionalism has, over the years, coated it with a provincial gloss. Testaccio's youthful energy and Esquilino's driven immigrant population point the way to an entirely different, if not yet settled, future. But Rome isn't Bilbao or Berlin. The Rem Koolhaases come and go, but the city endures, its surface serving as a palimpsest while the locals carry on with their feasting and loving and scheming. Before departing, we visit friends, an American/Italian couple who are about to have a baby boy. I look out their tiny bathroom window, which captures the rump of Esquilino's Santa Maria Maggiore cathedral, where one can confess in Ukrainian, Czech, Norwegian, and Tagalog. I can't imagine what a spanking-new infant will make of it all, but I'm guessing that now more than ever it's a heady time to be a Roman bambino.

Pina, a fortune-teller in Esquilino.

Princess Elena Wolkonsky Cicognani, an Esquilino resident.

Travelers' Guide to Hidden Rome

WHEN TO GO
In the neighborhoods of Esquilino and Testaccio, chances are you'll be safe from summer's stampede of tourists, but you'll still have the heat to contend with. Avoid both by visiting in late fall or early spring.

GETTING THERE
Delta, US Airways, Continental, and Alitalia fly direct to Rome from New York. Alitalia also flies between Rome and Boston, San Francisco, Los Angeles, Atlanta, Chicago, Montreal, and Toronto, usually via Milan.

While in Esquilino...
Arch of Gallienus **6**
Auditorium of Maecenas **10**
Domus Aurea **12**
Museo Nazionale d'Arte Orientale **9**
Piazza Vittorio Emanuele II **8**
San Martino ai Monti **1**
San Pietro in Vincoli **2**
Santa Maria Maggiore **4**
Santa Bibiana **7**
Santa Prassede **5**
Santa Pudenziana **3**
Sette Sale **11**

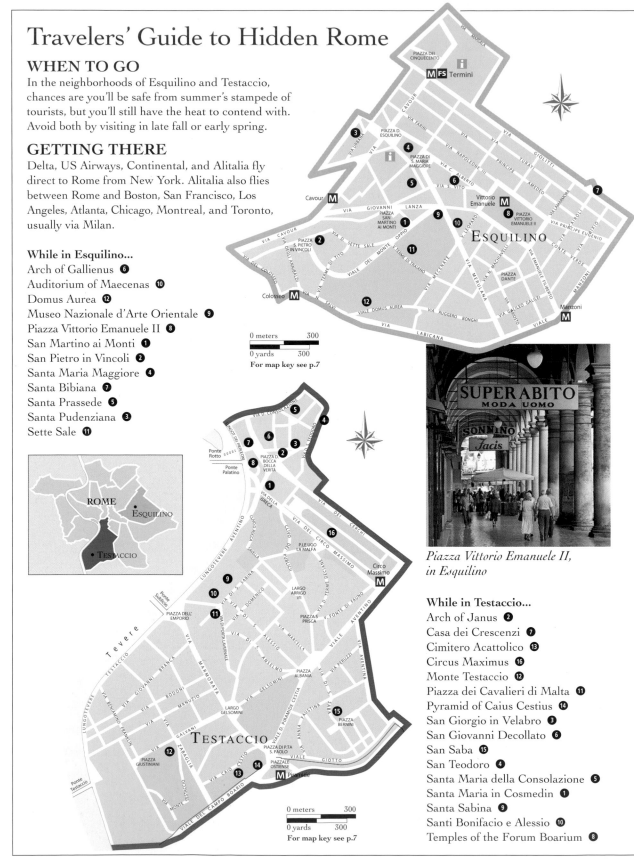

Piazza Vittorio Emanuele II, in Esquilino

While in Testaccio...
Arch of Janus **2**
Casa dei Crescenzi **7**
Cimitero Acattolico **13**
Circus Maximus **16**
Monte Testaccio **12**
Piazza dei Cavalieri di Malta **11**
Pyramid of Caius Cestius **14**
San Giorgio in Velabro **3**
San Giovanni Decollato **6**
San Saba **15**
San Teodoro **4**
Santa Maria della Consolazione **5**
Santa Maria in Cosmedin **1**
Santa Sabina **9**
Santi Bonifacio e Alessio **10**
Temples of the Forum Boarium **8**

WHERE TO STAY

Casa Howard
Affordable design hotel a short taxi ride from Testaccio and Esquilino.
18 Vin Capo Le Casa, Piazza del Popolo; casahoward.com; 39-06/6992-4555; doubles from $$.

Radisson SAS Es Hotel
171 Via Filippo Turati; 39-06/444-841; rome.radissonsas.com; doubles from $.

WHERE TO EAT

IN ESQUILINO

Osteria degli Artisti
6 Via G Sommeiller; 39-06/701-8148; dinner for two $$.

Trattoria Monti
13 Via di San Vito; 39-06/446-6573; dinner for two $$$.

IN TESTACCIO

Augustarello
98 Via Giovanni Branca; 39-06/574-6585; dinner for two $$.

Bottiglieria DOC
9 Via Beniamino Franklin; 39-06/574-4236; dinner for two $$.

Checchino dal 1887
30 Via di Monte Testaccio; 39-06/5740-6318; dinner for two $$$.

Da Bucatino
84/86 Via Della Robbia Luca; 39-06/574-6886; dinner for two $$.

Da Felice
29 Via Mastro Giorgio; 39-06/574-6800; dinner for two $$$.

Sora Rosa
A typical "old man bar," with simple Italian fare.
7 Via Galileo Ferraris.

Volpetti Deli
47 Via Marmorata; 39-06/574-2352.

WHAT TO DO

IN ESQUILINO

Chiesa di Santa Bibiana
154 Via Giovanni Giolitti (near Termini).

MAS store
11 Via dello Statuto (off Piazza Vittorio).

Piazza Vittorio Orchestra
orchestradipiazzavittorio.it.

Santa Maria Maggiore
Piazza Santa Maria Maggiore.

IN TESTACCIO

Cimitero Acattolico
5 Via Caio Cestio; 39-06/574-1900.

Metaverso
38A Via di Monte Testaccio; 39-06/574-4712; metaverso.com.

Museo d'Arte Contemporanea di Roma (MACRO), Mattatoio
A branch of Rome's modern-art museum, housed in a former slaughterhouse on Monte Testaccio.
Piazza Giustiniani.

Pyramid of Caius Cestius
Piazza di Porta San Paolo.

Testaccio Market
One of Rome's liveliest.
Piazza Testaccio.

Zoobar
1 Via Bencivenga; 39-339/272-7995.

Piazza Santa Maria Maggiore, in Equilino.

PART TWO
Places to Stay

*The traditional grounds of
Byblos Art Hotel Amistà.*

A bird's-eye view of the
hill town of Asolo.

Villas of the Veneto

JUST OUTSIDE OF VENICE ARE SIX OF THE REGION'S BEST HOTELS, LURING
VISITORS WITH ILLUSTRIOUS ARCHITECTURE AND VERONESE FRESCOES.
BY CHRISTOPHER PETKANAS

The Veneto should need no
introduction, or if it does,
maybe you shouldn't let on—is it possible you're not
as well-traveled as you think? I know too many
people who've been to Venice a hundred times and
never made good on vows to drag themselves out of
Harry's Bar to tour the backcountry. Is this you? If

so, what a pity. Or you could look at it another way:
You still have the discovery of the Veneto ahead of
you. If this slice of the former Repubblica Veneziana
has always played handmaiden to Venice, so much
the better. However breathtaking, Venice is a
casualty of its own enshrinement. The Veneto has no
such worries. Its main provinces—Padua, Treviso,

Photographs by Andrea Fazzari   69

Villa Pisani proprietress Mariella Bolognesi Scalabrin and Robert, her borzoi, in the hotel's courtyard.

The Red Room at Villa Pisani, in Vescovana.

Verona, Vicenza—are models of sustainable cultural tourism. Palladian villas attract the architecturally aware. Soave and Valpolicella vineyards draw wine pilgrims. And you would have to work very hard to find a restaurant proposing anything but regional home cooking, a canon with a core of risotto, polenta, beans, *baccalà*, and culty vegetable dishes like forced, blanched radicchio and castrated artichokes.

Beyond the Veronese frescoes and great food, luxury shopping and great food, and genius *barchesse* (read on) and great food, the Veneto has some extraordinary hotels. Many are grand, which here never rhymes with stuffy. Among the possibilities are a former shooting lodge with a hotly contested Byron connection, a Renaissance estate with a primo cooking school, and a 15th-century villa pumped with contemporary art. They're unique to the Veneto, which no one has ever confused with Venice.

VILLA PISANI, VESCOVANA
Of all Andrea Palladio's houses, Villa Barbaro, in Maser, is probably the most popular. But to see its Veronese frescoes you have to cope with tour buses and wait your turn until someone liberates a pair of the slippers that are required of all visitors.
You can endure all that, or just spend the night in woozy majesty at Villa Pisani, where Mariella Bolognesi Scalabrin has some sensational Veroneses

of her own. (The Pisani dynasty was one of the noblest in the Venetian Republic, which looked to it for ambassadors, generals, and doges.) If you want to pass the afternoon studying Veronese's portrait of Cardinal Francesco Pisani, who built the villa in 1552, Scalabrin will hardly be the one to discourage you.

Wistful for an era when being well-born, landed, and Italian coincided with a life of little exertion, she runs her eight-room bed-and-breakfast with a light touch. Some might call her style disinterested, but it is the reluctance of the villa's mistress to involve herself, her melancholy remove, that is so engaging. And chic.

Though not the work of Palladio, Scalabrin's house, located 15 miles south of Padua, incorporates an alluring and hardworking device identified with the architect. *Barchesse*—arcaded barns—are attached to the estate's residential block, designed as places to do farmwork that were out-of-doors yet protected. Today, they set the mood of a stay here: curtains of vines sweep the ground, an AirPort Internet terminal sits defunct in a corner, and winged garden furniture looks as if it was designed by the same madman who created Peggy Guggenheim's eyeglasses.

What does one call Vescovana? A town? A village? A hamlet? None of these satisfactorily suggests the place, which has a single main artery, flanked by the sort of houses—cubic, stuccoed, unlovely—that no Italian province has the monopoly on. It takes 90

A staircase at Villa Pisani.

seconds to drive through Vescovana before it dissolves into fields. Commercial activity is confined to a fruit stand and a *caffè-tabacchi*. Whether because of these limitations or despite them, Vescovana is charming.

The villa sits unbothered in a country setting that features a celebrated garden, all rigorous symmetry and geometry, planted in the 19th century by the last Countess Pisani—the colorful and cultivated Evelina. Born to an English doctor who treated Byron, and a Turkish mother reputedly raised in the sultan's harem, Evelina ordered her bulbs from England and received everyone from Henry James to one Margaret Symonds. In 1893, Symonds published *Days Spent on a Doge's Farm*, her diary of holidays at the villa: "The garden is the sole creation of a modern English fancy, and has nothing to do with the old Pisani nobles. It is natural that the strong English instincts of the new Contessa should have made her shudder at the general sunbaked and unsoftened aspect of this huge farmhouse…She needed flowers, as English women do, and shade…then the roses would grow and the birds would come."

Breakfast is taken in full view of Evelina's chef d'oeuvre, though Signora Scalabrin might try a little harder with the morning meal. The garden is seen to yet better advantage from the guest rooms, especially Irina, which is laden with needlepoint, velvet, satin, and lace, and has enchanting allegorical frescoes by Palladio's collaborator Zelotti.

Critic Witold Rybczynski settles the score between the two artists in *The Perfect House*. "There is no doubt that Veronese…was the more accomplished painter," he writes. "But in many ways Zelotti was a better decorator…more sensitive to the architecture and more interested in the purely ornamental aspects of his art." Stay at Pisani and never choose.

HOTEL VILLA CIPRIANI AND ALBERGO AL SOLE, ASOLO

In the foothills of the Dolomites, 40 miles northwest of Venice, Asolo projects prosperity, privilege, self-satisfaction. It has a lot to crow about, so the air of superiority is forgiven. The triumph of Asolo is what Guido Rosada, an archaeologist from the University of Padua, calls its rational simplicity. Certainly it is gorgeous, a snaking medieval burg with two good hotels, Albergo al Sole and Hotel Villa Cipriani; a Roman past; pitched, arcaded streets; a lively café life, centering on the 1796 Caffè Centrale; and a cultural legacy bequeathed by Robert and Elizabeth Barrett Browning, Eleonora Duse, Gabriele D'Annunzio, and Freya Stark. All were compelled to live in Asolo.

Pope Pius X received the tonsure in the town's cathedral in 1850, and a famous antiques fair is held the second Sunday of every month, except July and August. Landscapes seen from the walled perimeter put you in mind of Titian. Municipal fathers are happy to spend whatever it takes to keep Asolo sparkling. Palladio's Villa Barbaro is minutes away. Others of his masterpieces—Godi, Cornaro, Emo— are within easy driving distance.

You can walk to everything you want to see in Asolo from both the Albergo al Sole and Villa Cipriani, though deciding between them is no simple coin-toss. A country house once owned by Robert Browning, the 31-room Cipriani was managed by Giuseppe Cipriani, founder of Hotel Villa Cipriani, before being acquired by Starwood. Hidden behind a high wall on the edge of town, Villa Cipriani is rather fuddy-duddy, a quality I actually admire. The retro bar has grid paneling, equestrian prints, and the stylish undersize armchairs native to this genus of hotel. Hotel Villa Cipriani's terraced garden fades into a meadow, and the views are of the Asolan countryside. Life came cruelly close to imitating art, or at least to the Anita Brookner novel I was reading, when I spied two bitter old English birds supping wordlessly on chateaubriand with béarnaise sauce in the dining room.

Lunch on the patio at Villa Cipriani, in Asolo.

*Hotel Villa Cipriani's terraced garden fades into a meadow,
and the views are of the Asolan countryside*

Villa Cipriani at dusk.

73

Al Sole is younger, looser, fresher, perkier, and cheaper by about half. It also feels more integrated into the life of Asolo, because of its central location. Folded into a freestanding, foursquare 19th-century building with a rosy ocher façade, the hotel has 23 rooms, but if you can't secure 101, 102, 201, or 202, juggle your dates so you can. Asolo is all about the views, and these are the only accommodations that look directly on the town. Snappy service and bathrooms with slipper tubs have put the Cipriani on notice.

It would take a week to eat your way through Asolo's destination restaurants (while perfectly okay, Al Sole's is not one of them). At Hosteria Ca' Derton's annex, I built a late supper of herby rabbit terrine with marinated vegetables; *bigoli* (thick-strand pasta) with duck sauce; Asiago, served at three stages of ripeness with onion jam, green apple, and mustard fruits; and another, grassy cow's-milk cheese, Morlacco, that is made only for a short time in summer. Barolos are a third what you pay at home for the same wine by an inferior producer. At Al Bacaro the next day, I ordered a salume board of prosciutto, speck, lardo, mortadella, porchetta, pancetta, and soppressa, then sailed on to a giant plate of *trippa alla veneziana*, whispering nutmeg and bound with lots of creamy melted onions.

Asolo must have more jewelry shops per capita than even Rome. (The town's population is 8,836, basically what it has been since 1951. A good sign, it means Asolans aren't fleeing to the cities and the Milanese aren't eating up all the real estate for second homes.) The boutiques sell not costume stuff but $155,000 diamond bands, as at Antichità Conzada Nascimbene. Berdusco Daniele has Ballantyne cashmere polo shirts in colors—poison green with a pink collar—that there is no point trying to find anywhere else. Marta Stradiotto makes custom shirts with princess seams—for men. Opulent home-furnishing silks are woven on chattering wooden looms at Tessoria Asolana. Linens are embroidered by angels at Scuola Asolana Antico Ricamo di Anna Milani, founded by the Brownings' son, Pen.

I could go on, and will, because I still haven't mentioned the one shop I fell for hardest. I can die tomorrow without stepping foot in another lighting shop because I know none could please me more than Ernesto Di Lazzari's, which sells the ceramic saucer-shaped ceiling fixtures on pulleys that you've admired

A southwestern view of the countryside outside Asolo, from the terraced garden at Villa Cipriani.

Manicured gardens at Villa Giona, in San Pietro in Cariano.

in a million Italian kitchens. It's another reason to go to Asolo, if you need one.

VILLA GIONA, SAN PIETRO IN CARIANO

Despite her annoyingly arid personality and the fact that I witnessed a cigarette ash almost fall from her lips into a pot of risotto (this was 20 years ago, at the cooking school she then ran in Bologna), I am a huge fan of Marcella Hazan. So imagine my excitement when, having reserved a room at Villa Giona, a hotel and vineyard in Valpolicella country outside Verona, I learned that Marcella's son Giuliano had hosted a celebration for her 80th birthday there in 2004. If Giona was good enough for Marcella and all her fancy international friends—Adrienne Vittadini! Bryant Gumbel!!—how could it not be good enough for me?

It was and it wasn't. Giona is a place of which Americans in less blasé times would have said, "This is what we come to Europe for," the remark reflecting an uncomplicated appreciation of the villa's age (it was built in the 16th century), gorgeous patina, and crazy grandeur.

Do you long for simpler trips and times, to shed your inured self? Then consider Giona, where potted lemon trees and a phalanx of garden statues with their noses whacked off invite you to reconnect with your traveling past. Remember thrilling to an attic guest room where you had to crouch to see out the ocular windows? Or dining on a curtained loggia? Giona renews these pleasures.

The romantic loggia was almost, but not quite, enough to make up for the breakfast (Alpine Lace, bread that tastes like it was made in a machine— what would Marcella say?) and the absence of wine in the mini-bars. Not only was I in a region of Italy whose identity comes largely from wine, but the villa grows grapes that are made into a Bordeaux-style *vino da tavola* by Allegrini. When room service finally got it together, the white it delivered was from Umbria, as if Soave weren't right down the road.

Though Giona will always lack the infrastructure of a full-tilt hotel, I'm sure I would have received better attention if it hadn't been in the jaws of a wedding. With persistence, I dug out a staffer who produced recommendations for two amazing restaurants. Amid a vineyard in Fumane, Enoteca della Valpolicella serves the truest, most chaste risotto—flavored with red wine or herbs, but never the two together—and polenta so silky it flowed through the tines of my fork. At Dalla Rosa Alda, in the barely awake hilltop village of San Giorgio Ingannapoltron, I ticked two items off my checklist of local dishes: *patissada de caval*, horsemeat spiced with cinnamon, nutmeg, and cloves and braised in Amarone, a jammy red made from partially dried grapes; and *pissota*, a lemony olive-oil cake baked by a *nonna*, in a pan with an overturned bowl in the middle to obtain the signature ring shape.

When I go back to Giona, it will be to stay in Mantegna. The hotel's only (duplex) accommodation in a *barchessa*, it has a brick floor, roughly plastered walls, 1778 engravings depicting the stations of the cross, and a surprisingly successful mix of heavily carved antique furniture and Corbusier seating. I'll also return to take Giuliano Hazan's cooking course. But however much he insists that he and his mother are not the same person, for me he will always be her in pants, with a beard and without the pearls. If you want a hit of the old Marcella purity and clarity, now that she has retired to Longboat Key, Giuliano's the next-best thing.

BYBLOS ART HOTEL VILLA AMISTÀ, CORRUBBIO DI NEGARINE

This peacock of a debutante is down the road from Giona, but they are so opposed, they could be on different planets. The 60-room Amistà was conceived

Villa Giona's romantic breakfast loggia.

the former ballroom, now the lobby, a monumental space with coffered wooden ceilings, a ravishing terrazzo floor, and exquisite trompe l'oeil moldings.

Most of the guest-room furniture—including cartoonishly baroque headboards in crazy colors—was designed by Alessandro Mendini, whose work is housed in New York's MOMA. Many of Mendini's designs for the hotel are part of the retail collection Byblos Casa. At the villa, descriptive notices tell guests everything they want to know about the chairs they're sitting on, though good luck if you don't read Italian.

Fancy food like foie gras with violet cream is the last thing I go to Italy to eat, but if I did I wouldn't look further than Amistà's restaurant. I was much happier in Verona at Locanda Castelvecchio, where an epic trolley of roasted and boiled meats is accompanied by *salsa verde*, mustard fruits, grated horseradish, and a curious, porridge-like sauce, *pearà*, made with fresh bread crumbs. Antica Bottega del Vino, also in Verona, is the place for *baccalà vicentina*, a preparation that—however unlikely it seems on paper (salt cod, anchovies, milk…and parmesan)—is the most sophisticated dish in salt-cod cookery. Near Amistà, Trattoria Rosa serves an unreconstructed version of yet another regional specialty, *tagliolini in brodo*, topped with chicken livers.

As a modest trattoria, Rosa is sure of its identity in the Veneto landscape. The same is not true of Amistà, which, even given all the visual fireworks, offers a strangely flat experience. The place is so admiring of Philippe Starck, it already feels old (irony waits for no one). Still, the Amistà has the bones of a good hotel. The right pro could fix it.

as an upstart showcase for modern art and design inserted into a 15th-century villa with pretty gardens and a glamorous swimming pool. The hotel is in the countryside, 15 minutes outside Verona, hence the necessity for an hourly shuttle service that also happens to be efficient and free.

The owners are the family behind Byblos, a ready-to-wear label that had a moment in the eighties but means little now. Out of the spotlight, they launched the Amistà, which features works by Sol LeWitt, Cindy Sherman, Sandro Chia, Robert Indiana, and Takashi Murakami. Among the lighting and furniture are classics by Eero Saarinen, Frank Lloyd Wright, Ettore Sottsass, and Verner Panton. Some of the furnishings are silly, torturously uncomfortable, or both, but it's hard not to crack a smile at Dalí's big kiss of a sofa, cast in the form of lips in homage to Mae West's.

The suites and the public rooms have the lock on the most sensational pieces. The contrast between these and the aristocratic setting is shocking in a good way, at least for the first couple of hours (after that it can seem gimmicky). Giant photographs of nude armies of ghostly women, taken by Vanessa Beecroft during her VB 43 performance pieces, are hung in

CA' ZEN, TAGLIO DI PO

The mailman pulled out through the hissing avenue of poplar trees at Ca' Zen, on the Po River an hour south of Venice, as I pulled in. Elaine Avanzo Westropp Bennett, the bed-and-breakfast's Anglo-Irish owner, normally has a deliciously skeptical sense of humor, but a letter she had received put her in a sour mood. Someone was challenging Ca' Zen's literary pedigree, insisting that Byron never rendezvoused here with Teresa Guiccioli. Alessandro Guiccioli had exiled his sparky wife from Venice to tame her, but she did not cooperate.

Ca' Zen is secreted in the Parco Regionale del Delta del Po, a 70,000-acre puzzle of tidal flats, swamps, rice farms, lagoons, canals, and estuaries.

*The poplar-lined approach to
Ca' Zen, near the Po River Delta.*

79

"Even today," says Avanzo, "this is considered a remote part of Italy." The delta has a brusque, untamable flavor similar to that of France's Camargue, plus good riding, even better biking, and some of the finest fish restaurants in the country.

Built in the early 18th century as a shooting lodge, Ca' Zen ballooned into what Byron knew as a palazzina. The house is fractionally shorter than the 33-foot-wide, 180-foot-long *aia*, or brick threshing terrace, that hugs the south façade. Avanzo's daughter, Maria Adelaide—a leggy beauty, horsewoman, and law-school graduate—will offer to set your breakfast table here, overlooking a 15-acre park. (One morning she spoiled a guest with her personal stash of Fortnum & Mason orange pekoe, cooing, "You look like you'd appreciate it.") Ca' Zen has just seven rooms and a cottage, so even when it's full there's as much danger of crowding as of getting hit by a bus.

The rooms are sentimental repositories of hourglass slipper chairs, pious imagery, flouncy dressing tables, and blackamoors proffering trays of musty potpourri. Most of this trove was handed down to Pericle Avanzo, Elaine's late husband, who taught her the ins and outs of the Venetian kitchen. Served in an intimate dining room with silver domes on the sideboard and a florid, ecclesiastical candelabrum on the chimneypiece, dinner at Ca' Zen is partially prepared over a wood fire, stronger on *primi* (risotto with zucchini, zucchini flowers, and *gamberetti*) and *dolci* (lemon *torta*) than on *secondi* (whole branzino)—and ridiculously copious.

By checkout, Avanzo had answered her doubter in the Byron matter. She wrote the woman how the river that inspired his "Stanzas to the Po" was in Byron's time visible from the *salone*. She also outlined how Ca' Zen had passed from the cuckolded Alessandro Guiccioli to her mother-in-law's family, the Casalicchios, in the 19th century. When her husband's aunt died last year at age 100, Avanzo continued, she was still remembering how the Guicciolis visited the room where Byron had slept even after the house had been sold: "The Casalicchios are the last people to invent such a story: they remain a totally non-frivolous, non-snobbish kind of family, with a much keener interest in their land and children than in a passionate love affair between an English poet—however famous—and young, beautiful, spoiled Teresa! And yet they have always spoken about Byron and Teresa in Ca' Zen with such certainty that I have absolutely no reason to doubt it. Nor has anyone else, until now."

Dinner for two, served in the formal dining room at Ca' Zen, in Taglio di Po.

Ca' Zen's owners, Maria Adelaide and her mother, Elaine Avanzo Westropp Bennett.

The cobblestoned back porch at Ca' Zen.

Travelers' Guide to the Veneto

WHEN TO GO

The Veneto is mild most of the year; winters are damp and can be foggy. Summer, as elsewhere in Italy, is high season: expect a commensurate increase in crowds and, in some cases, prices.

GETTING THERE

Delta flies nonstop to Venice from Atlanta and New York/JFK; US Airways flies nonstop from Philadelphia from May to October. It's almost always cheaper to fly into Milan's Malpensa airport, then drive the roughly two hours to the Veneto. Or take a train from Milan's Central Station to Padua or Vicenza; visit trenitalia.com to get schedules and purchase tickets.

EXPLORING THE VENETO

The flat landscape of the Veneto plain is dramatically offset by the spectacular Dolomite mountains that form the northwestern border of the region. To the west is the vast expanse of Lake Garda, while to the south are the ports and beaches of the Adriatic, which provide a contrast with the area's gently rolling countryside and its many ancient towns.

While in the Veneto...

Asolo ❹
Bassano del Grappa ❸
Belluno ❿
Brenta Canal ❾
Castelfranco Veneto ❺
Conegliano ⓫
Cortina d'Ampezzo ⓭
Euganean Hills ❽
Lake Garda ❷
Padua (Padova) ❼
Treviso ❿
Venice (Venezia) ⓮
Verona ❶
Vicenza ❻

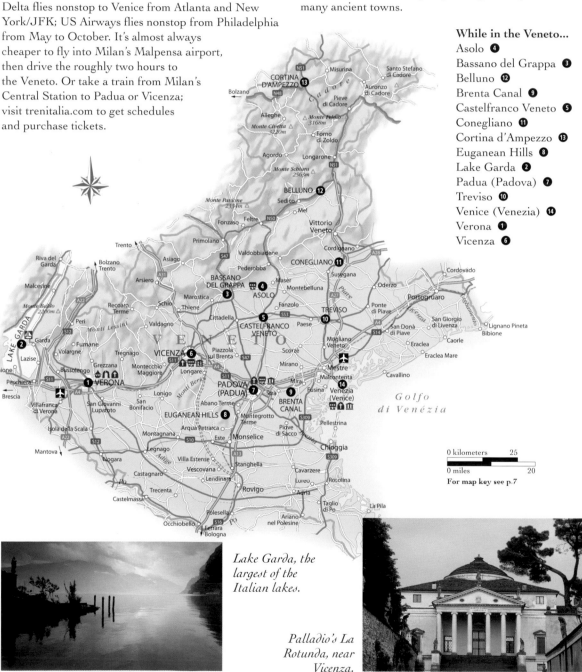

Lake Garda, the largest of the Italian lakes.

Palladio's La Rotunda, near Vicenza.

WHERE TO STAY

Albergo al Sole
33 Via Collegio, Asolo
39-0423/951-332;
albergoalsole.com;
doubles from $$$$$, including
breakfast.

Byblos Art Hotel Villa Amistà
78 Via Cedrare,
Corrubbio di Negarine,
39-045/685-5555;
byblosarthotel.com;
doubles from $$$$$$$.

Ca' Zen
Taglio di Po;
39-0426/346-469;
tenutaca zen.it;
doubles from $$$, including
breakfast.

Hotel Villa Cipriani
298 Via Canova, Asolo;
39-0423/523-411;
starwoodhotels.com;
doubles from $$$$$$$.

Villa Giona
8 Via Cengia, San Pietro in Cariano;
39-045/685-5011;
villagiona.it;
doubles from $$$$$,
including breakfast.

Villa Pisani
19–25 Via Roma, Vescovana;
39-0425/920-016;
villapisani.it;
doubles from $$$$$.

WHERE TO EAT

ASOLO
Al Bacaro
165 Via R. Browning;
39-0423/55-150;
dinner for two $$$$$.

Hosteria Ca' Derton
11 Piazza G. d'Annunzio;
39-0423/ 529-648;
dinner for two $$$$$$$.

*Piazza delle
Erbe, in Verona.*

FUMANE
Enoteca della Valpolicella
45 Via Osan;
39-045/683-9146;
dinner for two $$$$$$$.

SAN GIORGIO INGANNAPOLTRON
Dalla Rosa Alda
4 Via Garibaldi;
39-045/770-1018;
dinner for two $$$$$$$.

VERONA
Antica Bottega del Vino
3 Vicolo Scudo di Francia;
39-045/ 800-4535;
dinner for two $$$$$$$.

Locanda Castelvecchio
21A Corso Castelvecchio;
39-045/803-0097;
dinner for two $$$$$$$.

Trattoria Rosa
21 Via Brennero;
39-045/772-5054;
dinner for two $$$$.

WHERE TO SHOP

ASOLO
Antichità Conzada Nascimbene
186 Via R. Browning;
39-0423/952-784.

Berdusco Daniele
224 Via Regina Cornaro;
39-0423/952-303.

Ernesto di Lazzari
179 Via R. Browning;
39-0423/952-073.

Marta Stradiotto
21 Via D. Alighieri;
39-0423/529-490.

**Scuola Asolana Antico Ricamo di
Anna Milani**
333 Via A. Canova;
39-0423/952-906.

Tessoria Asolana
321 Via A. Canova;
39-0423/952-062.

WHAT TO SEE

Architecture by Andrea di Pietro
della Gondola, known as Palladio
(1508–89), himself a native of
Padua. Villas not to miss are Emo,
Cornaro, and Almerico Capra
(also known as La Rotunda).
Go to cisapalladio.org for maps,
details, and visiting hours, or call
39-0444/323-014.

SEE ALSO
For Venice:
Eat Like a Venetian pp.126–127

Puglia Rustica

WHETHER YOUR TASTES RUN TO 15TH-CENTURY CONVENTS OR 21ST-CENTURY RESORTS, THERE'S NO SHORTAGE OF PURE BEAUTY IN PUGLIA. NOT TO MENTION SOME OF ITALY'S BEST FOOD. BY CHRISTOPHER PETKANAS

Being able to identify the unspoiled destination is a useful talent—as far as it goes. The real trick is catching the unspoiled destination at just the right moment, when rumblings of interest have given rise to a comfortable infrastructure for knowing travelers, but the crowds are at least a few years off. That's Puglia right now.

The heel of the Italian boot, Puglia humbly holds out its rich and varied portfolio of assets. Five hundred miles of Adriatic and Ionian coastline front landscapes—plains in the south, mountains in the north—with a stark, primal, almost troubling beauty. Brilliantly whitewashed towns, their cubic houses locked together like pieces in a puzzle, are a reminder that North Africa is a near neighbor.

Aristocratic cities celebrate the delirious excesses of Baroque architecture.

New hotels so swooningly stylish that they're often destinations in their own right are imaginatively folded into *masserie*, ancient fortified farmhouses. Puglia is also home to Italy's most uncorrupted, brawniest, least known vernacular cuisine. It's a cuisine of the sun, drawing energy from one of the most punishing summer climates on the continent.

Remember Tuscany in the eighties? Umbria in the nineties? This is Puglia's moment. It's a place on the verge.

IL CONVENTO DI SANTA MARIA DI COSTANTINOPOLI, MARITTIMA DI DISO

The news arrived on heavy card stock, cream with solemn *sang de boeuf* lettering. No, it wasn't a royal birth notice.

"Athena McAlpine is happy to announce the opening of Il Convento di Santa Maria di Costantinopoli, a very special bed & breakfast in the southernmost tip of Italy."

It wasn't just the Smythson announcement that caused those who received it to stop in their tracks and call their best girlfriends. There was also the

The 15th-century Masseria San Domenico, in Savelletri di Fasano.

The church façade at Il Convento
di Santa Maria di Costantinopoli,
in Marittima di Diso.

find yourself casually holding or looking at or sitting on is museum quality. Other connoisseurs turned hoteliers might have held back the best things for themselves in some roped-off wing of the house, but not the McAlpines, who saw no reason to have even their own sitting room. No space is off-limits. Ask Lord McAlpine to walk you through the library. You won't have access to a private one like it anytime soon. There are 14 tons of books.

Wags assume that Santa Maria's potent cross-cultural magic is all the work of its celebrated and unlikely master. Not true. Athena McAlpine is one of the new wave of domestic goddesses you've been hearing about. Her husband knows a prize lot of Ethiopian pilgrim staffs when he sees one, but it's Athena who gives them decorative purpose, massing the bony Y-form sticks against the creamy rendered walls of the cloister.

The convent's mistress also knows how to run a house, ordering in reserves of his (Castile) and hers (Artemisia) toiletries from Penhaligon's, choosing the books that go on the night tables (*The Collected Dorothy Parker*, say, plus biographies of Eleanor Roosevelt and Bruce Chatwin), and making sure the cook arrives on time with the savory portion of your breakfast (béchamel and tomatoes enclosed in flaky pastry, from the Marittima bakery).

name. If you read *Harpers & Queen* and those sorts of publications, you know that five years ago Alistair McAlpine—sexagenarian lord, treasurer of the British Conservative Party under Margaret Thatcher, and one of the world's great collectors—married a vivacious Greek beauty who had trained as an actress and was some 30 years his junior. Could this be she? It could.

From Annabel's to the House of Commons to the nail salon at Harvey Nick's, London was gripped by the idea that the McAlpines had opened nine rooms in their 15th-century convent to paying guests. Some just figured it could only mean that Lord McAlpine had lost his considerable fortune (not the case). Others could not understand why the couple had chosen Puglia. Tuscany would have made sense—at least there's a big English community. But a B&B in the deepest, darkest south?

Calling Santa Maria a B&B is like calling Amandari an inn. Located 30 minutes south of Lecce and a half-mile back from the Adriatic, the convent is a dramatic repository for Lord McAlpine's collections of tribal textiles, Moroccan carpets, Nigerian carvings, Aboriginal art, Zulu ceramics, Madrasi paintings on glass, and terra-cotta statuettes of yogis. Much of what you as a guest

In the kitchen at Il Convento.

*The entrance to the Masseria Torre Coccaro,
in Savelletri di Fasano, near Bari.*

With lunch—and laundry service!—included in the room rate, some guests have whispered that Santa Maria may be underselling itself. "What they don't understand is that this is Puglia, not the Amalfi Coast," says Athena McAlpine. In any case, she is not interested in shortcuts. "Some of our beds are so big and elaborate, it takes three people to make them up, and I don't mind if one of those is me. The sheets are ironed twice: first on a board, then finished directly on the bed. It's the only way. The sheets are from Rossella Casa, this amazing shop in Lecce. We didn't have to toss in wine with lunch, but we've built up an incredible cellar, so…as Alistair says, we're not going to let bookkeeping get in the way."

MASSERIA TORRE COCCARO, SAVELLETRI DI FASANO

Because I like antiques and old-fashioned service, and because I have a fear of molded-plastic pod chairs, I'll always choose an old hotel over a new one. So imagine my surprise when I checked into the Torre Coccaro to find trendy graphics and a hip concept that had not meant an abandonment of tradition.

You can tell there are marketing minds at work here. With *masseria* hotels opening in Puglia more quickly than the regional tourist board can pump out press releases trumpeting them, the owners of Coccaro know that success lies in a sharply delineated property that nobody would confuse with any other. While the 33-room resort is much younger and far more laissez-faire than the San Domenico (*page 95*) and definitely livelier than Il Melograno (*page 91*) it offers a bit more structure and diversion than Borgo San Marco (*page 92*).

Indeed, filling the day is no hardship at Coccaro, which has a well-designed cooking program and a sensational one-of-a-kind Aveda spa dazzlingly inserted in a grotto. You can conk out under a *palapa* on the "beach" (a pool with one of those gimmicky but amusing "shorelines"), or in a hammock strung across a path between an almond and a pomegranate tree in the vast fruit and vegetable garden. Or settle into the pastel petit four of an 18th-century chapel and say a little prayer that the heat will let up. Local girls still dream of getting married in this tiny pink-and-blue confection.

If all that sounds too much like work, you can simply collapse in your room—which resembles the

Crowds in Piazza Sant'Oronzo, in Lecce.

home of a very stylish, visually aware farmer—and admire the decoration. Nos. 21 and 22 are the most desirable doubles, 19 and 24 the best junior suites. They all have nearly double-height tray-vaulted ceilings; glassy, deliciously cold stone floors; and bathrooms that wed charm to function. The furnishings are ratcheted-up, idealized versions of things that have been kicking around the Italian countryside forever, from painted wardrobes to bobbin-pedestal tables. Headboards borrow their design from shutters, the sheets are crisp hemstitched linen (the only way to survive summer in Puglia), and the crunchy cotton coverlets are by Blanc d'Ivoire. Starched white organdy curtains roll up rather than pull to the side, and giltwood mirrors are draped by the thoughtful housekeeper with olive branches. Whoever the farmer is, he certainly knows about color. As soon as I have a minute I'm going to redo my New York bedroom in straw, cream, gray-blue, and oxblood.

I'll also be making the *aperitivo* nibble I learned to prepare one morning when I wandered into the hotel kitchen. The chef called me over to the stove, where he was frying unrehydrated dried fava beans in very hot olive oil. He served them that evening, salted, with a brittle white wine, and they were as fantastically

The coastline at Polignano a Mare, on Puglia's Adriatic coast.

Piazza Vittorio Emanuele, in Cisternino.

The Basilica di San Nicola, in Bari.

connections (lots of nail-biting lunch talk of Jeremy Irons and whether he'll be signing with HBO).

Of course, Il Melograno didn't become famous just by being first. The hotel is a spectacular labyrinth. Until you get the hang of it, you don't always know where you are or where you're going, which lends your acquaintanceship with the place a beguiling element of mystery. The main courtyard is as big as a public piazza and veiled in the erotic, sugary scent of jasmine. Only birdsong and a gardener scratching around in his flower boxes interrupt the silence.

The gaze of diners in the sunken poolside loggia is on the same level as the water, a lovely conceit. The breakfast buffet is so elaborate, so copious, that two enormous tables are needed to display all the flatbreads, platters of fragrant white peaches and baseball-sized figs, and flaky sour-cherry turnovers. The restaurant features silver chargers, tuxedoed waiters, breathtakingly high prices, and good if unsensational versions of local specialties: *panzotti*, plate-sized ravioli, is here filled with ricotta and walnuts and topped with chopped fresh tomatoes. Sprinkled throughout the hotel are old maps, engravings, and a dotty assortment of *pugliese*

crunchy and satisfying as you would imagine a fried unrehydrated dried fava bean to be. The chef acquitted himself again the next day with a dish of tender cavatelli, white beans, and sweet thumbnail-sized mussels, all in a bonus puddle of wonderfully starchy broth.

Of course, there aren't a dozen new hotels in Italy as fresh and original as Torre Coccaro. But it is exciting to imagine what it might beget.

IL MELOGRANO, MONOPOLI

Before the San Domenico swaggered onto the scene, Il Melograno was the only status option if you had your heart set on staying in a *masseria* in Puglia. People still perk up when you mention it, partly because Il Melograno is such a legend (it bowed in 1987) and partly because it's a member of Relais & Châteaux. The property's owners were indeed brave pioneers, but they seem dangerously slow to react to competing hotels that have opened since they first led the way.

And yet you can't count Il Melograno out. It has a devoted constituency, from rich Greeks over for a quick weekend, to lean and mean signore of a certain age (with their puppy-dog husbands), to fortyish couples from England with vague Hollywood

Diners at Osteria Perricci, in Monopoli.

91

*The church at Borgo
San Marco, Fasano.*

antiques, some of which you might kill for, and some of which are for sale. I'm sure I should have struck a deal for that giant marquetry urn in the salon.

With so much to recommend it, where is Il Melograno going wrong? Like dowagers who neglect to refresh their face powder, the 37 rooms are looking tired. And you know something's up when the front-desk manager snaps at you over the phone, "I'm alone at the moment. Can you call back?"

When Il Melograno started, it had the field to itself. Now it's time to play catch-up.

BORGO SAN MARCO, FASANO

I was checked into Borgo San Marco and shown around for an hour by an excitable wild-haired man whom I assumed was the owner but who turned out to be…the gardener.

"How long has the *masseria* been in your family?" I asked as we toured the chapel, where touch-up work was being carried out on a magnificent 17th-century fresco.

"*Mia famiglia*?" the gardener laughed, pointing through the chapel door at the immense courtyard. There stood a patrician man in his late forties, Alessandro Amati. You didn't have to be a genius to figure out he was San Marco's owner. It was late evening, and he was wrapping up a cell-phone conversation about the price carobs had brought that day. Amati grows carobs, figs, and almonds, but he is best known as an olive-oil baron. Staying known among Puglia's crowded stable of producers of first-quality, ever more specialized olive oils is no part-time job. A museum devoted to the subject, created by Amati at neighboring Masseria Sant'Angelo de' Graecis, helps keep his Borgo San Marco oil out front.

"Built by the Knights of Malta in the fifteenth century, San Marco was uninhabitable when I inherited it in 1981, but it took me until now to figure out what to do with the place," says Amati. "I already had enough houses, so there was no point in restoring it for me and my small family. Besides, I wanted the property to pay for itself." Transforming San Marco into a 15-room hotel gave Amati the reason he needed to rehabilitate it. The hotel offers everything you want in the *masseria* experience—the monumental foursquare architecture, the piquant air of exoticism—but with a difference. San Marco is the bohemian *masseria alternativa*. Guest rooms surrounding the former farmyard are done in sheer embroidered-patchwork textiles from Egypt and

in rich man–poor man combinations of baby-blue silk grosgrain and tobacco-colored linen burlap. Mattress platforms and headboards (crowned with finials modeled on San Marco's roof ornaments) are of plastered masonry and, this being Puglia, slathered in whitewash. Canal tiles fashioned into wall lights and amber beads strung into curtains that chatter in the breeze dot the i's of a look that's bright, fresh, and just a tad enigmatic. Knowing that some people would find traditional furnishings less of a challenge, Amati has appointed rooms in the main house with painted iron beds, night tables with blousy pom-pom–fringed skirts, and antique walnut armoires.

As at all *masseria* hotels, eating is a central part of the experience. Amati says his most important hire for the property was Peppino Palmisano, who ran a popular restaurant in Fasano and rose to local celebrity on the wings of his eggplant Parmesan, a dish with roots in Puglia, and oven-roasted sea bream

A Bari street scene.

An antique-painting gallery in Bari.

with black olives. If they're not on the menu, he'll happily make them for you the next day. The San Marco is that kind of hotel.

MASSERIA SAN DOMENICO, SAVELLETRI DI FASANO

Of all of Puglia's *masseria* properties, San Domenico is the one that feels most like a destination resort—make that a luxury destination resort. While the competition pretends to luxury, only the San Domenico, which opened in 1996, truly delivers. Before going to Puglia I assumed it was too much of a backwater to have a slickly run, you-want-it-you-got-it–style hotel. I don't like to be proven wrong, but the San Domenico can hold its own, and more.

With a dead straight, magnificently groomed 1,600-foot drive leading to a pair of electronic gates, you know the P&S (privileged and special) factor is going to be pretty high even before the 15th-century *masseria* looms into sight. On the way to your room, you can't help remarking on the grandiose sense of space. Each courtyard seems more massive than

the one before it, and the sea is teasingly glimpsed over the treetops. The other thing you notice is the obsessive tidiness. There's not a blade of grass out of place. Wow, you think, am I going to be happy here or what?

Wealthy northern Italians are. Historically, as everyone knows, many Italians from the north have a complex relationship with the south. Their attraction to it is tempered by wariness and—how else to say it?—feelings of superiority.

What they like about the San Domenico is the slightly whitewashed version of the *masseria* hotel experience the place offers. It's Puglia without tears. Everyone dresses for dinner and exudes an air of bourgeois self-satisfaction. Children not yet in their teens have their own cell phones, the men all sport Panerai watches, and some of the women have big hair. No one shouts "*Ciao, bella!*" across the bar or minds that a Negroni costs $18 (it's a very good Negroni). There's a perfume war going on, and Fendissime seems to be winning.

While the 50 guest rooms play to the San Domenico's core clientele, who place comfort above looks, I have to say they were a bit on the plain side for my taste. A touch of decorative provocation would go a long way here. Those offering the best value are the 14 junior suites, whose patios give glamorously onto ancient olive groves that seem to stretch to infinity. With just a bit of tweaking, by the way, those cute little patios could fulfill their promise of privacy.

Not that anyone spends much time hanging around their rooms. In the great tradition of upscale Italian resorts, many guests are content to park themselves beside the saltwater pool, oil up (skipping the sunblock, *certo*), and stay put the entire day. The free-form pool, landscaped with boulders and palms and spiky vegetation, is somebody's improbable idea of an oasis. It's hokey, but it works.

Only when the sun is at less than maximum tanning strength do you see anyone on the new 18-hole golf course or at the spa, the best in the region. The 2,220-square-foot knockout facility has an encyclopedic menu of treatments, many of them using hydrotherapy or Carita products. It would take weeks and many thousands of euros to work through them all. Guests do manage to unstick themselves from the pool for perfectly okay plates of fresh egg noodles with tomato sauce, green beans, and grated ricotta. Personally, I found the food at the San Domenico too fancy. But I'm sure I was the only one.

The Cattedrale di
San Sabino, Bari.

Travelers' Guide to Puglia

GETTING THERE

There are a number of direct flights to Bari from New York, Miami and Toronto. Alternatively, fly to Rome or Milan and pick up a connecting flight to Bari or Brindisi, or travel via London's Gatwick or Stansted airports or Frankfurt in Germany.

EXPLORING PUGLIA

Puglia is the "heel" of the Italian boot, and the spectacular Gargano Peninsula, with its lovely coastline, is its "spur." Just below Gargano is the fertile Tavoliere plain, and further south a series of plateaux (the Murge) descends towards the dry Salentine Peninsula and the Adriatic. Puglia has glorious architecture, particularly the chuches and castles of the north. The curious *trulli* houses in central Puglia, the florid baroque of Lecce, and the Levantine atmosphere of its merchant cities complete the picture of an ancient land subject to more influences from outside the Italian peninsula than from within it.

While in Puglia...

Alberobello	❶	Lecce	❼
Bari	❷	Lucera	❽
Castel del Monte	❸	Otranto	❾
Galatina	❹	Ruvo di Puglia	❿
Gargano Peninsula	❺	Taranto	⓫
Isole Tremiti	❻	Trani	⓬
		Troia	⓭

WHERE TO STAY

Hotels without description appear in this story

Borgo San Marco
33 Contrada Sant'Angelo, Fasano;
39-080/439-5757;
borgosanmarco.it;
doubles from $\$$$\$$.

Il Convento di Santa Maria di Costantinopoli
Via Convento, Marittima di Diso;
44-7736/362-328;
doubles from $\$$$\$$$\$$.

Il Melograno
345 Contrada Torricella, Monopoli;
39-080/690-9030;
melograno.com;
doubles from $\$$$\$$$\$$.

La Sommità Relais Culti
An intimate, 10-room retreat in the town of Ostuni's restored Palazzo Palmieri.
7 Via Scipione Petrarolo;
39-0831/305-925;
lasommita.it;
doubles from $\$$$\$$$\$$.

0 kilometers 50
0 miles 25
For map key see p. 6

Castel del Monte, on the summit of a low hill.

A street in Vieste, on the Gargano Peninsula.

Masseria Montelauro

Many of the 29 rooms have their own entrances to the garden, where guests mingle over evening aperitivi.
S.P. Otranto, Uggiano, Località Montelauro; 39-0836/806-203; masseriamontelauro.it; doubles from $$$.

Masseria Pagani

An orange grove scents the air at this farmhouse in Lecce, where late Italian tenor Tito Schipa summered in the 1940s.
Via Leopizzi Filomena, Nardò, Lecce; 39-0833/872-524; agriturismo.it/masseriapagani; doubles from $$.

Masseria San Domenico

379 Strada Litoranea, Savelletri di Fasano; 39-080/482-7769; masseriasandomenico.com; doubles from $$$$.

Masseria Torre Coccaro

8 Contrada Coccaro, Savelletri di Fasano; 39-080/482-9310; masseriatorrecoccaro.com; doubles from $$.

Masseria Torre Maizza

This 16th-century watchtower has 26 spacious guest rooms. Suites feature fireplaces and satin sheets.
Contrada Coccaro, Savelletri di Fasano; 39-0804/827-838; masseriatorremaizza.com; doubles from $$$$.

WHERE TO EAT

Throughout the region, the antipasto is fun because you don't know how many dishes you'll be getting, or what they're going to be. In general, expect deep-fried veal balls, which taste like gunshot; zucchini-and-ricotta-plumped fritters; and breaded and fried balls of ricotta forte.

Al Fornello da Ricci, Ceglie Messapica

Antonella Ricci is a talented chef, but a conflicted one, offering cucumber mousse for the Michelin inspectors and grano pestato *in rabbit-flecked tomato sauce for disciples of* cucina povera.
Contrada Montevicoli; 39-0831/377-104; dinner for two $$$$.

Alle Due Corti, Lecce

The menu is in a dialect most Italians find impenetrable, which tells you everything you need to know about this restaurant's commitment to pugliese culinary traditions. Loud, bright, and frill-less, this is the place for real-deal tajeddha *(layered potatoes, rice, and mussels) and* ciceri e tria *(boiled and crisp-fried pasta with chickpeas).*
1 Corte dei Giugni; 39-0832/242-223; dinner for two $$.

Aria Corte Sapori Antichi, Marittima di Diso

With bridles and yokes supplying the decoration, this village restaurant is an unprepossessing monument to down-home pugliese cooking. Antipasti swing from silky fried peppers with capers and mint to timbales of fresh anchovies with tomatoes and bread crumbs. Athena and Alistair McAlpine ate here almost daily for months while restoring their convent.
32 Via Roma; 39-0836/920-272; dinner for two $$.

Whitewashed and sunbaked trulli in Alberobello.

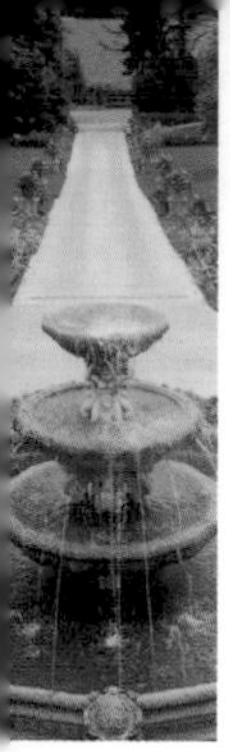

Il Frantoio, Ostuni
If you like excess, you'll love this storybook masseria, *whose eight-course dinner makes it a must-stop for collectors of Eating Experiences. Like many degustation menus, Il Frantoio's goes on too long, with authoritative dishes (chickpea soup with fresh borage pasta) jumbled in with lesser ones (green beans in cheese baskets). Still, the goodwill is palpable, and it's hard to argue with an all-women kitchen. Thirteen homely guest rooms are several notches above those of other* agriturismo masserie.
S.S. 16, Km 874;
39-0831/330-276;
dinner for two, with wine, $$$.

Macelleria Demola Vincenzo and Arrosteria del Vicoletto, Cisternino
This town's butchers don't merely sell meat—they roast it and serve it, whether right in their shops or, as at Demola, in a neighboring arrosteria. *The drill's the same for housewives shopping for dinner as for those who continue on to Vicoletto: step up to the counter, chat with the butcher about what's best, and make your choice. People headed for the* arrosteria *mix it up with a pork chop, a scallop of veal with a bread crumb–parsley–Parmesan filling, a couple of sausages, and a handful of* gnomarelli. *Mamma threads them all onto skewers, then walks them up to Vicoletto, where you take a seat on a hard bench at a bare table while your order sputters in the wood-burning oven.*
2 (*macelleria*) and 16 (*arrosteria*) Via Giulio II;
39-080/444-8063;
dinner for two $$.

Osteria Perricci, Monopoli
Puglia has a more evolved antipasto culture than perhaps any other region in Italy. At proto-rustic Perricci, you can't get away with less than salt-cod fritters, boiled octopus, anchovies, tomato bruschetta, and raw cuttlefish. For full-blown antipasto, multiply the number of dishes by two—then follow with a buttery grilled sarago.
1 Via Orazio Comes;
39-080/937-2208;
dinner for two $$.

Ristorante ai Portici, Martina Franca
The custom of having crudités for dessert never made the crossing to the United States. Neither did gnomarelli*—bits of liver, lung, heart, or spleen bound in intestines. They're for fans of organ meats but also for those who've sworn never to eat them. At Portici, on one of the most romantic* piazze *in Puglia, the brochettes are part of an* arrosto misto *that includes sausage and baby kid chops. If you want to look like you belong, finish with raw vegetables and dip them in salt. If you want to look like you just got off the plane, dip them in olive oil.*
6 Piazza Maria Immacolata;
39-080/480-1702;
dinner for two $$.

Ristorante Alberosole, Bari
Alberosole exudes prosperity, with bankers in Brioni suits dining on pea pod–shaped pasta with anchovies, pine nuts, and mint. The dining room has a contemporary feel that marries handsomely with the old stone floor and cathedral ceiling.
13 Corso Vittorio Emanuele;
39-080/523-5446;
lunch for two $$$.

Trattoria Cucina Casareccia, Lecce
Casareccia's version of that most emblematic of pugliese dishes—braised wild chicory with a purée of (boiled) dried fava beans—is epic. The trattoria used to be a private house, and it still feels like one, with patterned cement floor tiles, paneling, and a desk piled with bills and letters. I've lived in France for 22 years, but it took traveling to Puglia to hook me on horsemeat, which is sweeter than beef and is done here in a salsa piccante.
19 Via Colonnello Costadura;
39-0832/245-178;
dinner for two $$.

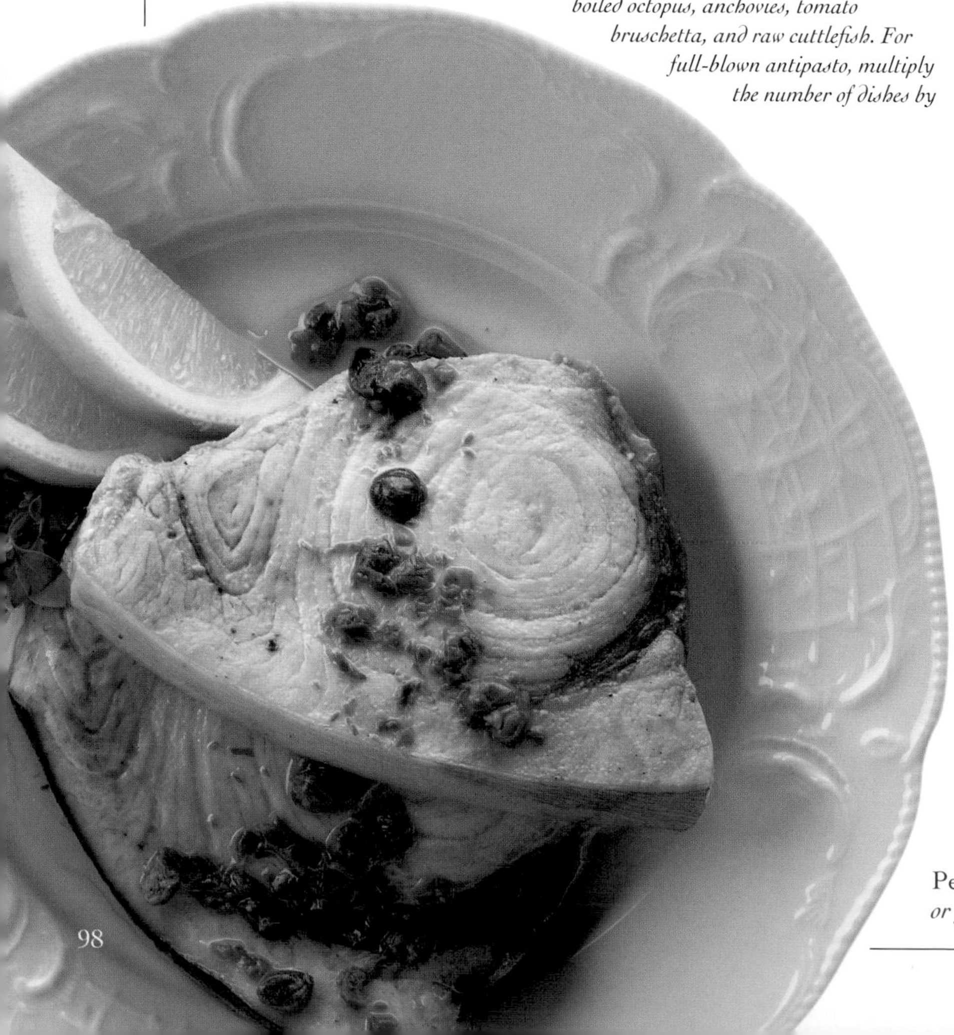

Pesce spada—*swordfish pan-fried or grilled with lemon and oregano.*

LECCE: A BAROQUE EYEFUL

Lecce is famous for some of the most rapturous and energetic Baroque architecture in Italy, but what nobody tells you about the city is how young it is. I drove in on a hot steamy night in late June, and every café, every storefront was draped with the supple, preening form of a languorous *ragazzo* or *ragazza* practicing the twin arts of *far niente* and *la dolce vita*.

For first-time visitors, Lecce is a revelation. Beginning in the 1500's, dozens of churches and palazzi were erected in local honey-colored stone in a cutthroat spirit of ornamental one-upmanship. The softness of the stone encouraged the carving of voluptuous scampering putti, caryatids, portal crests, masks, garlands, fruit, corbels hoisted by

Detail from the Baroque façade of Lecce's Santa Croce church.

grotesques, and lyrical scrolls. For anyone strolling the city's golden pedestrian streets today, the buildings are pure eye candy.

Don't agonize over where to stay: Starwood's Patria Palace Hotel (13 Piazzetta Gabriele Riccardi; 39-0832/245-111; starwood.com; doubles from $$) is the only game in town. The renovation of the old, distinguished palace is sadly clunky, but the service is expert, and though you'd never guess it from the hard look of Atenze, the hotel's restaurant, the food is amazing, according to Athena McAlpine. The second-floor rooms with little Juliet balconies and bang-on views of the rose window of the Basilica di Santa Croce are the ones to snag.

BOOMTOWN BARI IS BACK

Travelers wanting proof that Bari, the capital of Puglia, is no longer also the region's purse-snatching and car-break-in capital should talk to Roberta Guerra Watkins. In the late 1990's, Watkins—the well-born part owner of the hotel Il Melograno—moved to the Città Vecchia district with her Canadian husband and their two children to participate in Bari's great civic renaissance. In the

years before that, she says, she wouldn't have set foot in the place without a bodyguard.

"Thanks to our mayor, who envisions Bari as a kind of Italian Barcelona, everything has changed," notes Watkins. "The Old Town, where I live, used to be a ghetto, like the Bronx or Naples, only worse. If you dared go in, you were doomed to be robbed. But after an ambitious cleanup campaign, and commercial initiatives that gave breaks to young

people starting small businesses, the neighborhood is now full of restaurants, shops, and cafés. It's unrecognizable."

The Cattedrale di San Sabino and Basilica di San Nicola are important examples of Italian Romanesque architecture. The Old Town is a warren of immaculate cobblestoned alleyways like those in a Moroccan medina. The street life is rich, not to mention entertaining. The good women of the neighborhood think nothing of doing their ironing, rolling their pasta, and plucking their mustaches outside their front doors.

Bari makes a perfect day trip from Monopoli, Fasano, or Savelletri di Fasano. (It's also where you fly to from Milan, Rome, or London.) None of the city's hotels match the thrill of staying in a *masseria*, but if you want to spend the night, look no further than the Palace Hotel Bari (13 Via Lombardi; 39-080/521-6551; palacehotelbari.it; doubles from $$$).

Bari Castle, in the Città Vecchia district.

Overnight Sensations

IN FLORENCE, WHERE YOU CHOOSE TO STAY SPEAKS VOLUMES ABOUT WHO YOU ARE. TAKE YOUR PICK FROM THIS PRIMER ON GREAT HOTELS THAT MAKE THE DESIRED STATEMENT. BY CHRISTOPHER PETKANAS

Florence is such an engaging and romantic city, it hardly matters where you lay your head, right? Anyone who thinks that has obviously never spent the night in one of these long-lived, long-loved hotels. Their styles, from reassuringly traditional to briskly contemporary, couldn't be more dissimilar.

Neither could their constituencies, who swing all the way from scholars of E. M. Forster to subscribers to *Next*. You can spend your whole life looking for the perfect Florence hotel. Or you can read on.

GRAND HOTEL VILLA MEDICI

THE RETRO REDOUBT Though I should have been drafting a lawsuit—my bags had been left out on the tarmac in Milan for two hours in the rain—all I could think about was my reservation at the Grand Hotel Villa Medici. The place has my idea of a great reputation: it's known for being princely, stylish, and slightly démodé. But delays caused by a violent storm had made it almost certain that I would not be spending the night in Florence.

A room at the Hotel Helvetia & Bristol, in Florence.

Photographs by Edina van der Wyck 101

Then an angel appeared, in the form of the rare pilot who hadn't taken advantage of the bad weather and gone home to a spaghetti dinner and mamma's bosom. When the skies cleared, he flew me and a couple of other stragglers to Florence. It was midnight before I finally pulled up to the Medici, an early-18th-century palazzo that became a luxury hotel in 1961, but the night manager was there to greet me with an easy smile. "Welcome!" he exclaimed, knowing who I was without asking. "No need to register right away. You have two friends waiting for you in the bar. Why don't you relax and join them for a drink?"

You have to hand it to a hotel that can make you forget that your three favorite Borrelli linen suits have just been reduced to used paper towels. The barman matched the kindliness and efficiency of the manager with a model Negroni (the trick is the vermouth—it must be sweet). Urns of gladioli and little wedding reception–style bouquets had been set out on the tables, and piped-in, terrifically schlocky old-school Italian pop music filled the bar. As more of the Medici's decorative details began to kick in—effete blackamoors, life-sized ceramic greyhounds balancing potted ferns, ceilings painted with cloudscapes—it hit me that the hotel had not been oversold.

Size and location also recommend the Medici, a haven for travelers of a certain age with a layered knowledge of Florence and no need of a scene. With 103 guest rooms, the hotel is neither so big that the concierge looks at you blankly no matter how many dinner reservations he's made for you, nor so small that you always have the same nattering neighbors at breakfast. The hotel is a block from the Arno and a 10-minute, million-dollar walk from the Duomo. In other words, it's perfectly central, minus the notorious foot traffic that ensnarls many of the city's best-situated hotels.

A charmingly biomorphic swimming pool is snuggled in a walled garden furnished with teak lounges. Seduced by the garden as a setting for lunch, but not expecting much of the food, I was knocked out by white-bean bruschetta draped with satiny, nearly liquid ribbons of *lardo*, creamy fatback that had been infused with herbs in a marble box. Room-service breakfast had arrived with a lid (porcelain, not

paper) thoughtfully placed atop my *caffè doppio*. When I called for the morning papers, and forgot to remove the Do Not Disturb sign, the bellhop shyly apologized for bothering me.

Only in Italy.

HOTEL SAVOY

THE DESIGN DIVA Is there any more glamorous introduction to Florence than the Hotel Savoy? Not likely. Arrive by cab and you are greeted by a young man who does not look the least bit ridiculous in a top hat and long, dove gray coat. Either he's the greatest actor since Mastroianni or he really is thrilled to see you. Folded discreetly in his hand is a

At the Savoy, the doorman knows your name.

Set on a side street just west of the Piazza della Repubblica, the Helvetia is still the best place in Florence for starring in your own mini-production of A Room with a View

paper with the names of expected arrivals. Would the gentleman by any chance be Signor Petkanas? You bet he would.

The Savoy, which Rocco Forte Hotels refurbished for $17 million, does not disappoint. Its location, on the Piazza della Repubblica, Florence's main square, is unimpeachable. The Duomo and Prada, the Uffizi Gallery and Etro, the Arno and Cellerini—all are in luxurious roll-out-of-bed proximity, making the Savoy a natural base of operations for heat-seeking career shoppers. (Those beds, by the way, are made up with wonderfully starchy linen sheets, coverlets that are a cross between a moving quilt and a Provençal *boutis*, and both foam and down or feather pillows.) If your dream of Italy involves staying in the thick of a nonstop, A-list *passeggiata*, no other hotel will do.

Forte's sister Olga Polizzi is in charge of the Savoy's visuals, and that contagious International Boutique Hotel Sensibility comes through, with explicit references to French design idol Christian Liaigre. Razor-tailored decoration has its day, and then some, in 102 guest rooms housed in a proudly unfrivolous 1893 building owned by the Ferragamo shoe family. Bathrooms come in two varieties of marble, white or rich brown, and have ravishing mosaics and high-tech glass Soehnle scales. Shame about the Savoy's art, though. It could have been bought by the yard. Aren't we in Florence?

As for the service, it's probably the best in town, provided by a crisp, fresh-faced team whose idea of a good time is to turn on a dime. The nimble guest relations manager, who fairly bristles with finesse, missed his calling. He should have been a diplomat. "We won!" exclaimed the concierge after heroically securing an eleventh-hour Sunday lunch reservation at La Fontana, the proto–Tuscan hill restaurant in nearby Prato.

The Savoy's own food is better than it has a right to be and certainly better than you'd expect. (Hotels this design-centric often think decent food is beneath them.) Surely there is no more heavenly Florentine experience than dining on the pretty parasol-shaded platform, set out on the hotel's piazza, and engulfed by flower boxes and topiaries. A casual question about the Parmesan risotto unleashed an eloquent explanation from the waiter about how the dish is prepared (the secret: the cheese is cut into chunks,

not grated, and melts as the rice cooks). Obliquely ridged penne, tossed with a sauce of crumbled shrimp, tomato, and dill, was 10 times more than the sum of its parts. Better than dessert, the Marchesa Pucci walked by in vintage Pucci.

HOTEL HELVETIA & BRISTOL

THE MERCHANT-IVORY MOMENT A century ago, Florence was a must stop for members of the British cultured classes on the Grand Tour, and the Helvetia & Bristol was one of their favorite hotels. What could be nicer, after an exhausting day decoding the Maestà altarpiece at the Uffizi, than to return to the Helvetia for tea in the *giardino d'inverno*, with its delightful arched glass ceiling and profusion of plants? Those art-hungry ladies in Edwardian plumage and men in starched collars had no way of knowing it then, but they were living a Merchant-Ivory moment.

Built in the 19th century as a private palazzo, and set on a side street just west of the Piazza della Repubblica, the Helvetia is still the best place in Florence for starring in your own mini-production of *A Room with a View*. Afternoon tea remains a civilized ritual in the palm-decked winter garden, a terrific spot for reviewing today's shopping spoils and for planning tomorrow's museum assault. The lobby is a residential mix of the creamy terra-cotta tiles with ruddy highlights from Vietri on the Amalfi Coast, *pietra serena* pillars with the girth of hundred-year-old plane trees, Persian carpets, lovely antiques, and burnished-oak bookcases with glazed fronts. The most enveloping wing chairs offer the perfect perch for polishing off Mary McCarthy's classic primer, *The Stones of Florence*. Amazingly, in a city that is always drawing you outside, the Helvetia's public spaces are places where you want to idle.

The hotel's complete lack of interest in anything chichi or gratuitously up-to-date extends to the 67 guest rooms, which are freighted, typically, with wildly shaped baroque beds, overstuffed sofas trimmed in furry moss-green fringe, and the framed fans of some forgotten *principessa*. The rich damasks and brocades for which Florence has been known for centuries have been fashioned into wall coverings, bedspreads as heavy as the pope's chasuble, and elaborately shaped pelmets. It's all very moody, very *fin de siècle*. The guests, an uncommonly civilized

*The Hotel Helvetia
& Bristol's entrance.*

group who live by *politesse*, are a responsive audience.

Service at the Helvetia attains heights of formality that would seem absurd elsewhere. In the restaurant, disarmingly dressy preparations—so different from the straight-shooting dishes one eats almost everywhere else in Tuscany—arrive under silver cloches lifted by waiters in white jersey gloves. The night I was there, the flourish that revealed turbot-and-salmon rolls made a couple of young, wide-eyed newlyweds from Pennsylvania nearly swoon. Perhaps to assure themselves that it wasn't all a dream, the honeymooners gave each other a good squeeze.

GRAND HOTEL & WESTIN EXCELSIOR

THE DOYENNES These old-world institutions not only face each other in a kind of stand off across a wide-open Renaissance *piazza*, but they share a parent company, Starwood Hotels & Resorts— at least for the moment. Starwood has put both properties on the block, though it hopes to continue to manage them under the next owner, whoever that might be. On paper, the Excelsior and the Grand can be a little difficult to tell apart, but staying at them proves the opposite point: they're as different as *perciatelli* and *pappardelle*. This is true even though the hotels share many top personnel; shuttling between them, the general manager and

The winter garden at the Grand Hotel.

executive housekeeper wear out an awful lot of shoe leather. According to Starwood, this synergy isn't just cost-efficient: it gives the company an advantage over the competition.

At right angles to the Arno, the 171-room Excelsior (where Napoleon's sister lived) and 107-room Grand (designed by Brunelleschi as a palazzo in the 16th century) are a maddeningly complicated lesson in modern hotel-branding. The Grand is part of the Luxury Collection; of Starwood's nine groups, only the St. Regis is higher. The Excelsior is a Westin but, just to confuse things, also a member of Luxury, its dual designation placing the hotel a notch below a purely Luxury property. One thing you're paying extra for at the Grand is the service: it's more attentive and nuanced.

But it's not just the hotels that have differing profiles—so do their clienteles. Guests at the Grand seem to have a few more calendar years, fatter portfolios, less of a mission to do business, and more of a desire to unwind. Relaxing in the hotel's public spaces became a lovelier proposition with the transformation of the lobby—from a turbulent,

The Hotel Excelsior's staircase.

workaday corridor to a proper, elegant sitting area that invites sustained lingering—in 2003. As former general manager Michele Frignani says, "It was always felt that the lobby wasn't up to our winter garden, with its stained-glass ceiling and breakfast mezzanine. Now one space flatters the other."

The restaurant represents another big change. It was moved from under the loggia in the winter garden (diners didn't love the nearness of the bar crowd, apparently) to the former luggage hold, a handsomely scaled room off the lobby. And a swatch of parking space on the Piazza Ognissanti was reclaimed for an intimate little drinks-and-dining terrace. It's a low-key spot for observing mailmen zipping across the square on their scooters in the morning, and for watching the streetlamps come on along the Arno in the evening.

That's the good news. The bad news is that the Grand is having an identity crisis. If the hotel stands for one thing, it's tradition. But the straining-to-be-hip restaurant, InCanto, is a complete disconnect. To remind myself why I have been coming back to the Grand for 25 years, I settled in for tea among the palms, statuary, and cut-velvet sofas with gilded pinecone finials in the winter garden.

The new butler floor, like the rest of the hotel, offers rooms in two styles: Empire, and what the Grand calls Florentine. The latter is a hokey cocktail of flame-stitched curtains and bedcovers, fleur-de-lis–patterned carpets, freshly minted frescoes of maidens on horseback, and loopy wrought-iron chandeliers. With their nod to the early 19th century and their heady whiff of Napoleonic splendor, the Empire rooms are a lighter, livelier bet.

One difference between the Grand and the Excelsior is the difference between grand and grandiose. That's not a dig at the Excelsior. Indeed, with its monumental quadruple-width staircase, columns in multicolored marble, and painted ceilings divided into hundreds of coffered squares, the hotel gives flamboyance a good name.

Unlike the Grand, the Excelsior confines most of its antiques (including quintessentially Florentine X-form Savonarola chairs detailed with lions' heads) to the public areas and suites. But the guest rooms still look plenty pedigreed. Swooping headboards are carved with scrolls and shells. Walls are lavishly upholstered above the dado and

edged with passementerie rope. Sofas are extra deep. Bathrooms are equipped with a crucial accessory that, despite its obviousness, most hotels overlook: a shoehorn.

I have a fantasy. I am the owner of a Tuscan villa. The Excelsior is my Florence pied-à-terre.

THE FERRAGAMO COLLECTION

THE STYLE-SETTERS Florence's First Family of Fashion is as big a force on the local hotel scene as they are in shoes and ready-to-wear. The owners of Lungarno Hotels, the Ferragamos run four well-bred properties. All of the city's riverside hotels have streets separating them from the Arno—except the genteel, 73-room Hotel Lungarno, which is poised directly on the embankment. With 74 rooms and a contemporary boutique sensibility, the Gallery Hotel Art is the family's bid for a younger, more design-aware customer. Unfortunately, you could be anywhere. The discreet Lungarno Suites, whose 44 rooms all have kitchens, is tailored to independent travelers seeking an apartment rather than a hotel experience. If your idea of hell is having to greet an army of personnel before setting out every morning, this place is for you. The small reception area is the only public space (though guests have privileges at all the group's hotels), and room service is supplied by the Fusion Bar Shozan Gallery, at the Gallery Hotel Art. The sleek, fifties-flavored 43-room Continentale, at the foot of the Ponte Vecchio, may not be for seekers of calm, but fashion hounds are pronouncing it heaven.

Fusion Bar Shozan Gallery, at the Gallery Hotel Art.

Travelers' Guide to Florence

GETTING THERE

Alitalia, Delta, and Continental fly to Florence from New York or Newark via Rome or Milan. And Delta now flies direct to Pisa from New York.

TOP SIGHTS IN FLORENCE

Duomo Group ❼

Florence's religious heart: Giotto's belltower, the Baptistry's Gates of Paradise and Byzantine mosaics, Brunelleschi's dome, and a museum full of Michelangelo and Donatello sculptures.

Galleria degli Uffizi ❸

The world's greatest collection of Renaissance art, with masterpieces from Giotto and Botticelli through Michelangelo, Raphael, and Leonardo da Vinci to Titian, Caravaggio, and Rembrandt.

Galleria dell'Accademia ❶

Michelangelo's *David* (1501–4) stands at the end of a corridor lined by the artist's *Slaves*. The plaster casts crowding one long room hint that this is still a fine-arts academy.

Il Bargello ❾

This sculpture gallery, installed in a medieval town hall and prison, has early Michelangelos, Giambologna's *Flying Mercury* (1564), and a prize collection of works by Donatello.

Palazzo Pitti ❹

The late Renaissance mansion was a royal home from 1560 until the 1860's, when Florence did a stint as Italy's capital. Backed by the elaborate Boboli Gardens, the palace's seven museums include the Galleria Palatina of late Renaissance/early Baroque art.

Palazzo Vecchio ❻

Arnolfo di Cambio's mighty town hall (1299–1302) is still Florence's seat of government.

Piazza della Signoria ❽

Florence's public living room and outdoor sculpture gallery, with copies of Donatello's *Marzocco* (Florence's leonine symbol) and *Judith*, and Michelangelo's *David*.

For map key see p.7

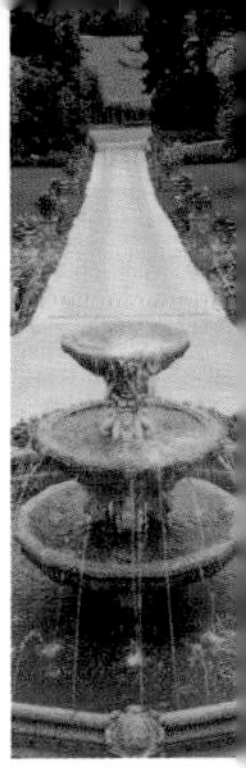

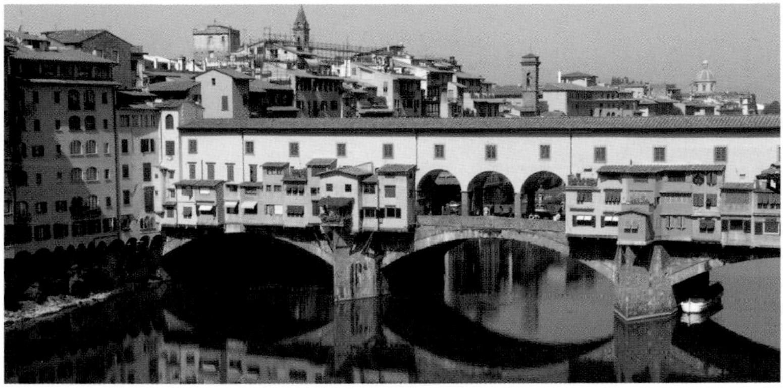

Ponte Vecchio, the city's oldest bridge, retains many original features.

Ponte Vecchio [5]
The shops on Taddeo Gaddi's 1354 "old bridge" have housed gold- and silversmiths since Ferdinando I evicted the butchers in the 16th century (his private corridor from the Uffizi to the Pitti ran overhead and he couldn't stand the smell).

San Marco [2]
Cosimo I (Il Vecchio) de' Medici commissioned Michelozzo to build this Dominican monastery in 1437. Fra Angelico frescoed the cells with devotional images and altarpieces.

Santa Croce [10]
The Gothic church contains the tombs of Michelangelo and Gallileo, and Giotto frescoes. Off the cloisters are the Pazzi, a chapel designed by Brunelleschi, and a small museum containing a *Last Supper* by Taddeo Gaddi and Cimabue's *Crucifix*.

WHERE TO STAY

Continentale
6R Vicolo dell'Oro;
39-055/2726-4000;
lungarnohotels.com;
doubles from $$$.

Gallery Hotel Art
5 Vicolo dell'Oro;
39-055/2726-4000;
lungarnohotels.com;
doubles from $$$.

Grand Hotel
1 Piazza Ognissanti;
800/325-3589 or 39-055/288-781;
starwoodhotels.com;
doubles from $$$$$.

Grand Hotel Villa Medici
42 Via Il Prato;
39-055/277-171;
villamedicihotel.com;
doubles from $$$$.

Hotel Helvetia & Bristol
2 Via dei Pescioni;
39-055/26651;
hotelhelvetiabristolfirenze.it;
doubles from $$$$.

Hotel Lungarno
14 Borgo San Jacopo;
39-055/2726-4000;
lungarnohotels.com;
doubles from $$$.

Hotel Savoy
7 Piazza della Repubblica;
800/223-6800 or 39-055/27351;
roccofortehotels.com;
doubles from $$$$.

Lungarno Suites
4 Lungarno Acciaiuoli;
39-055/2726-4000;
lungarnohotels.com;
doubles from $$$$.

Westin Excelsior
3 Piazza Ognissanti;
800/325-3589 or 39-055/264-201;
starwoodhotels.com;
doubles from $$$$$.

SEE ALSO
For more on Florence:
Master Class pp.166–167

WHERE TO EAT

Garga
Small linked dining rooms hum with fun, glamour, and deft, friendly service. Try the asparagus risotto or scaloppine di vitella al limone *(veal scallops with lemon).*
48R Via del Moro;
39-055/239-8898;
dinner for two $$$.

Simon Boccanegra
Mottled stone walls, mismatched wooden tables, and an adventurous Tuscan menu ensure that this tiny trattoria across from the Teatro Verdi is always packed.
124R Via Ghibellina;
39-055/200-1098;
dinner for two $$$.

Trattoria Armando
The chef's forte is making standbys like ribollita *(cabbage-and-bean soup) and* trippa alla fiorentina con fagioli *(tripe with cannellini beans) taste delicious.*
140R Via Borgognissanti;
39-055/216-219;
dinner for two $$$.

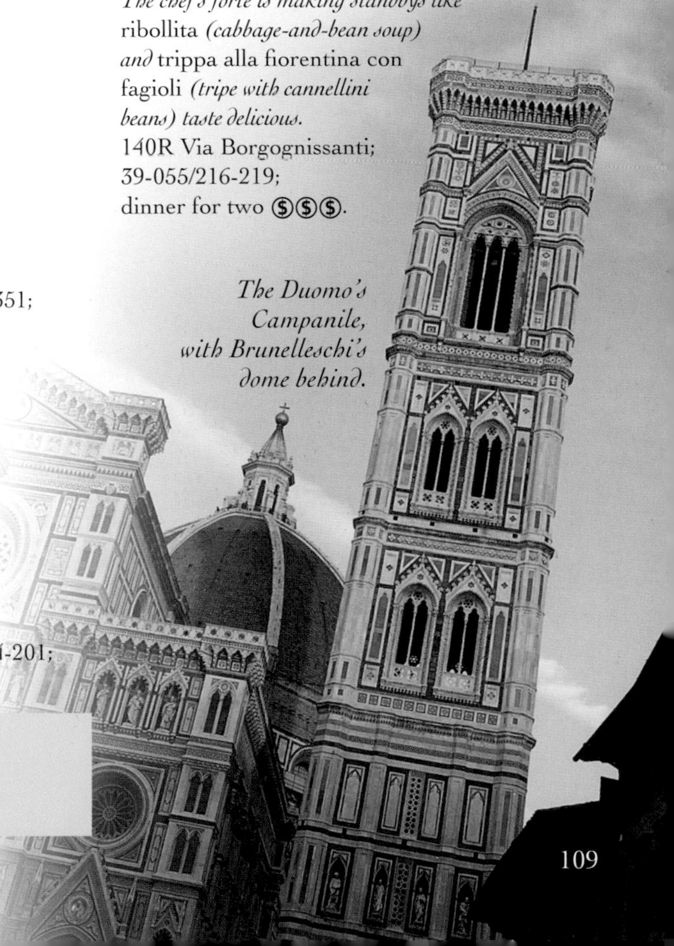

The Duomo's Campanile, with Brunelleschi's dome behind.

PART THREE
Food and Drink

Plin de seirass
—an agnolotti pasta
traditionally served on a
bed of dried grasses.

TUSCANY

On the Tuscan Trail

FROM *SALUMI* MAESTROS IN GREVE IN CHIANTI TO A STAR VINTNER IN MONTALCINO, TRACE A PATH BETWEEN THE BEST ARTISANAL PRODUCERS IN NORTHERN ITALY. BY NILOUFAR MOTAMED

The creator of the world's most expensive olive oil is standing in a dusty parking lot beside Tuscany's autostrada, hurling glass bottles against a concrete wall. *Thwuck…doink. Thwuck…doink.* Remarkably, not one breaks. "See?" Armando Manni says proudly. "I had these made specially in the Veneto—the

Chianti's Molino di Grace winery.

bottle is a half-inch thick. The manufacturer thought I was crazy."

Crazy is certainly one way to describe Manni, an Italian film director who happened upon an unexpected second career in 1997. "When my son, Lorenzo, was born, I wanted to give him the healthiest food I could find," he says. Immersing

himself in research, Manni realized that what manufacturers call extra-virgin olive oil is often of an inferior grade, compromised by exposure to sunlight and oxygen long before it's consumed. With the help of scientists, Manni was able to bottle a "live" oil, which he claims contains more cancer-fighting agents. He keeps his product from oxidizing by topping it off with nitrogen; the bottle's thick black glass protects it from sunlight. Portions are small (only 3.4 ounces) so the oil stays fresh from start to quick finish, and each comes marked with a vintage and a "best before" date. Charlie Trotter,

Michel Troisgros, and Thomas Keller are a few of Manni's devoted clients, each happy to pay $6 an ounce for this ethereal liquid gold.

Brimming with passion and possessed of impeccable taste, Manni embodies the term *gusto*, in both senses. (In his Comme des Garçons suede jacket and handmade leather boots, he also looks uncannily like Robert De Niro.) The Rome native—who spends half his time in Tuscany, where his olives are grown—recently opened his black book and took me on a tour of the Italian countryside.

We tracked down vintners, cheesemakers, and *salumai* who share Manni's intense enthusiasm and rigorous devotion to craft, as well as family-owned restaurants that still do things the old-fashioned way. The culinary treasure trail starts here.

HONEY AND JAM

TENUTA LA PARRINA At this rustic farmstead B&B south of Grosseto, the air is scented with the same herbs and flowers that flavor its wild honey—a heady conflation of rosemary and eucalyptus made even more intense by the strong sunshine. ("We need to find shadow," Manni murmurs as we pull in. He's carrying precious cargo—two cases of oil—and doesn't want it to overheat in the parked car.) *Agriturismi* have proliferated in Italy lately; Tenuta La Parrina is one of the few selling high-grade products that are every bit the equal of the setting. We stop at the farm stand to buy jars of house-made jams (kiwi, kumquat marmalade, lemon-and–golden apple), as well as organic lettuces and herbs grown on the property. The owners also create fantastic cheeses, including an 18-month-aged *caprino* that's rich and dense. A tasting room for pairings of wine, cheese, and jams makes it easy to decide which to take home.

Pecorino stagionato, *ready for aging at Caseificio Seggiano.*

PAPPA REALE

RISTORANTE PETRONIO "Maremma is like Texas," says Petronio Scalabrelli, dressed in blue jeans, plaid shirt, and suspenders. At his humble restaurant in the heart of Italy's cowboy country, the walls are covered with sepia-toned photographs of ranch life in the early 1900's. The meal begins with fava beans and purple baby *carciofi*, which Scalabrelli plucked from his garden an hour earlier, served raw with a drizzle of salted olive oil. Next comes the signature *pappa reale*, a pillow-shaped potato pasta resembling an oversized, airy gnocchi, lightly swathed in a tart pork-and-beef *ragù*. It's followed by a grass-fed Florentine steak, seared on lava rock. Eggy, almond-dotted biscotti and house-made limoncello signal the end of the show. And that's just lunch.

CHEESE

CASEIFICIO SEGGIANO As we drive north, wild fennel overtakes guardrails, and forests of Mediterranean pine are replaced by endless fields of red poppies. We are heading to see the Fabbri and Governi families, who together produce some of Italy's best

Dino Fabbri, tending Caseificio Seggiano's goats.

The road to Montalcino has sweeping vistas of the Tuscan countryside: ocher-hued villas on hilltops, cypress trees, neon-green expanses

Stefano Falorni, an eighth-generation salumaio.

pecorino di fossa, aged for seven months in wells lined with straw. Their small factory creates coveted, one-of-a-kind cheeses, including a mellow *pecorino dolce* that inspires compulsive eating. Visit in the early morning to get a bite of the still-warm, buttery ricotta just after it's made.

SALUMI

ANTICA MACELLERIA FALORNI Falorni is an institution: its *salsicce* and prosciutto have been made artisanally for eight generations. To walk into the *salumeria* is to walk into a world where all things porcine are prized. The intoxicating scent of pepper and smoked meat permeates the space; prosciutto with the tail still on hangs from the ceiling. A place of pride is reserved for products from the *cinta senese*, an indigenous wild black boar. The jovial, mustachioed co-owner, Stefano Falorni, can be

found behind his fire engine–red Berkel slicer giving customers tastes of garlicky *capocollo* or paprika-tinged *salame piccante*. But the signature sausage of the *macelleria* is the *finocchiona sbriciolona*, a richly marbled salami spiced with wild fennel seeds. Accompanied by a bottle of Chianti, Falorni's velvety *prosciutto Toscano* is ideal for a picnic in the piazza.

PINCI

VINERIA LE POTAZZINE We wander Montalcino's winding cobblestoned streets, and after a stop at the medieval fortress, we come upon the family-owned Osteria Le Potazzine. Manni quickly secures the last available outdoor table (that Italian charm) and we order a *gran piatto di affettati tipici del territorio* (a platter of cured meats) from Carlo Pieri, an area *salumaio*. The sausages are spicy, well balanced, and flavorful. Next up, Manni suggests a local specialty: *pinci fatti a mano*, pasta rolled by hand to resemble thick spaghetti. The *pinci* arrive perfectly al dente, in a fresh *pomodoro* sauce redolent of basil. I can't say for sure that this is the best plate of pasta I've ever eaten, but having it in a square, with church bells tolling in the distance, makes it a contender.

Artisanal prosciutto on sale at Falorni, in Greve in Chianti.

Sylvester Anthony's Grape Bearers, *in the Molino di Grace vineyard, in Chianti.*

BRUNELLO

SIRO PACENTI The road to Montalcino has sweeping vistas of the Tuscan countryside: ocher-hued villas on hilltops, cypress trees, neon-green expanses. As we approach a long driveway, Manni raves about Siro Pacenti's wines, which he loves so much that he bought a case for his son's future cellar when he was born. The standout Brunello di Montalcino is a complex Sangiovese with powerful spice and red-fruit flavors, a precise marriage of grapes from several plots of land in Montalcino. It is aged for two years in Sylvain and Taransaud oak barrels, and then for another two in Pacenti's cave.

CHIANTI

IL MOLINO DI GRACE Manni drives with the abandon that only Italians can pull off, often overtaking cars on the hairpin turns. We are heading to Panzano to meet Frank Grace and his wife, Judy, who are living out the Tuscan dream: owning a winery in Chianti. Avid art collectors and travelers, they have shaken up the Italian wine establishment. In their eighth year of production, they received a prestigious Gambero Rosso award for best emerging winery. Il Molino's powerhouse is the 100 percent Sangiovese Super Tuscan, Gratius, the kind of wine you want to chew rather than sip. Save room for a bottle (or two) in your suitcase.

STEAK

ANTICA MACELLERIA CECCHINI It's not often that you run across a butcher who wears Prada shoes and spouts Dante and poetry while slicing meat in a book-lined space. Dario Cecchini's shop doubles as the town hall in Panzano. Sure, people come here to buy *bistecca panzanese*, or Florentine beefsteak, but they mostly come to gossip and catch up on the town's happenings. Though his personality may not win you over (he admits to not liking American visitors because they don't buy enough), he is nonetheless the consummate host. Bowls filled with olives with sliced oranges and free glasses of Chianti greet customers.

Giovanni Napolitano, the cantiniere, *at work in the aging room at Chianti's Il Molino di Grace.*

*The town of Montalcino, home
to the Siro Pacenti winery.*

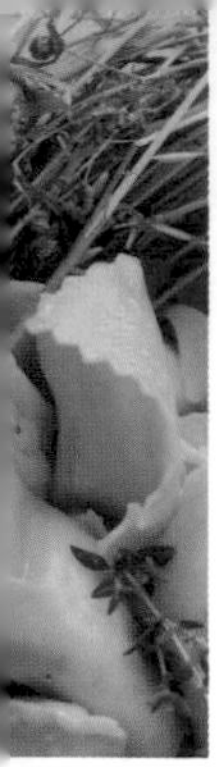

Travelers' Guide to Tuscany

GETTING THERE

Alitalia, Continental, and Delta all connect through Rome or Milan to Florence or Pisa.

EXPLORING TUSCANY

Tuscan cities such as Florence, Siena, and Pisa, together with smaller towns like Lucca, Cortona, and Arezzo, contain some of Italy's most famous artistic treasures. The medieval village of San Gimignano, with its famous towers, and Pienza, a tiny Renaissance jewel, sit at the heart of the glorious pastoral countryside for which the region is equally renowned.

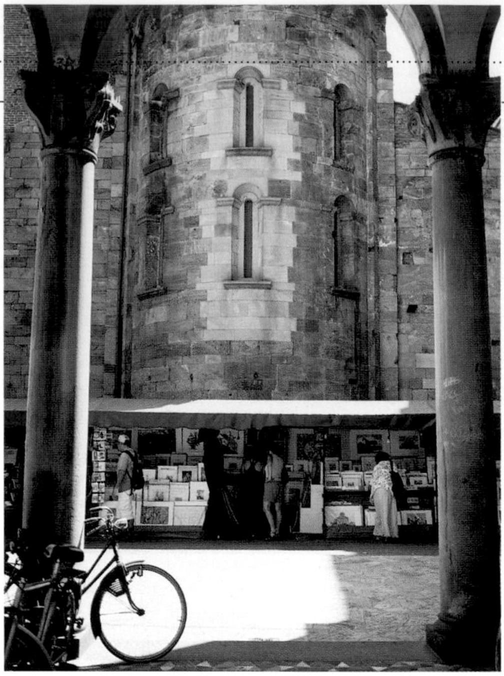

A Lucca street market.

While in Tuscany...

- Arezzo 14
- Artimino 11
- Bagna di Lucca 3
- Carrara 1
- Chiusi 17
- Cortona 16
- Crete Senesi 21
- Elba 28
- Fiesole 13
- Florence 33
- Garfagnana 2
- Lucca 6
- Maremma 31
- Massa Marittima 27
- Montalcino 20
- Monte Argentario 32
- Montepulciano 18
- Monteriggioni 23
- Pienza 19
- Pisa 7
- Pistoia 9
- Pitigliano 30
- Prato 10
- San Galgano 26
- San Gimignano 24
- San Miniato 12
- Sansepolcro 15
- Sienna 22
- Sovana 29
- Torre del Lago Puccini 5
- Viareggio 4
- Vinci 8
- Volterra 25

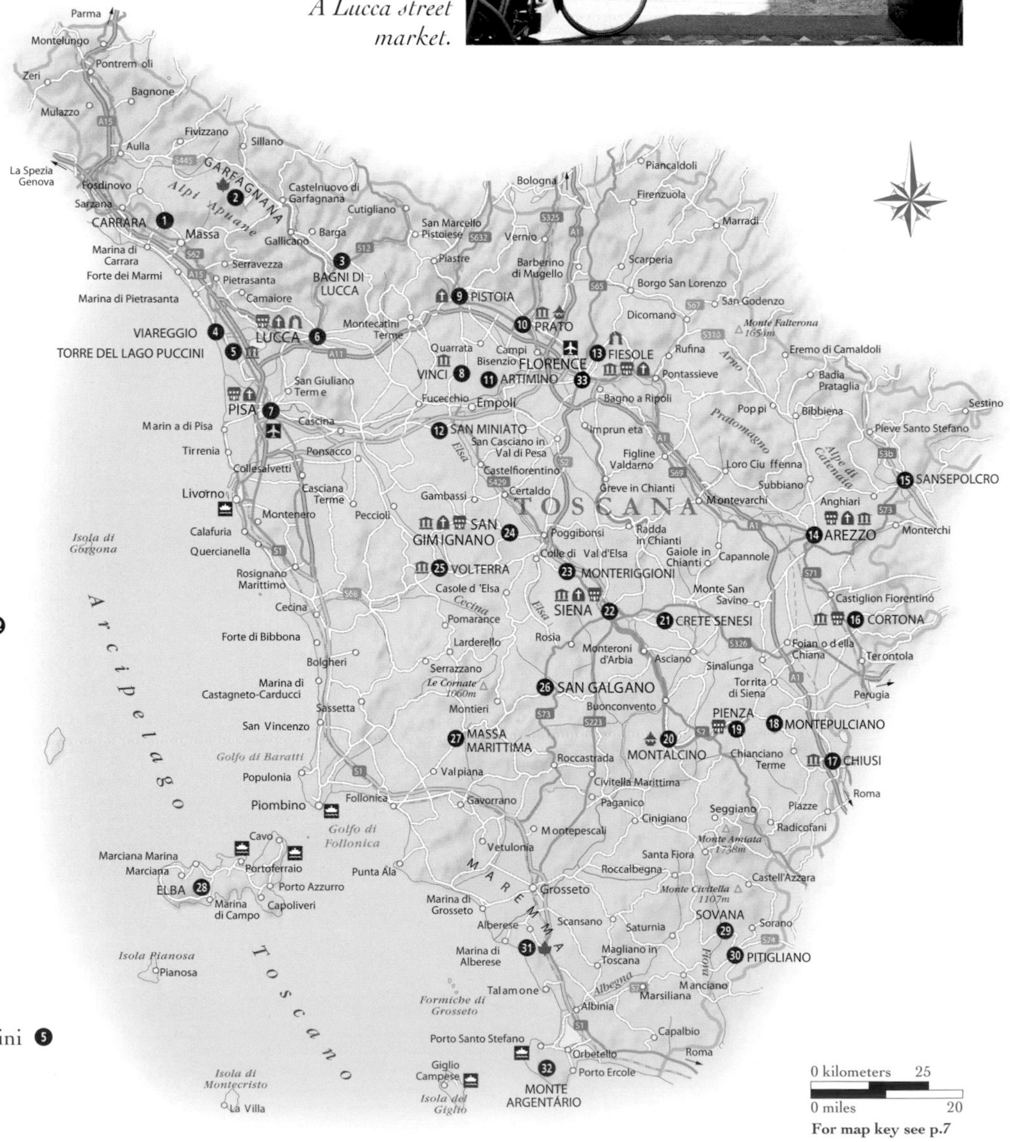

Parma
Montelungo
Pontremoli
Zeri
Bagnone
Mulazzo
Aulla
Fivizzano
Sillano
La Spezia
Genova
Fosdinovo
Sarzana
CARRARA 1
GARFAGNANA 2
Alpi Apuane
Castelnuovo di Garfagnana
Cutigliano
Massa
Gallicano
Barga
Marina di Carrara
Forte dei Marmi
Serravezza
Pietrasanta
Marina di Pietrasanta
Camaiore
3 BAGNI DI LUCCA
VIAREGGIO 4
TORRE DEL LAGO PUCCINI 5
LUCCA 6
San Giuliano Terme
PISA 7
Marin a di Pisa
Tirrenia
Cascina
Pontsacco
Collesalvetti
Livorno
Casciana Terme
Montenero
Peccioli
Isola di Gorgona
Calafuria
Quercianella
Rosignano Marittimo
Cecina
Forte di Bibbona
Bolgheri
Marina di Castagneto-Carducci
Sassetta
San Vincenzo
Golfo di Baratti
Populonia
Piombino
Follonica
Golfo di Follonica
Cavo
Marciana Marina
Marciana
Portoferraio
Porto Azzurro
ELBA 28
Marina di Campo
Capoliveri
Punta Ala
Isola Pianosa
Pianosa
Isola di Montecristo
La Villa
Arcipelago Toscano
Bologna
Pianca ldoli
Firenzuola
San Marcello Pistoiese
Vernio
Marradi
Piastre
Barberino di Mugello
Scarperia
Borgo San Lorenzo
9 PISTOIA
Dicomano
San Godenzo
Montecatini Terme
10 PRATO
Monte Falterona 1654m
Quarrata
Campi Bisenzio
FLORENCE
13 FIESOLE
Rufina
Eremo di Camaldoli
VINCI 8
11 ARTIMINO
33
Pontassieve
Badia Prataglia
Fucecchio
Empoli
Bagno a Ripoli
Poppi
Bibbiena
Sestino
12 SAN MINIATO
Impruneta
Pieve Santo Stefano
San Casciano in Val di Pesa
Figline Valdarno
Pratomagno
Castelfiorentino
Loro Ciuffenna
Alpe di Catenaia
Certaldo
Greve in Chianti
Subbiano
15 SANSEPOLCRO
Gambassi
TOSCANA
Montevarchi
Anghiari
SAN GIMIGNANO 24
Poggibonsi
Radda in Chianti
14 AREZZO
Monterchi
Colle di Val d'Elsa
Gaiole in Chianti
Capannole
25 VOLTERRA
23 MONTERIGGIONI
Casole d'Elsa
Monte San Savino
Castiglion Fiorentino
Pomarance
SIENA 22
21 CRETE SENESI
16 CORTONA
Larderello
Rosia
Monteroni d'Arbia
Asciano
Foiano della Chiana
Terontola
Serrazzano
Sinalunga
Le Cornate 1060m
26 SAN GALGANO
Torrita di Siena
Perugia
Montieri
Buonconvento
PIENZA 19
18 MONTEPULCIANO
27 MASSA MARITTIMA
20 MONTALCINO
Roccastrada
Chianciano Terme
17 CHIUSI
Valpiana
Civitella Marittima
Roma
Gavorrano
Paganico
Cinigiano
Seggiano
Piazze
Montepescali
Monte Amiata 1738m
Radicofani
Vetulonia
Santa Fiora
MAREMMA
Roccalbegna
Castell'Azzara
Grosseto
Monte Civitella 1107m
Marina di Grosseto
Alberese
Scansano
Saturnia
SOVANA 29
Sorano
Marina di Alberese
31
Magliano in Toscana
30 PITIGLIANO
Talamone
Manciano
Marsiliana
Formiche di Grosseto
Albinia
Albegna
Capalbio
Porto Santo Stefano
Orbetello
Roma
Giglio Campese
32 MONTE ARGENTARIO
Porto Ercole
Isola del Giglio
0 kilometers 25
0 miles 20
For map key see p.7

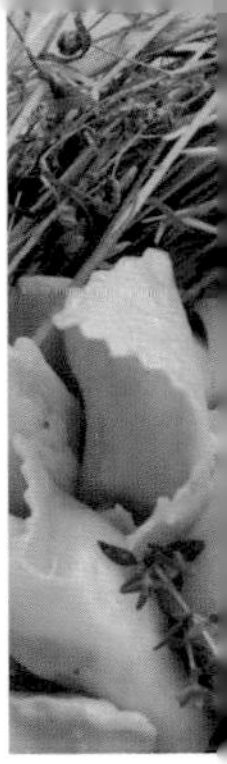

WHERE TO STAY

Il Pellicano
A Relais & Châteaux property on the Maremma coast. Sunset drinks on the terrace and a dip in the saltwater pool are a must.
Porto Ercole;
39-0564/858-111;
pellicanohotel.com;
doubles from $$$$$, including two meals.

Tenuta Villa Gaia
Idyllic three-suite inn on the slopes of Mount Amiata. Rooms overlook olive groves and medieval villages in the distance.
Seggiano;
39-0564/950-642;
tenutavillagaia.com;
doubles from $$$.

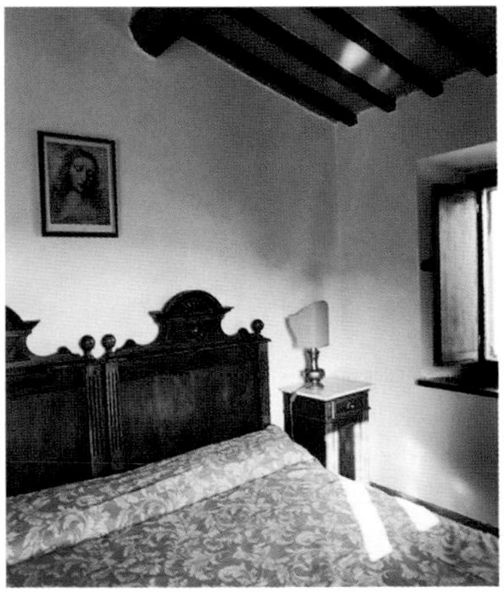

A bedroom at Tenuta Villa Gaia.

Castello di Spaltenna
This medieval castle has a bell tower dating back to the year 1000. The courtyard is a lovely spot for dinner.
Gaiole in Chianti;
39-0577/749-483;
spaltenna.it;
doubles from $$$.

SEE ALSO

For Florence:
Overnight Sensation pp.108–109
Master Class pp.166–167
For Arezzo:
On Pierro's Trail pp.182–183

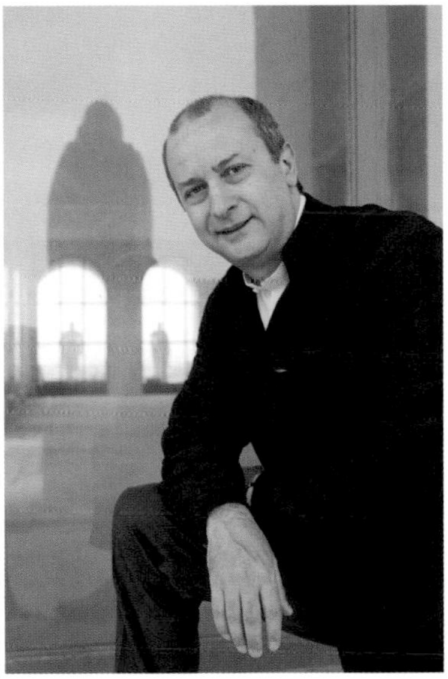

Cult olive-oil maker Armando Manni.

WHERE TO EAT

Ristorante Petrono
74 Strada Statale, Marsiliana;
39-0564/606-345;
lunch for two $$$.

Vineria le Potazzine
10 Piazza Garibaldi, Montalcino;
39-0577/846-054;
lunch for two $$.

Panzanella, a typical Tuscan dish.

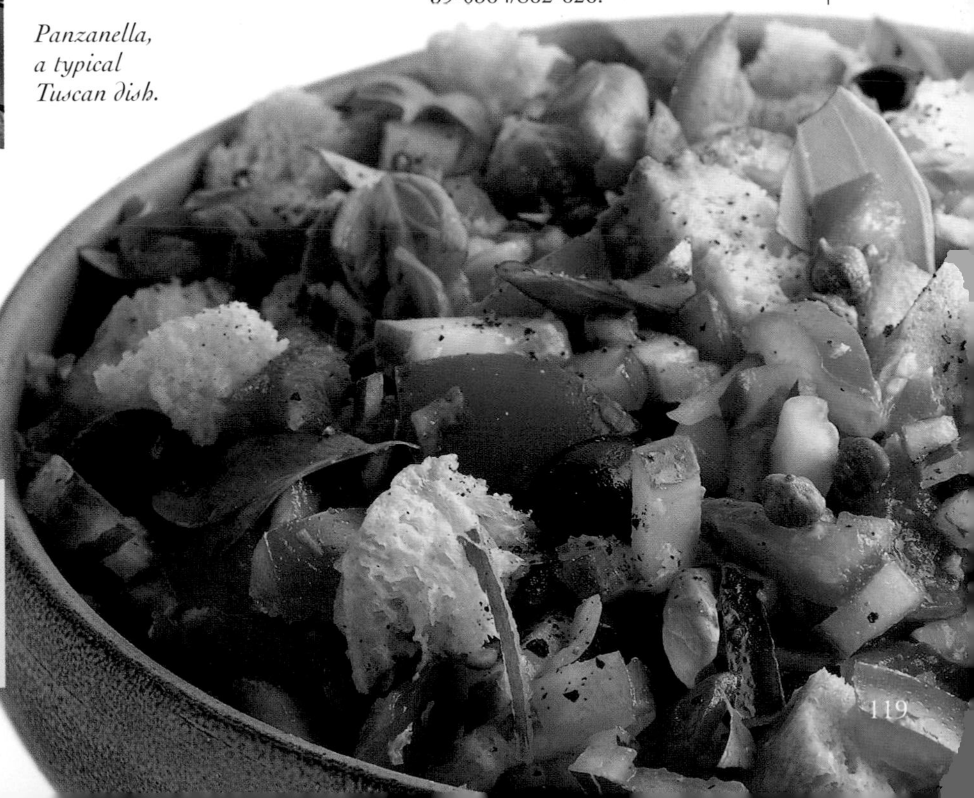

WHERE TO SHOP

Antica Macelleria Cecchini
11 Via XX Luglio, Panzano;
39-055/852-020.

Antica Macelleria Falorni
71 Piazza G. Matteotti, Greve in Chianti;
39-055/853-029.

Caseificio Seggiano
Via Privata, Seggiano;
39-0564/950-034;
tours by appointment only.

Il Molino di Grace
Località il Volano, Panzano;
39-055/856-1010.

Manni Extra Virgin Olive Oil
39-06/9727-4787;
manni.biz.

Siro Pacenti
1 Località Pelagrilli, Montalcino;
39-0577/848-662;
tours by appointment only.

Tenuta La Parrina
Km 146, Via Aurelia, Albinia;
39-0564/862-626.

Outside Il Refolo, on the San Polo Canal, in Venice.

Photographs by Lisa Linder

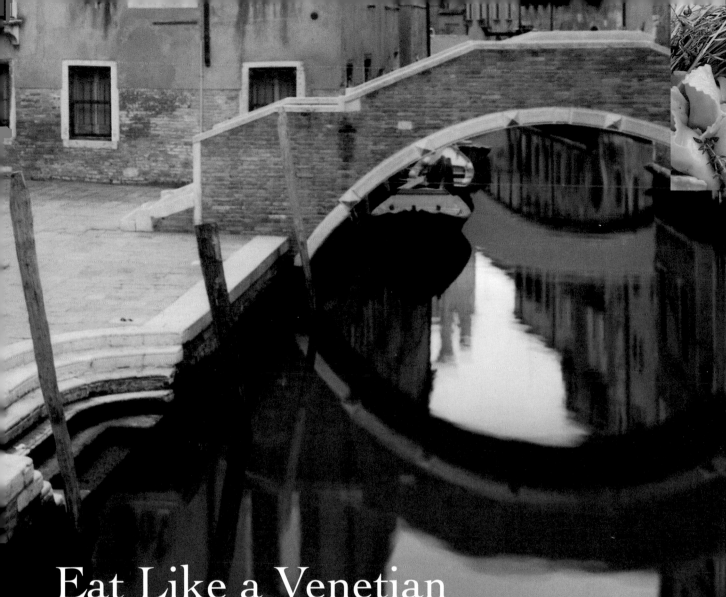

Eat Like a Venetian

IN A CITY THAT OFTEN CONFOUNDS FOOD LOVERS, THE ADVICE OF SOME TRUSTWORTHY LOCALS LEADS THE WAY TO TEN OF VENICE'S MOST MEMORABLE MEALS. BY GAEL GREENE

VENICE

Not everyone falls in love with Venice at first sight; certainly not at first bite. For all its mythic enchantment, its wondrous changing light and shimmering reflections, its haunting intimacy, Venice can seem indifferent to the casual visitor, and it's never been known for noteworthy cuisine. The popularity of certain ferociously expensive (especially for those of us toting the diminished dollar) dining perennials suggests Venetians love overcooked fish and thrive on the gluey black ink of the cuttlefish. My partner, Steven, and I are on our fourth extended sojourn here, and I'm happy to report that there are dishes to savor, and restaurants from which the fussiest mouths emerge smiling. All it takes to eat well in

Venice are walking shoes, a vaporetto pass, and reconnaissance. For the latest table buzz, I count on all manner of Venetians, including transplants from elsewhere in the Veneto and expats from Austria, Boston, and Los Angeles, and right away we find ourselves eating the way these passionate locals do, as inexpensively as possible without skimping on what's essential: great food.

WORTH THE SPLURGE

We've been going to Fiaschetteria Toscana for years, and once showed up with Marcella and Victor Hazan, so the owners know us. But that doesn't seem to matter. Sometimes the staff is rude (especially upstairs) and sometimes they kiss our toes. But the

Franz Kosta, a local student, dining on scallops at La Cantina.

Martin opened their simple neighborhood wine bar, and even those of us who discovered it in later years in the international spotlight, are shocked by how fancy and how expensive it is now. Steven and I decide to go for broke, and are amazed by one of the best meals of our stay: tuna carpaccio, cut like sashimi for optimal mouth-feel; overabundant saffron-scented pappardelle with oysters; a masterly fritto misto; and a dessert that still haunts me—stingingly tart lemon *sorbetto* dusted with pulverized licorice.

Young locals rave about the bargain lunch at Muro Vino e Cucina—a glass-walled wine bar with a sleek gray-and-black-themed dining room—an unlikely 21st-century sight in the historic Rialto district. We go in the evening, shouldering our way through crowds downing wine and flirting outside, despite the chill. Upstairs in the small dining room, the genial waitress keeps bringing warm olive rolls every few minutes. At first the clumsy English menu translations put me off. But an antipasto of "deer with truffle foam" proves to be carefully grilled venison, enough for three to share. Argentine steak, chewy but flavorful, is paired with roasted potatoes and a bowl of immaculate baby greens in a splendid vinaigrette. Since bottled water and cover charge are included, and a waiter will open a bottle to pour wine by the glass, the tab is less steep than we expected.

THE BEST BACARI

Denizens of Venice are fiercely loyal to their local *bacaro* (wine bar), where *cicheti* (small plates) can be a nibble before a meal or dinner itself. At a neighborhood wine and beer joint like Enoteca do Colonne, two or three *tramezzini*—sandwiches in soft dark bread, here filled with pork or salami—and perhaps a shared plate of such rough-hewn classics as *musèto* (a fatty sausage made mostly from pig's snout) or *nervèti* (boiled veal tendons with parsley and vinegar) would be dinner for a young working couple.

Ca' d'Oro dalla Vedova does two kinds of meatballs, both of them delicious; an equally well-prepared squid with potatoes; and whole grilled *seppie*. Choose from the display at the counter, where wine is red or white and nondescript, poured into teeny goblets. Around eight, packs of locals and tourists begin trooping in, claiming bare wooden tables in the simple, informal *osteria* for unusual Venetian dishes such as polenta with cuttlefish in black ink and the deftly fried fritto misto.

food—Venetian, not Tuscan, as you might think—is always good (except when the chef oversalts his signature fried seafood, *frittura della Serenissima*). "Ask the chef not to use too much salt," I beg Claudio, the English-speaking waiter. He shrugs. "I can tell him, but if he's mad at his wife, who knows?" Try spaghetti with clams, whole wheat *bigoli* (thick noodles) in salsa (a must for anchovy fans), and don't miss an unexpected French touch: the luscious tarte Tatin.

When we fly in with only a few days, we want the best at any price. And the best for aquatic creatures is Alle Testiere. After a hill of buttery sautéed razor clams and the most impeccably cooked swordfish I've had since the time I bought it on a beach and cooked it myself, I have to admire the audacity of the satiny rare tuna, with balsamic tempering the sweetness of fresh berries. The tiramisu is a revelation. (Request it when you reserve.) Why are there so few Venetians in Testiere's 22 seats? Maybe it's because co-owner Luca Di Vita recites the menu in five or six languages to a global clientele, reminding Venetians how demoralizing it can be to owe your livelihood to tourism.

Those who knew the consistently top-rated Da Fiore almost 30 years ago, when Mara and Maurizio

An antipasto of seafood bollito misto *with octopus, calamari, scampi, crayfish, and mantis shrimp, at Alle Testiere in Castello.*

Muro's minimalist interior.

Sarde a beccafico, sardine rolls with bread crumbs and pine nuts.

market offerings, focusing on meat and vegetables: wonderfully light potato *gnocchetti*, tossed with artichoke and slivers of smoked ricotta; classic liver and onions. Grilled vegetables accompany the small steak, which is smartly caramelized and modestly priced. We share homey spiced pear cake and fudgy chocolate triangles anchored on caramel streaks.

Venice can be unkind to pizza. After a couple of leathery pies, we are ready to give up. But friends are high on Il Refolo, an upscale pizzeria created by the duo at Da Fiore for their son Damiano, with Mamma coaching the kitchen. Sitting at an umbrella-shaded table with a view of the canal, I give high marks to the *azazel* pie and its layers of spicy sausage, mozzarella, and chopped tomato, with the extra garlic we requested. But lamb chops and a simple side of penne with tomato sauce are even more impressive.

Two friends—he's an Italian architect, she's an American juggling jobs—lead us to Enoteca Mascareta, where Mauro Lorenzon, an actor and wine connoisseur, keeps a serious cave with champagne and wine by the glass, drawing regulars nightly till 2 a.m. We share platters of *salumi* with cheese and a scattering of tiny pickles at a small cramped table while Lorenzon snaps off the neck of a bottle with a sword and pours a free round of bubbly for all.

Our budget-minded Venetian pals often stake out a table in the back room at La Cantina, where Francesco slices cured salamis, raw fish, cheeses—everything to order, even the bread. Platters are priced by weight. Francesco's creative crostini are full of surprises—tongue piled high under fresh horseradish shavings, salted beef with smoked ricotta and chopped pickle. But we pay the price for his fame and obsessiveness with waits that seem endless. Francesco can be temperamental, and when he's in a really bad mood, the place is closed. On a recent visit, he was sipping red wine and singing along to Sinatra. The pilgrims simply drink, laugh, and patiently wait.

A TRATTORIA FOR EVERY MOOD

Even Venetians who don't need to pinch euros are enamored of La Bitta, a new mom-and-pop act in a small storefront off the Campo San Barnaba. The menu, propped on a wooden table easel, mirrors

Alle Testiere, in Castello.

125

Travelers' Guide to Venice

WHEN TO GO

There's no such thing as a "bad" time to visit Venice. Every season has its attractions, whether that be hot summer days with balmy evenings; melancholic autumn with its fog; crisp winter with its snowbound Alps as a backdrop, or mild spring with its photogenic sunsets.

GETTING THERE

Venice's Marco Polo Airport is located at Tessera, 5 miles north of the city, on the edge of the lagoon. Delta Airlines fly from New York to Venice. Alternatively, visitors can travel via Rome or Milan, or connect through London, Paris, Amsterdam, or Frankfurt.

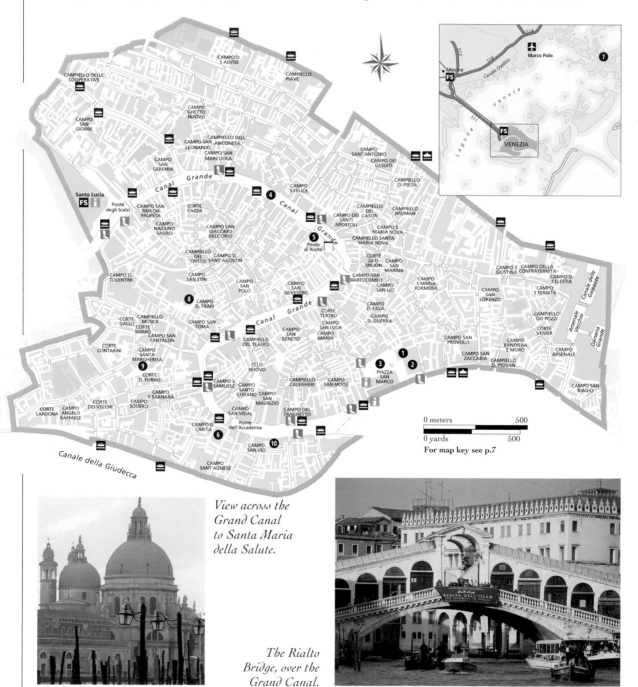

View across the Grand Canal to Santa Maria della Salute.

The Rialto Bridge, over the Grand Canal.

0 meters 500
0 yards 500
For map key see p.7

Venice's Piazza San Marco, with its Byzantine Basilica, the focal point of the city.

TOP SIGHTS IN VENICE

Accademia Galleries ❻
An unsurpassed collection of Venetian paintings, with masterpieces by Titian, Bellini, and Giorgione. A must, not only for art lovers.

Basilica di San Marco ❶
Venice's fairytale cathedral is pure Byzantine, while its façade and interior have been embellished with resplendent mosaics and works of art through the ages.

Campo Santa Margherita ❾
A wonderful square, bustling with life day and night thanks to its market stalls and outdoor cafés. The multiple architecture styles are a bonus.

Grand Canal ❹
The city's majestic watercourse swarms with all manner of boats, while its embankments feature a dazzling succession of palaces dating back as early as the 13th century.

Island of Torcello ❼
Escape the city crowds with a ferry ride over the vast expanse of the lagoon to this peaceful, lush island, the site of Venice's original settlement.

Palazzo Ducale (Doge's Palace) ❷
This was the powerhouse of the city's rulers for nearly 900 years, from the ninth to the 18th centuries.

Passing through a maze of rooms gives visitors an insight into the sumptuous lifestyle that so often accompanied state affairs.

Peggy Guggenheim Museum ❿
Italy's leading museum for 20th-century European and American art, the collection is housed in a one-floor palace on the Grand Canal.

Piazza San Marco ❸
This magnificent square—called "the most elegant drawing room in Europe" by Napoleon—is surrounded by monuments that testify to Venice's glorious past, such as the Basilica and its campanile.

Rialto Market ❺
This Mediterranean fresh-produce market has enlivened this quayside since medieval times.

Santa Maria Gloriosa dei Frari ❽
A Gothic interior with grandiose works of art lies in store behind this church's brick façade.

WHERE TO EAT

Alle Testiere
Calle del Mondo Novo, Castello 5801; 39-041/522-7220; dinner for two $$$$

Ca' d'Oro dalla Vedova
Ramo Ca' d'Oro, Cannaregio 3912; 39-041/528-5324; dinner for two $$$

Da Fiore
Calle del Scaleter, San Polo 2202A; 39-041/721-308; dinner for two $$$$

Enoteca do Colonne
Cannaregio 1814/c; 39-041/524-0453; dinner for two $$

Enoteca Mascareta
Calle Lunga Santa Maria Formosa, Castello 5183;

39-041/523-0744; dinner for two $$$

Fiaschetteria Toscana
San Giovanni Grisostomo, Cannaregio 5719; 39-041/528-5281; dinner for two $$$$

Il Refolo
San Giacomo dell'Orio, Santa Croce 1459; 39-041/524-0016; dinner for two $$

La Bitta
Calle Lunga San Barnaba, Dorsoduro 2753A; 39-041/523-0531; dinner for two $$$

La Cantina
Campo San Felice, Cannaregio 3689; 39-041/522-8258; dinner for two $

Muro Vino e Cucina
San Polo, 222 Rialto; 39-041/523-7495; dinner for two $$$$

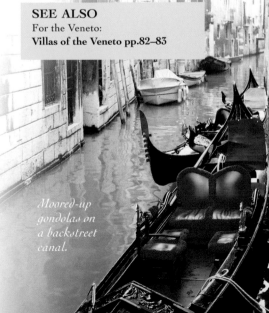

SEE ALSO
For the Veneto:
Villas of the Veneto pp.82–83

Moored-up gondolas on a backstreet canal.

Flavors of Piedmont

PIEDMONT

FOR A PAIR OF DEDICATED GASTRONOMES, NORTHERN ITALY'S TRADITIONS OF SLOW FOOD, LONG LUNCHES, AND BOLD RED WINES MAKE FOR THE CULINARY JOURNEY OF A LIFETIME. BY MATT LEE AND TED LEE

Due lanterne (two lanterns) was what the man watering his window boxes at dusk had said when we asked for directions to I Bologna, a trattoria in or around the stucco settlement of Rocchetta Tanaro. At least that is as much as we, with our semester of college Italian, had understood. Still, two lanterns (and two left turns—we'd gotten that, too) seemed more promising than what the elderly man in the town square had volunteered: *Chiuso*. (Closed.)

And now we were at an intersection: to our left was a building, shuttered, with an unlit lantern on each side of the front door; to our right, the lonely road out of town.

We had no intention of skipping dinner that evening, or on any other evening during our culinary foray through Piedmont. The day before, we'd landed in Turin, the area's largest metropolis, to begin an itinerary that would take us south to the wine-making towns scattered among the vine-covered hills of Asti and Alba for six days of tasting and sipping. Even if Tuscany's remote Maremma region seems to be garnering much of the foodie cred nowadays (due largely to the opening of Alain Ducasse's L'Andana resort), for people who scratch out a living writing and fantasizing about food and wine, a trip to Piedmont will always be the Holy Grail.

Photographs by Oberto Gili

In many ways, Piedmont is Italy's gastronomic capital, thanks to the frenzy that surrounds white-truffle season each fall. But it is also here that the grapes for austere, elegant Barolos and Barbarescos (as well as fizzy, bubble gum–fresh Moscatos) have been cultivated for centuries. It is here, too, that you find Cherasco, a hilltop town with a reputation for having the tastiest snails in the world. And there's Bra, the seat of Slow Food, that international movement of people dedicated to preserving the tradition of handmade, artisanal cuisine. Oh, and there's cheese. It was Carlo Petrini himself—the Slow Food founder—who years ago told us with utter sincerity that the "flavor of the future" will be Castelmagno, a rustic Piedmontese cheese turned out by a handful of farmers who allow their cows to graze on the grassy, vertiginous lower slopes of the Alps.

Piedmont has a certain buzz. The 2006 Winter Olympics in Turin left businesses flush with money and expansion plans. The proprietor of the family-run, 10-table L'Agrifoglio—Turin's most beloved restaurant, hands down—was positively giddy at the prospect of taking the summer off and finding a new location come fall, as the restaurant has occupied its handsome room on the Via Accademia for 12 years. And sleek Grom, the *gelateria* with a Slow Food sensibility that wine-making scion Guido Martinetti and Federico Grom opened in 2003, has taken flight, expanding to nine more Italian cities plus New York over the past four years.

A view of Castiglione Falletto.

Seasonal produce for sale at Alba's morning market.

There's even a frisson of *Hello!* magazine glamour in Piedmont these days, spurred by the return of the House of Savoy, the dynasty that ruled this region from the 14th to the mid-19th centuries. Exiled to Switzerland in 1946 on the founding of the Italian republic, the family was forbidden to set foot in Italy until 2002. Now, young Prince Emanuele Filiberto of Piedmont and Venice, a dashing Swiss hedge-fund manager, and his French film-star wife, Clotilde Courau, are frequenting the wine region around Alba. (True to script, the prince's father, Crown Prince of Italy Vittorio Emanuele, was charged with corruption by the Italians shortly after his return to the country.) But few people here seem to resent a flashback to the time when Piedmont was the seat of power for the entire country.

Before leaving for Italy, we'd contacted some friends in high places for advice. The I Bologna we had in our sights came highly recommended by Lidia Bastianich, the Istria-born restaurateur famous for her authentic regional Italian cooking. She is also known for the unwavering discipline of the kitchens she runs, so when we followed that desolate road out of Rocchetta Tanaro and found, not 200 yards from the man who'd given us directions, a carriage house with two lanterns ablaze and a lot full of black German luxury sedans, we were ecstatic and not entirely surprised.

I Bologna had, in fact, been closed for renovation but reopened just two weeks before we'd arrived, according to the stout gentleman with silver hair and goblet-sized glasses—an Italian Ed McMahon—who welcomed us. Later, it was he who ushered us into the wine room to choose what we wanted to drink when our Italian—and his English—failed us. In short order, his son, Giuseppe Bologna, in starched chef's whites, joined us in the glassed-in wine "cave." He is the executive chef of the operation but counts on his mother to make the pasta. In fact, she'd just finished the *agnolotti del plin* for the evening. Wouldn't we like to see them, and to meet her?

Those *agnolotti* were a kind of angel food entrée—no more than a postage stamp's worth of paper-thin, tender egg pockets stuffed with minced pork, veal, cheese, and summer truffles. The *guanciale di cavallo* (horse cheeks) were described to us with such glowing enthusiasm that we couldn't pass them up. They were undeniably delicious, with the beefy richness of oxtails and the pull-apart tenderness of pork shoulder. From a cheese course of sheep's-milk

Robiola, which had the texture of a soufflé, to the sparkly dessert wine Brachetto d'Acqui, which erupted with the scent of wild roses, our meal was exactly the kind of taste experience we'd sought in Piedmont: focused and uncluttered—even simple—yet entirely new (to us) and exceptional.

And we had a newfound appreciation for a chef with a strong, singular personality. Bastianich had warned us that in larger cities, we'd see kitchens caught between the impulse to prepare meticulous renditions of classic Piedmontese foods like *vitello tonnato* and *tajarin*, and the desire to keep up with the Spanish new wave's foams, airs, and gelées. At our first meal in Turin, we'd been presented with that split personality writ large: a *menu creativo* and a *menu tradizionale*. Whichever you decide on, and however good the results, it's easy to feel as though you're missing out on something special. The success of our first insider's tip encouraged us to follow an itinerary the next day that Mario Batali, the larger-than-life chef-restaurateur–TV host, had laid out for a market morning in Alba, the city that serves as the urban center for the wine-making towns of Le Langhe, as the region of hills that stretches out around it is called.

Turin's Caffè al Bicerin.

Truffle hunters, in Bra.

Piedmont wine country isn't like Napa and Sonoma, with their come one, come all policy and tasting rooms à go-go. There are very few Italian wineries that welcome impromptu tours, and the ones that do generally don't make wines you'd go out of your way to drink. Thankfully, most wine-making towns feature *enotecche regionale*, wineshops with tasting rooms that carry many, if not all, of the wines from the region.

The *enoteca* in the town of Barolo is one of the region's most impressive: a long, vaulted brick chamber in a grand, turreted castle where sommeliers in black tie and long black aprons pour generously from about 60 different Barolos. Despite the $20 tasting cost, the place attracts a mixed throng of Milanese on vacation, Japanese in Commes des Garçons, French people in bright stripes, and Americans in college T-shirts and shorts.

Although great labels are offered at the *enoteca* (we sampled lovely, complex wines from Einaudi, with herby notes of eucalyptus and thyme), all of the wines available during our trip were from the 2002 vintage, considered, because of heavy rains, to be the weakest for Barolo in the last decade—so much so that the best winemakers didn't bother to make their wine that year. Fortunately, the town includes a few other wineshops (and a snazzy corkscrew museum), among them a charming *enoteca* called Il Bacco, presided over by a bookish couple and their cat, that offers all the best labels of Barolo and the better vintages.

We bought a few souvenir bottles but didn't taste too deeply. We needed our faculties intact to find the Cappella di Sol LeWitt–David Tremlett, an architectural work of contemporary art in the middle of a vineyard owned by the Ceretto family. We knew only that the chapel was very colorful and that you had to take a dirt road south of La Morra to get to it. After a couple of wrong turns, we spotted four thirtysomethings in a late-model Audi stealing cherries from a roadside tree, and we deduced that we were on the right path.

Vineyards spilled out from the narrow gravel track, which steeply descended the slope from La Morra but afforded ravishing views across one of the major valleys that arc back toward Alba. Finally, in the near distance, a psychedelic church appeared in a field. Built in 1914 as a chapel and a shelter for vineyard workers during storms, the one-room *capella* was never consecrated. In 1999, the Cerettos asked the artist Sol LeWitt to paint

Batali had advised us to head early to Antico Caffè Calissano, a baroque tea hall with vaulted ceilings, gilt, and pink marble, for a *caffè corretto*—a wonderfully syrupy espresso "corrected" with a splash of grappa (which we desperately needed after spending a half-hour idling while waiting for a parking space). It was Saturday, and the town was teeming with old-timers stuffing their mesh shopping bags with opal-colored baby artichokes, the local ricotta variation called Seirass, and black Livornese hens. The truffles for which the town is most famous wouldn't begin appearing until October.

But the narrow stone side streets leading away from the market center in Alba were comparatively calm, and we soon found the serene La Bottega del Vicoletto, an utterly contemporary take-out deli Batali had recommended for assembling a brunch picnic. We were headed up the hills to Barolo that afternoon to do a bit of wine tasting, so we bought some of the sweetest roasted peppers we've ever had (Bastianich had alerted us to those), slippery and cold and perfect on a hot morning, and a dish of *polpette di tacchino*—turkey meatballs studded with carrots and herbs and bathed in a delectable white-wine gravy. Unable to defer gratification, we proceeded immediately to the shade of the Piazza Savona and ate our brunch, washing everything down with a half bottle of plummy Barbaresco as we watched the traffic rotate around the square.

Freshly picked porcini mushrooms.

Beneath a vine-covered pergola
at the Marchesi Alfieri castle
and winery, in Asti.

Piedmont wine country isn't like Napa and Sonoma, with their come
one, come all policy and tasting rooms à go-go

the exterior in his trademark geometry of vibrant colors. David Tremlett, a British artist, painted the interior in a moody, more contemplative palette. The cherry pickers arrived soon after we did, to take pictures, and so did a local couple, out walking their Irish setter.

From the door of the chapel, across the valley, hilltop burgs can be seen, set at regular intervals along the ridgelines. When we arrived in Cherasco, we knew we'd found the most picturesque of them all. The town is home to the Istituto Internazionale di Elicicoltura—a research facility dedicated to the farming of snails—and its restaurants are said to serve the tastiest *lumache* in Italy. We headed straight for Osteria de la Rosa Rossa, figuring that if we arrived toward closing time, we might snag a table. Reservations here are notoriously hard to get, both because of the restaurant's size—12 tables—and its reputation: the real deal in a tourist town.

The place had settled into a late afternoon's quiet roar when we arrived, and after a short wait, our patience was rewarded with terrific snail dishes—one with wild mushrooms, another with tomatoes and chiles. We discovered that the *osteria* also turns out some memorable plates that don't involve *lumache*, such as a gnocchi made with a velvety sauce of cream and Castelmagno, fruity tang tempering buttery richness; a simple, beautiful plate of cured leg of lamb with arugula, sweet cherry tomatoes, extra-virgin olive oil, and lemon juice. There was an antipasto we'd never seen, which the waiter called *carpione*, a piquant chicken dish with batons of zucchini; the bird had been pickled for two days in white wine vinegar and water and was served just slightly chilled—a delicious refresher on a humid afternoon.

The dining rooms and the cooking at La Rosa Rossa are casual enough that you could make it your daily canteen (we drank a juicy, inexpensive Dolcetto d'Alba from legendary winemaker Renatto Ratti), but the place offers enough indulgences that you might be inclined to spoil yourself on occasion. It made total sense that the local couple behind us were celebrating their 45th anniversary there in the company of a few friends—at 4 p.m.

That evening, we checked into the Hotel Castello di Sinio, restored by Americans James Russell and Denise Pardini, who describe themselves as two refugees from the Internet boom. Their castle is an impressive brick mass that dominates the town square in minuscule Sinio, and near the front entrance it features what is becoming a hotelier's most prized possession: a framed note from the Crown Prince of Savoy on his official letterhead,

thanking the castle's keepers for a recent stay. The Castello's tranquil terrace pool and chaises longues hover over the main square, just out of eyeshot of everything except the town's bell tower.

Before they bought the castle, Russell and Pardini guided winery tours in Piedmont. They know all the wine players in Le Langhe and can arrange for private tastings and tours for their guests at most of the wineries that keep low profiles—a relationship we imposed upon in short order after tasting that night a 1985 Barolo from Paolo Scavino, a wine that left us wanting to taste more, and know more: we had to make a pilgrimage to the winery.

Before we checked out the following morning, Pardini had secured us an appointment with Enrica Scavino, Paolo's granddaughter, for a tour and tasting the following day. We drove into Bra feeling triumphant, but the town seemed to be waking up only lazily. (Slow Food's logo is, after all, a stylized snail.) So we downed a quick *macchiato* at the Caffè Converso and headed off to explore Pollenzo, a Roman-era town in a riverside plain just a few miles away. Bra may be the administrative seat of Slow Food, but it is in Pollenzo that the future of the movement seems to be taking shape.

In a vast, sprawling, neo-Gothic estate on the edge of the town that in the 1830's was home to Savoy's King Carlo Alberto, a consortium of public and private entities has pooled its capital to create a gastronomical campus called the Agenzia di Pollenzo. Within the complex are a sleek new four-star hotel; an accredited graduate school for food studies called the University of Gastronomic Sciences; the Banca del Vino, an "archive" of Italian wine; and a restaurant, Guido Pollenzo, run by the Alciati, an esteemed family of restaurateurs.

When we arrived at the walled compound, a chic wedding party was descending on the hotel, and in the building's main courtyard a gaggle of students loitered outside the entrance to the university cafeteria. The harried "welcome" we received at the front desk made us wonder whether warmth and hospitality had escaped into the ether of the Agenzia's constelled mission.

No matter. We had a reservation at Guido, housed in a separate building, a minimalist restoration of a 19th-century granary, with soaring, two-story brick arches. It is here that the Agenzia's potential is embodied, in Piero Alciati, who as soon as we sat down poured us eye-opening glasses of a cold Langhe white wine that had all the jasmine-scented richness of a Viognier, married to the racy citrus flavors of a Sauvignon Blanc (and which had been made, to our

At Ristorante Guido, in Pollenzo.

great delight, by the Scavinos). We sipped it with an amuse-bouche that was a lesson to all those conceptual "bites," "shooters," and "spoons" that come unbidden at the beginning of fancy meals these days. Here were shaved onions and carrots, lightly pickled, served chilled, with a drizzle of superb olive oil and a sprinkling of sea salt. "Coleslaw" may have been invented in Holland, but the Italians have perfected it.

There were other highlights: a pinwheel of sweet red shrimp nestled on a tangle of thinly sliced eggplant that had been marinated in herbs and olive oil; a steamed hunk of cod dressed with a pesto made of lettuces; a veal shank cooked in a broth of milk and Moscato d'Asti for eight hours and served with a spoon; and an interpretation of a classic Piedmont *finanziera*, a stew of veal sweetbreads and brains, that proved that hearty comfort food can seem light, elegant, and uplifting.

Which was crucial, because our afternoon excursion was to Castelmagno, two hours away — a heroic distance in the condensed geography of Piedmont. We skipped a cheese course — in the hope that we'd be nibbling on a hunk of Castelmagno's namesake in a couple of hours — but inhaled the quince ice pops and cream-filled macaroons Alciati set down with the check.

After we'd driven about a half-hour due west through wide-open flatlands, the delicate tracery of the Alps became visible on the horizon, and with every passing minute, the mountains loomed larger.

At Caraglio, we took a hard left, and the road began climbing along ledges that were lush and green, with grassy slopes below and a fringe of snow above, on the loftiest peaks.

The road steadily became narrower and steeper, a track of back-to-back double-hairpin turns, without any guardrails whatsoever. And just when we'd be thinking the road couldn't get any narrower, an obstacle like an asphalt-paving crew or slow-climbing cyclist would show up around the next blind curve.

When, finally, we arrived, we found that the locus of Petrini's "flavor of the future" resides in just a few houses built into the mountain, which rings with the sound of cowbells clanging on distant slopes. One house we passed had a hand-lettered sign reading FORMAGGI, so we pulled into that driveway, past sleeping dogs and pecking chickens. Soon the cheese maker's mother stepped forward. She rewarded our ascent with an enthusiastic guided tour of the spotless cheese-making rooms, where bulbous mesh bags of curds hung, dripping whey, from a rack; the not-so-spotless barn, where a few calves were dozing in the hay; and the dark, damp cave where the cheese was aged.

We bought a large wedge and broke off chunks on the ride down the mountain. This Castelmagno, fresh from the source, had an almost chalky texture, not as farmhouse-funky as it had seemed when served in the gnocchi at I Bologna. It also had a pleasant tartness balanced by nutty notes, and a taste of the mountain grass that surrounded us. But it would require some time to reach its full potential.

We were happy to have seen the cows up close, and they reminded us that Patrick Martins, a Slow Food member and co-owner of Heritage Foods — a New York–based company that scours American farms for the most flavorful meat from humanely raised rare breeds of cattle, pigs, and poultry — had told us about a small, quiet, in-the-know kind of place in Alba called LaLibera, where serious food lovers congregate.

Judging by the international crowd that had assembled there at noon, word had clearly gotten out about LaLibera, a pretty set of salons strung together in the sleepiest corner of the bustling southern end of Alba. The kitchen — so small that a sous-chef was peeling potatoes in an open courtyard behind the restaurant — didn't miss a beat: grilled sardines came on caramelized Piedmontese peppers, with a scoop of *bagna cauda* gelato; a spit-roasted pigeon had green garlic and rosemary; and veal fillet,

perfectly medium rare, was served with a scattering of capers and chopped tomatoes over the top.

Before catching our plane back from Turin to the States, we needed—in the august tradition of all tourists—to find out who was making the best gelato in Italy. Since the arrival of Grom, which we'd heard about from Faith Heller Willinger, an American author and educator who lives in Italy and writes about Italian cuisine, the Turin gelato wars have become particularly intense. Everyone has taken sides, and even the concierge at our hotel added her two cents: "Fiori"—an esteemed *gelateria* that's been around for ages—"is the more better."

It would be hard to top what we sampled at Grom, which was an outstandingly rich, smooth *gianduja* made with intense Tonda Gentile hazelnuts from Le Langhe, and a *stracciatella* made with chocolate from Turin's finest chocolatier, Guido

Gobino. There was also a raspberry gelato whipped up from organic berries so sweet that just a hint of sugar had been added.

But for comparison's sake, we hustled over to Fiori, in the heart of the pedestrian-choked university district. Fiori was making no big deal about its flavors or ingredients, just working as fast as it could to make a dent in the line stretching out from the streetside window. We got six small cups to try (two flavors in each cup), and in short order, the cups were empty. The pistachio was genuinely nutty, deserving of its name.

Caught up in the heat of the competition, we then jogged over to Gelateria Silvano, on the Via Nizza. It was our incredible good fortune, before anything got out of hand, to find a sign in the window: CHIUSO. In our book, every guest should leave something for the sequel.

A field of poppies on the road to Alba.

Travelers' Guide to Piedmont

WHEN TO GO

Early fall—when temperatures hover just above 70 degrees—is the ideal time to visit this part of northwestern Italy. September is particularly delightful, and the cooler autumn months of October and November bring the Barbera and Moscato wine harvests, along with the crowds who arrive for white truffle season.

GETTING THERE

The towns around Alba and Asti, the gastronomic heart and soul of Piedmont, are about two hours from Turin, the region's largest metropolis. Fly to Turin International Airport (TRN) and rent a car, a must for touring the hills of the Langhe. Flights from North America connect through Rome, Milan, Paris, Frankfurt, or Munich.

The 17th-century Basilica dell'Assunta, in Varallo.

While in Piedmont...

- Asti ❶
- Avigliana ⓫
- Basilica di Superga ⓯
- Bossea Caves ❷
- Cuneo ❸
- Domodossola ⓱
- Garessio ❹
- Lake Ceresole Reale ❼
- Lake Orta ❺
- Novara ❻
- Pinerolo ⓬
- Sacra di San Michele ❿
- Santuario d'Oropa ⓰
- Stupinigi ⓮
- Susa ❾
- Turin (Torino) ⓭
- Varallo ⓲
- Vercelli ⓳
- Via Lattea ❽

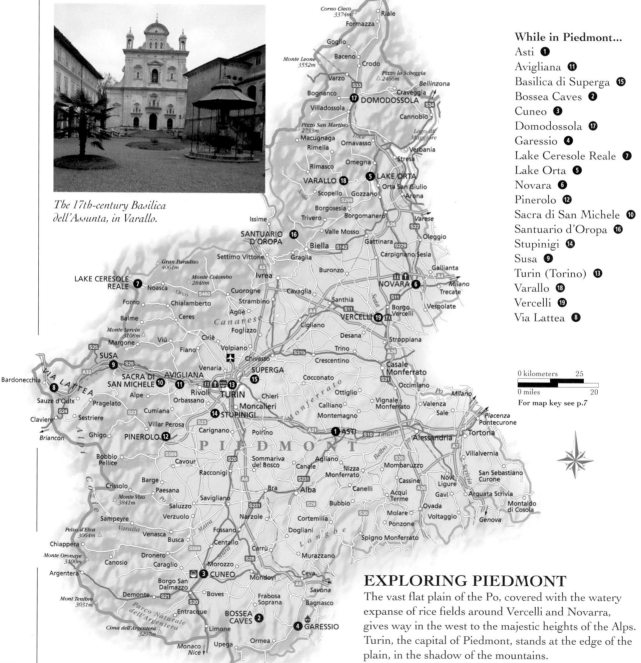

0 kilometers   25
0 miles   20
For map key see p.7

EXPLORING PIEDMONT

The vast flat plain of the Po, covered with the watery expanse of rice fields around Vercelli and Novarra, gives way in the west to the majestic heights of the Alps. Turin, the capital of Piedmont, stands at the edge of the plain, in the shadow of the mountains.

WHERE TO STAY

Castello di Verduno
The enormous Baroque rooms of this shabby-chic castle on a hill south of Alba go a long way toward helping guests overlook the spartan amenities (there's no TV—or phone).
9 Via Umberto I, Verduno;
39-0172/470-125;
castellodiverduno.com;
doubles from Ⓢ.

Hotel Castello di Sinio
A luxurious base camp for exploring the Langhe region, run by a knowledgeable American couple with a passion for the food and wine of Piedmont.
1 Vicolo Castello, Sinio;
39-0173/263-889;
hotelcastellodisinio.com;
doubles from ⓈⓈ.

Marchesi Alfieri
A spacious, tastefully appointed agriturismo with outstanding views, on the grounds of a winery famed for its Barbera d'Asti.
28 Piazza Alfieri, San Martino Alfieri, Asti;
39-0141/976-015;
marchesialfieri.it;
doubles from Ⓢ;
to purchase Marchesi Alfieri Barbera d'Asti in the United States, call 425/747-9241.

The paddy-field region around Vercelli and Novarra, Europe's rice capital.

Relais San Maurizio
At the summit of steep, vineyard-covered slopes, this former monastery, decked out in grand florals and Murano glass chandeliers, features a Caudalie spa.
39 Località San Maurizio, Santo Stefano Belbo;
39-0141/841-900;
relaissanmaurizio.it;
doubles from ⓈⓈⓈ.

The courtyard at Marchesi Alfieri castle and winery, in Asti.

SEE ALSO

For more on the Langhe, plus a map:
The Best Wine in the World?
pp.154–155

Sardines and caramelized red peppers with bagna cauda *gelato at LaLibera.*

WHERE TO EAT

Antico Caffè Calissano
In the vaulted arcade of Alba's Piazza Duomo, this 18th-century confection of pink marble and gilt is the preferred first stop for truffle hunters on market mornings in November.
3 Piazza Risorgimento, Alba;
39-0173/442-101;
coffee and pastries for two Ⓢ.

Caffè al Bicerin
The signature bicerin *(melted chocolate, coffee, and cream) has been served at this Turin landmark since 1763.*
5 Piazza della Consolata, Turin;
39-011/436-9325;
pastries and hot chocolate for two Ⓢ.

Caffè Converso
You, too, might spy Slow Food founder Carlo Petrini downing an espresso at this turn-of-the-19th-century café and bakery.
199 Via Vittorio Emanuele II, Bra;
39-0172/413-626;
coffee and pastries for two Ⓢ.

La Ciau del Tornavento
(For details, see p.155)

Carlo Petrini, Slow Food founder, at Bra's Caffè Converso.

Grom
This new-school gelateria carefully sources all ingredients—from cream and eggs to add-ins like cornmeal cookies and coffee.
1D Piazza Paleocapa, Turin;
39-011/511-9067;
gelato for two Ⓢ.

Guido Ristorante Pollenzo
(For details, see p.155)

I Bologna
Owned by members of an esteemed Bologna winemaking family, this trattoria cooks fresh, flavorful renditions of esoteric regional classics.
4 Via Nicola Sardi, Rocchetta Tanaro;
39-0141/644-600;
dinner for two ⓈⓈⓈ.

La Bottega del Vicoletto
A great place to stock up for a picnic, this shop cooks up dishes to go and offers local cheeses and prosciutto crudo di Parma.
6 Via Bertero, Alba;
39-0173/363-196;
picnic for two ⓈⓈ.

L'Angolo di Paradiso
Chef Cesare Giaccone's signature capretto, *or roast baby goat, is cooked on a spit in an open fireplace in the restaurant.*
12 Via Umberto, Albaretto Torre;
39-0173/520-141;
dinner for two ⓈⓈⓈⓈ.

Osteria de la Rosa Rossa
A casual, homey osteria *serving seriously delicious snails. Make sure you book early.*

Piedmontese white truffles have an earthy, garlicky aroma and flavor.

31 Via San Pietro, Cherasco;
39-0172/488-133;
dinner for two ⓈⓈ.

Osteria LaLibera
This sleek corner room attracts an international crowd for its inventive take on market-to-table fresh ingredients.
24A Via Elvio Pertinace, Alba; 39-0173/293-155;
dinner for two ⓈⓈⓈ.

Piazza Duomo
Enrico Crippa serves avant-garde Italian food made with rarely seen ingredients like hop sprouts and goat's beard.
4 Piazza Risorgimento, Alba;
39-0173/442-800;
dinner for two ⓈⓈⓈⓈ.

WHERE TO SHOP

Enoteca Regionale del Barolo
Sommeliers pour wine from a cross section of Barolo's producers.
Castello Falletti, Barolo;
39-0173/56277;
baroloworld.it;
Ⓢ for a flight of three wines.

Il Bacco
A superb, tiny boutique cellar with some of the best wines in the region.
87 Via Roma, Barolo;
39-0173/56233.

I Piaceri del Gusto
This store's selection of books on Piedmontese wine and food complements a cellar of excellent, hard-to-find bottles.
23 Via Vittorio Emanuele II, Alba;
39-0173/440-166.

Tartufi Ponzio
A shoebox-sized shop with a wide selection of sauces, vinegars, and oils, many made with white truffles.
26 Via Vittorio Emanuele II, Alba;
39-0173/440-456.

Spacious arcades on Via Roma.

TOP SIGHTS IN TURIN

Armeria Reale ❺

Housed in a wing of the Palazzo Reale, on the northern side of the main square, this is one of the most extensive and breathtaking collections of arms and armory in the world.

Duomo ❷

The cathedral, built in 1497–8 and dedicated to St. John the Baptist, is Turin's only example of Renaissance architecture. The interior is filled with statuary and paintings.

Mole Antonelliana ❾

Alessandro Antonelli's 550-foot-tall Mole is Turin's signature building. It was originally designed as a synagogue, but on its completion in 1897 the city used it to house the Risorgimento museum; it is now the home of Turin's Museum of Cinema.

Museo Egizio/Galleria Sabauda ❼

Turin's Egyptian museum is one of the world's best, with monumental sculptures, reconstructed temples, and everyday objects. The Galleria Sabauda, in the same building, contains the House of Savoy's main art collection.

Palazzo Carignano ❽

With its magnificent brick façade and ornate rotunda, this Baroque building was designed by architect Guarino Guarini and built in 1679. Today, it houses the Museo Nazionale del Risorgimento, which tells the story of the reunification of Italy.

Palazzo Madama ❻

This palace began as a medieval castle, which itself incorporated parts of the Roman city walls. It was later extended and remodeled, and given a new façade in the 18th century. It contains the Museo Civico d'Arte Antica, with treasures from Greco-Roman times to the 19th century.

Palazzo Reale ❹

The Savoy royal family's seat from 1660 until Italian reunification in 1861. The austere façade hides richly decorated state apartments.

Porta Palatina ❶

The city's only surviving Roman gateway—one of the best examples to be seen anywhere—dates from the 1st century A.D.

San Lorenzo ❸

The interior of Guarini's fine Baroque church, begun in 1634, boasts an extraordinary geometric dome.

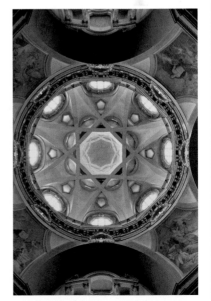

An interior view of Guarini's dome in the church of San Lorenzo.

The Best Wine in the World?

ON THE FERTILE HILLS OF ITALY'S LE LANGHE REGION, IN THE HEART OF BAROLO COUNTRY, TWO WINEMAKERS WITH RADICALLY DIFFERENT STYLES ARE HARVESTING GRAPES FROM THE FINEST VINES. BY BRUCE SCHOENFELD

LE LANGHE

The morning fog, or *nebbia*, of Italy's Piedmont region had long since cleared when I found my host, the winemaker Giorgio Rivetti, straddling the steep slope of the Gallina vineyard, inspecting nebbiolo grapes, which get their name and much of their distinctive character from that encompassing shroud. Shortly before, Rivetti and I had finished a lunch the length of a Bertolucci epic. It had involved course after course of local specialties—snails with leeks and apples, pasta stuffed with rabbit—tweaked for modernity and accompanied by multiple bottles of Rivetti's La Spinetta wines. Inspired, I had struck off alone to visit the grapes.

From the top of the vineyard, I had a panoramic view of the area's hilltop towns. Capped by medieval churches and fronted by vine-covered hillsides, each

A panoramic view of the hilltop town of Monforte d'Alba, from the Hotel Villa Beccaris.

stood in the foreground of the next until the soft purples and muted greens faded together at the horizon. It was a timeless scene. But I'd been listening to Rivetti describe the recent evolution — no, call it revolution — of wine making in Piedmont. I'd tasted the extraordinary wines produced in the neighboring communes of Barolo and Barbaresco since the mid-1990's. I understood that much of what was happening on those hillsides bore scant resemblance to what had gone before.

Short and dark-haired, Rivetti looks something like the actor John Cusack. He'd changed from his lunchtime clothes into a tattersall shirt worn untucked over camouflage pants. Now he looked up from his refractometer, a device he uses to measure the sweetness of the grapes, and greeted me without surprise. Where else but a vineyard would someone go after having sampled such wines?

"The best winemakers are farmers," he said, a notion that hardly sounds revolutionary. But until recently, most *piemontese* winemakers considered the region's vineyards little more than a source of raw material, mere office-supply stores for grapes. The wine making began at the winery door. Rivetti, along with perhaps a dozen other inspired and industrious viticulturists, helped change that mind-set. They snipped nascent grapes from the vines in June to give those that remained a better chance to develop character and power. They used modern technology to understand why some vines yielded better fruit than others. They harvested days after everyone else, waiting to ensure that their grapes were truly ripe.

Photographs by David Cicconi   143

Rivetti and his peers must have seemed like dangerous radicals, but by creating such coveted wines, they ultimately helped transform hobbies into businesses

Oak barrels full of aging La Spinetta.

These were common techniques in Bordeaux, not to mention the thoroughly modern Napa Valley. But in this corner of northwestern Italy, a static, insular, landlocked place where fresh ideas are about as common as fresh fish, they seemed heretical. The wines that resulted were both smoother and more potent than the old Barolos and Barbarescos. They were full of personality but without harshness, so they didn't need a decade or more of cellar time before they could be enjoyed. They appealed to a wide range of wine drinkers throughout the world, not just to locals who'd acclimated their palates to nebbiolo, and to a tiny coterie of Barolo and Barbaresco fanatics elsewhere.

Before long, these wines had altered the economics of the region. For most of the 20th century, young adults in this part of Piedmont, which is called the Langhe, would finish school and migrate from the picturesque but economically stagnant hilltop towns to nearby Turin for work in the Fiat factory. On weekends, they would return to tend their small vineyard plots—as their parents and grandparents had tended them—but with little knowledge or passion. Rivetti and his peers must have seemed like dangerous radicals, but by creating such coveted wines, they ultimately helped transform hobbies into businesses. "Everything changed," says Domenico Clerico, another of these iconoclasts-turned-icons. "Our entire way of life is different now."

These days, acclaim for the new Barolos and Barbarescos is attracting wine pilgrims to what has always been an inaccessible area, hidden behind an arc of mountains and a suspicion bordering on antipathy toward the outside world. Centuries-old villas have been converted into hotels that belong to one or another of the luxury associations. The culinary scene is thriving. Even nature has relented. After several decades of mostly uncooperative weather, a string of remarkable vintages—from 1996 to 2001—has made the wines of the Langhe as consistently great as any in the world.

Rivetti might still describe himself as a farmer, but the nebbiolo from the rarefied vineyards of Barolo and Barbaresco has become a spectacularly lucrative cash crop. His finest wines—three Barbarescos and a Barolo—sell for more than $100 a bottle on release. He dresses like a rock star, in designer shirts and leather jackets. He drives a Mercedes. And nearly every night when he isn't traveling, he eats at one of the growing number of

Michelin-starred or similarly accomplished restaurants in the area—such as Cervere's Antica Corona Reale da Renzo, where we'd had lunch—that use the finest ingredients, employ imaginative chefs of the highest order, serve the wine-making community and well-heeled tourists, and never could have existed here before now.

But as often happens when something is gained, something else has been lost. Pio Boffa is Rivetti's antithesis: a fourth-generation proprietor of a winery called Pio Cesare that does its best to resist the call to modernity. Boffa is just four years older than Rivetti, yet he dresses like a European of another time, with supple loafers buffed to a shine and sweater vests worn over striped shirts. "How you dress is important," he says. "You see kids today looking like…if I saw them in the middle of the night, I'd be scared."

Once upon a time, Boffa himself was regarded as a revolutionary. A 1982 clipping from *Wine Spectator* anointing him as such adorns a wall in the Pio Cesare winery, where both Boffa and his mother were born. Boffa was among the first in the area to ferment his wine in stainless steel; among the first to moderate the time it spent in contact with the skins, thereby limiting the amount of tannin that would be transmitted; and among the first to obsess about

Winemaker Giorgio Rivetti, with a glass of 2001 Barolo Campé.

Inside the cellar at Pio Cesare, in Alba.

cleanliness in his winery—and, by extension, in his wines. He spent time in Napa with Robert Mondavi, living at his house for several months.

But now Boffa stands as a guardian of a dying tradition. He believes the wines that Rivetti and the others are making taste too much like wines from all over the world. This doesn't make them bad so much as improper for a region that has something singular to offer. "There are so many areas that make wine that is approachable, easy to drink," he says. "I don't want to be one of those."

Boffa bemoans much of the modernization he sees around him. "We have made progress," he says, "but I think in many ways we've lost our integrity. We have made lots of mistakes, in terms of following too closely the modern trend." He's talking about wine, but also about culture. "I understand that this is the perspective of somebody with an older mentality," Boffa says, "and from a family that has been here forever. But why do I have to go to restaurants around here and see ostrich meat?"

The Langhe is small, and Boffa and Rivetti inevitably pass each other on the sidewalks of Alba or when driving one of the hairpin turns on the road to Serralunga or La Morra. Both love to eat well, so they periodically find themselves manning adjacent tables at one of the region's better restaurants. When that happens, Rivetti will order a bottle of Pio Cesare and Boffa will order a bottle of La Spinetta

as a sign of mutual respect. Each will enjoy the other's wine over their *vitello tonnato* or *carne cruda*, but with a nagging feeling that an opportunity has been squandered. Such talent, such formidable intelligence, such elite vineyards should be used in the service of making truly great wine, each will be thinking about the other. How unfortunate that someone who could be making some of the best wines around, should be so utterly, transparently, and irrevocably wrong.

On a map, Piedmont appears perfectly positioned at the center of Mediterranean Europe. The abundance of Liguria lies directly to the south, with France due west. Milan and the riches of Lombardy lie to the east, while the snowcapped peaks of Switzerland are almost visible to the north.

The truth is, for centuries the Langhe existed as a place out of time. Nobody came, almost nobody left, and the culture was turned inward for so long that it became almost impenetrable. The Piedmontese spoke their own dialect, which was only rudimentarily linked to Italian. Trade with the outside world was minimal, as was travel. "You ask a 70-year-old farmer here about the sea and he's never seen it," Rivetti says. "It's an hour away by car, but he's never seen it."

"Piedmont is in the middle of nowhere," Boffa volunteers. "There are no direct trains here. But the thing is, we like that. We're a very closed people. We like to stay by ourselves."

The Rivettis were different. In the mid-1800's, the family left for Argentina. Around 1920 Giorgio's grandfather, Giovanni, wandered to Brooklyn, where he seems to have found work in wine distribution, though alcohol sales were illegal in the United States at the time. Eventually, Giovanni's son abandoned New York for his ancestral home. Giuseppe Rivetti bought land in Neive, in the heart of Barbaresco, and started making wine. Unlike almost everyone else in the Langhe's wine industry, he hadn't grown up in the region. He wasn't doing things a certain way because his ancestors had. And when his youngest son, Giorgio, asked to spend two years working with the Bordeaux producer Château Margaux, Giuseppe was worldly enough to appreciate the opportunity.

Rivetti had already taken an undergraduate degree in Alba, and he would later study enology in Turin, but his real education came at Margaux. He was exposed to the viticultural and enological techniques used to make the world's most renowned

The vineyards and countryside of Neive, in the heart of Barbaresco.

147

Villa Tiboldi's main building.

wines, and he was able to taste those wines day after day. He came home in 1985 with a head full of ideas and a car full of bottles: French wines, from Bordeaux and farther afield. Soon after, he called friends and colleagues and invited them to a restaurant called Guido, in Costigliole d'Asti. He wanted them to sample the wines he'd brought back, alongside a selection of wines from the Langhe. "I wanted them to realize, 'Why would anyone buy *piemontese* wine when it tastes like this?'" Rivetti says now. "Old, dirty, oxidized. And the French wine was so approachable, so drinkable."

Many of the attendees of that tasting—Elio Altare, Luciano Sandrone, Roberto Voerzio, Enrico Scavino, and Domenico Clerico—now rank among the region's greatest winemakers. "We tried the wines to understand what is good, what is wrong, what is best," says Roberto Damonte, an enologist who studied with Rivetti and whose Malvirà wines are made just outside the Barolo appellation, in Roero. "We realized that Piedmont has too much tradition. Our wines weren't clear. They smelled wrong. After that, vintage by vintage, producer by producer, the wines changed."

The 1989 and 1990 vintages marked the first successes for some of the new and revitalized producers. Simultaneously, the Slow Food movement, founded as a reaction to the encroachment of McDonald's hamburger stands around the world and headquartered in the Piedmontese town of Bra, emerged to provide a

context. These wines were made in limited volume from nebbiolo, which is native to Piedmont and known for expressing the attributes of the *terroir* where it is grown. The grapes have a transparency of place that the Slow Food mentality cherished. Nobody could mistake a Barolo or Barbaresco for anything else.

Soon curious wine drinkers from Switzerland and Germany started to visit, driving down to taste for themselves the changes that were unfolding. Many had spent time in Bordeaux, Burgundy, and beyond, and when they began calling on the Piedmontese farmers and sampling wines in rudimentary tasting rooms, a curious thing happened. "They'd actually teach some of the producers," Rivetti says. "They'd say, 'These wines are good, but try doing this and they might be even better.' And the producers learned!"

By the time the first of the extraordinary run of vintages arrived, in 1996, both vines and mind-sets were ready. And as the wines began to sell, affluence crept into the region. That same year, Damonte and his wife, Patrizia, bought a hillside vineyard in Canale, near Alba. With the property came a dilapidated 18th-century villa that a Genoese lawyer had kept as a summerhouse. At the time, there was little commercial use for such a structure, but by 2003 they'd transformed it into Villa Tiboldi, a stunning hotel with a commanding view of the Roero. They marketed it first to clients who bought their wine, then pitched the property to their importers around Europe.

Now Villa Tiboldi sells itself. It is booked much of the year by Germans, Swiss, French, English, other Italians, and a smattering of Americans. With each morning's fog, Patrizia arrives bearing freshly laid eggs, and one by one guests throw open their shutters to the day. By lunchtime exquisite dishes such as roasted squab with grainy mustard and a marmalade of green tomato are served on the terrace.

Rivetti came to Villa Tiboldi one day to see Damonte and walked away with a girlfriend: a quick-witted, fair-haired German named Anja who now runs La Spinetta's business side. One evening I meet them in Pollenzo at a restaurant called Guido, on the campus of Slow Food's University of Gastronomic Sciences: an institution of higher learning that, by dint of its name alone, could exist only in Italy. This Guido is a direct descendant of the old Guido, where the 1985 tasting was held. The original Guido is gone but his sons now run the restaurant.

Patrizia and Roberto Damonte, owners of Villa Tiboldi.

Fourth-generation vintner Pio Boffa,
in the Pio Cesare tasting room.

Rivetti is wearing a white dress shirt unbuttoned at the cuffs, his third shirt of the day. ("We go through a lot of shirts," Anja says.) He eats at Guido often, yet each time he encounters the high wooden ceiling, with its arc of futuristic lights, or the row of wine glasses behind a translucent wall, visible only in silhouette, he can't help but marvel. "I remember being here back in 1998," he says. "It was an absolute mess."

The first Guido was one of the few places that employed sommeliers who were inquisitive about wine. The second has taken that to extremes, with two phone book–size lists for red wine alone. "Now winemakers come and drink wine from all over," Rivetti says. And this Guido is a departure from the old Piedmont in another way: the restaurant serves so much fresh fish that one of the two chefs specializes in it.

At Guido we eat beef tongue stuffed with cabbage and *bottarga*—preserved tuna roe. We eat *agnolotti* pasta filled with three meats, then rabbit with rectangles of puréed vegetables. Each of us at the table has chosen a wine to be served blind, and

we end up with two Barolos, two Barbarescos, and a Burgundy.

We agree unanimously on which is best. Lush and supple, it has a nose of cherries but the driving force of a Charlie Watts beat. It is more modern than traditional but exudes that sense of place that marks the world's finest wines. The bottle is revealed as the La Spinetta 1998 from Barbaresco's Starderi vineyard.

Rivetti, who had no idea that a wine of his was on the table, is overjoyed by our reaction, but even more by his own. "I never recognize my wine," he says. "But I always love it."

The memory of the Starderi still lingers when Pio Boffa collects me the next morning in Monforte d'Alba, where I'm staying. We wind past groves of pencil-thin trees toward Alba and his winery. The towns we pass through seem similar—each is built atop a hill and dominated by a church, with streets paved in square stones and red-shuttered houses topped by barrel-tile roofs, yet each has singularities. Monforte uses white-marble inlay instead of paint to mark its crosswalks, for example. We pass a man in a long coat shuffling along the street beside a dog; both look as they might have a century ago. "Truffle hunters," Boffa says.

Pio Cesare was founded in 1881 by Boffa's great-grandfather. The winery itself, which has a tiled courtyard, brick-domed ceilings, and other features of traditional Piedmontese architecture, dates back to the 1600's. Boffa takes me to see a Roman wall from 50 B.C. that cuts through the cellar, separating his fermentation tanks from his barrels. "If you have something like that in your winery, you must respect it," he says.

Accordingly, he uses large wooden casks, which impart less oak flavor, to age his wine. Unlike La Spinetta's labels, which feature Albrecht Dürer woodcuts of wild animals, Pio Cesare's look as if they've been handed down directly from the 19th century. And when Boffa spent about $10 million to renovate the winery's inner workings several years ago, he commanded the contractor to keep the place looking the same. "So if my late grandfather walked in, he'd not notice a difference," Boffa says. "I told them, 'I don't care about the cost. I don't care if it's not practical. Exactly the same.'"

The wines themselves have the same sense of being crafted to feel like heirlooms. "A glass of real Barolo, the first time you have it, it's hard to

The grapes at Pio Boffa's Gustava vineyard.

151

understand," he explains. "It's rude, it's rough, it's controversial. But sip by sip, it conquers you. It requires time to understand it, but when you do, you can't live without it. That's the kind of Barolo I try to make."

Earlier in the week, we'd eaten a traditional *piemontese* dinner cooked by Boffa's wife, Nicoletta, at their summerhouse in Treiso, a few miles away. Now, with lunchtime approaching, he takes me upstairs to a terrace off the living quarters, where his mother still resides. A red-and-white-checked tablecloth is spread over a table. We open bottles of Pio Cesare and eat preserved tuna, homemade bread, spaghetti with tomatoes from the garden, and peaches soaked in Barolo—all made by his mother, who is in her eighties. We gaze out over the buildings of Alba.

"I have been eating lunch and dinner here with my grandfather and my father for 51 years," he says. "The same view. The same table. The same food."

His manner is brusque, but I see that his eyes are moist. He gestures toward the hills, which glint in the sunshine. "You can see why we like to keep things the same."

I spend the next night with Rivetti at La Ciau del Tornavento, in Treiso. Perhaps the best restaurant in the area, it can't be more than a half-mile from Boffa's summerhouse. As I revel in chef Maurilio Garola's wry take on Piedmontese cuisine, I can't help thinking about the home-cooked meal Boffa is doubtless eating at the same moment.

Nicoletta Boffa's dishes aren't updated versions of anything, just traditional recipes served with the utmost sincerity. They aren't as exciting as what Garola creates at Tornavento, just as her husband's Barolos and Barbarescos don't thrill my palate quite as much as Rivetti's versions of those wines, yet I understand that it is vitally important that Nicoletta's food, like the Pio Cesare wines, continues to exist in its current form. If Rivetti and his cadre were

necessary to help pull Piedmont into the present day, Boffa is there to ensure that it doesn't get pulled too far. After a week spent between one winemaker and the other, I have come to perceive them as the twin halves of today's Piedmontese culture. One looks ahead, the other behind.

Except that this isn't exactly true. For my last dinner in the area, I meet Boffa in Rivoli, outside Turin. He has invited me to Combal.Zero, an avant-garde restaurant within a museum of contemporary art, where our meal is easily as surreal as any of the paintings hanging in the galleries. Spanish ham and frozen melon are presented in a hollowed-out book. A fish course arrives in a faux fossil, and we're asked to hammer away at the clay around it. Foie gras is sucked out of a hole in a balloon.

Boffa loves every course. It is like taking Gore Vidal to see the Three Stooges and watching him double over in hysterics. Flabbergasted, I ask Boffa how he can reconcile his fervor for the traditional, for that which exists without irony, with the most studiously ironic meal I have ever eaten. "This is provocative," he replies. "You go to traditional restaurants in La Morra, you have traditional dishes. You come here, you start talking."

At that moment, a bottle of his Dolcetto arrives at the table. It is a lighter, simpler wine than Barolo or Barbaresco, made from a different grape—an everyday beverage for the Piedmontese that, if anything, symbolizes the region even more than those expensive, exalted wines do. He tastes it and sighs with contentment. I tell Boffa that it is absolutely the last wine I would have ever imagined ordering at a place like this, and he looks at me with an expression—a mixture of defiance and pity—that seems to embody the whole of *piemontese* culture.

"I'm from Piemonte, what can I tell you?" he says, turning his palms toward the sky. "I love what I love."

*Pio Cesare's
L'Ornato vineyard.*

Travelers' Guide to the Langhe

WHEN TO GO

Fog blots out mornings for nine months of the year, but afternoons are generally gorgeous year-round, and the soft, understated landscape wears its seasonality well. June is particularly lovely, with highs of 70 degrees and the first evidence of grapes on the vines.

GETTING THERE

Alitalia and Delta fly direct from U.S. gateways to Milan's Malpensa Airport, which is a two-hour drive northwest of the Langhe. Alternatively, connect via Rome, Milan, Paris, Frankfurt, or Munich and fly to Turin. The drive to Alba takes about an hour.

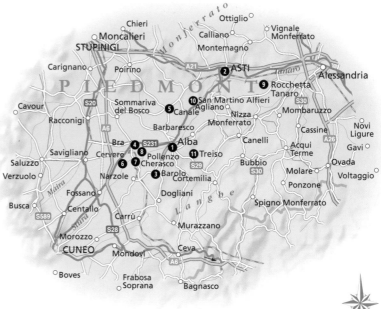

0 kilometers 00
0 miles 00
For map key see p.7

WHERE TO STAY

Villa Tiboldi
Atop a steep hill of vineyards outside Canale in the Roero appellation, this prototypical Italian villa—part of a working winery—was underrated until Paul Allen rented out all nine rooms for the 2006 Turin Winter Olympics.
127 Case Sparse Tiboldi;
39-0173/970-388;
villatiboldi.it;
doubles from $$.

Hotel Villa Beccaris
A beautiful (if somewhat soulless) 18th-century compound perched above Monforte. But beware: the bell in the adjacent cathedral sounds on the hour all night long.
1 Via Bava Beccaris, Monforte d'Alba;
39-0173/78158;
villabeccaris.it;
doubles from $$, including breakfast.

L'Antico Asilo
Spotlessly clean and family-run, this four-room inn on a Serralunga back street has a courtyard overlooking the hillside vineyards. Utterly charming, friendly, reasonably priced.
13 Via Mazzini, Serralunga d'Alba;
39-0173/613-016;
anticoasilo.com;
doubles from $.

WHERE TO EAT

Antica Corona Reale da Renzo
Home cooking—Piedmontese-style—at the Michelin-starred level, including perhaps the finest rendition of tripe anywhere in the world. Wine options are extensive and underpriced.
13 Via Fossano, Cervere;
39-0172/474-132;
dinner for two $$$$.

Combal.Zero
Castello di Rivoli, Piazza Mafalda di Savoia, Rivoli;
39-011/956-5225;
dinner for two $$$$.

While in the Langhe...
Alba ❶
Asti ❷
Barolo ❸
Bra ❹
Canale ❺
Cervere ❻
Cherasco ❼
Pollenzo ❽
Rocchetta Tanaro ❾
San Martino Alfieri ❿
Treiso ⓫

La Ciau del Tornavento
No restaurant in the area is more ambitious, nor as consistently rewarding. Interiors border on kitschy, but the view over a valley is stunning, the atmosphere elegant, and the wine list a work of art.
7 Piazza Baracco, Treiso;
39-0173/638-333;
laciaudeltornavento.it;
dinner for two $$$$.

Guido Ristorante Pollenzo
Not the warm, traditional trattoria of your Italian fantasy, but a modern culinary temple with deferential service and imaginative food on the grounds of Slow Food's University of Gastronomic Sciences.
19 Via Fossano, Pollenzo;
39-0172/458-422;
guidoristorante.it;
dinner for two Ⓢ Ⓢ Ⓢ Ⓢ.

WHERE TO SIP

Visiting wineries in the Langhe is like visiting a working farm in the United States. It can be done, and someone there will have plenty to show you, but he's likely to have done nothing to make the place look nice on your behalf—and you need to set up the visit before you arrive. That said, Barolos and Barbarescos (or, if you really want to sound Italian, *baroli* and *barbareschi*) rank among the world's finest wines, and the Piedmontese are fantastically generous. Try some wines before you go, pick a few favorites, call

A bottle of Pio Cesare 2005 Arneis.

ahead with a polite request, and have an unforgettable time, usually with the owner.

Pio Cesare Azienda Agricola
The only producer remaining in Alba, Pio Boffa's family winery brings more than a century of tradition (and a surprisingly open mind) to bear on some of the best vineyard sites in Barolo and Barbaresco.
6 Via Cesare Balbo, Alba;
39-0173/440-386;
piocesare.it.

La Spinetta
Giorgio Rivetti's wines are decidedly new wave, but so full of flavor and nuance that traditionalists can't help loving them, too.
1 Via Carzello, Grinzane Cavour;
39-0141/877-396;
la-spinetta.com.

Azienda Agricola Vigna Rionda (Massolino)
A small winery located on a hillside in Serralunga, it looks the way wineries have looked in Barolo for half a century, but

the wines are on the cutting edge.
8 Piazza Cappellano,
Serralunga d'Alba;
39-0173/613-138;
massolino.it.

WHAT TO READ
The Vines of San Lorenzo
By Edward Steinberg
The story of Barbaresco pioneer Angelo Gaja and his Sori San Lorenzo vineyard.

A Passion for Piedmont
By Matt Kramer
An interweaving of the history of the region with recipes and insights into Piedmontese wines.

Vino Italiano
By David Lynch and Joe Bastianich
This compendium of producers and their wines is a valuable resource.

SEE ALSO
For Piedmont:
Flavors of Piedmont pp.138–141

The pool at Villa Tiboldi, in Roero.

155

PART FOUR
Arts and Culture

The Fountain of Neptune in the Piazza della Signoria, Florence.

Florence's Galleria
degli Uffizi.

Photographs by Andrea Fazzari

Master Class

FROM MASACCIO TO MICHELANGELO, FLORENCE PRODUCED SOME OF
THE WORLD'S GREATEST PAINTERS. AT THE CITY'S ART SCHOOLS, STUDENTS
WALK IN THE FOOTSTEPS OF THESE NATIVE SONS. BY CHARLES MACLEAN

FLORENCE

Across the river, in the blue-collar Oltrarno district, where for centuries the art of Florence has been made and mended in neighborhood workshops and *bottegas*, I enter with some trepidation the oldest operating atelier in the city: Charles H. Cecil Studios. In continuous use as a drawing studio since the early 19th century, the Cecil Studios is also one of the last schools of fine art in the world that teaches pupils how to draw like the Renaissance masters.

The volatile fug of oils and turpentine thickens as I climb the steep marble stairs from the street. A pretty woman in Levi's and a dark turtleneck drifts by with an armful of small mirrors. "Weren't we expecting you…yesterday?" she asks vaguely in an English accent and with a distracted manner reminiscent of Warhol Factory personnel circa 1979. "He's working. I'll see if he can be interrupted."

She leads me through a complex of rooms lit by high windows; we're in the roof space of a former church. Blackout curtains are pulled aside, and Charles Cecil, interrupted, emerges, palette in hand. A tall sixtysomething man in faded denim, with strong, chiseled features and longish hair, he looks like everyone's idea of a master painter. Gravely exuberant (I half expect the shoulder clasp with which Charlton Heston greeted acolytes in *The Agony and the Ecstasy*), he welcomes me to the city of Michelangelo. On a whirlwind tour of the atelier—the cast room, the sculpture room, the *gipsoteca*, and the drawing studio where I will be joining the first-year life class—Cecil expounds on the importance of upholding the tradition of naturalistic figure painting. Cecil, who studied at Yale and apprenticed with two American painters, opened the school in 1983. He shows me some of his own works in

Students draw from casts before graduating to models.

progress. I'm struck by a Titianesque *Deposition from the Cross*.

Besides learning how to draw, I've come to Florence to fulfill another delayed ambition. Though my father grew up here, I have never stayed long enough to get to know the city. I want to discover the Florence that I dreamed about as a child, raised in Scotland on tales of the Medici and reproductions of Benozzo Gozzoli, whose *Procession of the Magi* hung above my bed. I want to see the houses where my grandparents Charlie and Gladys lived as part of a raffish, once glamorous Anglo-Florentine colony.

In the courtyard of a grand apartment building on Lungarno Amerigo Vespucci, their last address, the *portiere* bellows over the intercom that there's no one here called Maclean. When I explain that I'm talking about 40 years ago, she hangs up. Back at my hotel on nearby Via Montebello, I order a cup of tea with a nostalgic brand name, Sir Winston English Blend, that offers, absurdly, a soothing, if remote, connection to Charlie and Gladys. It was his lifelong friendship with Churchill that helped secure my grandfather, who had been disabled by wounds received at the Battle of the Somme in 1916, the post of British consul to Florence.

Following the daily route he took to the consulate, I wander up Via del Proconsolo to see the sculptures in the Bargello museum. Onto the crowded sidewalk I project a Merchant-Ivory vision of Charlie: straw hat, white suit, glint of a gold watch chain, walking with the help of a black malacca cane. A simple, soldierly character, he seems an unlikely gamekeeper for Florence's famously louche expat community.

In an upper room of the Bargello, I stand spellbound by Andrea Della Robbia's glazed-terra-cotta portrait of a young noblewoman. Her hair, scraped back into spiky plaits and adorned with rows of pearls, reminds me alternately of Beatrice's (I'm re-reading Dante's *La Vita Nuova*) and the retro-punk look favored by my teenage daughters. Her face, demurely reflecting the love it must have inspired, enchants me. I want to know who she was and whether her likeness in clay began life as a drawing…but I'm already late for my first class.

I pass through the *gipsoteca*—a silo-like space that soars 90 feet high—and enter the studio. There's a disquieting moment as I realize I'm the only male in a room full of women, one of them nude. Nobody else seems to notice or care. Throughout the studio, kept steamy as a sauna for the life-model's comfort, there is a hushed concentration.

With help, I set up my easel, and get to work. I learn the sight-size method—standing back from the easel, I visually fit the model onto the paper, using a piece of string as a plumb (perpendicular) line to take measurements. In the beginning, I find working on a vertical plane a challenge. (Though I've painted and drawn before, this is the first time I've used an easel.) But I soon get the hang of holding a pencil like a brush, walking back and forth between the plumb line position and the easel, making little marks on the paper that grow into a forest of coordinates as the image slowly takes shape.

The moment of truth comes when I look back through a mirror at what I've done. Maybe I stopped measuring and started connecting the dots too soon, but the mirror—*il vero maestro*, as Leonardo da Vinci called it—doesn't lie: the mistakes are glaring. I've no choice but to erase and start over.

For the next three hours I remain lost to the world. When the session ends, the studio empties fast. Leaving strips of tape on the floor to mark easel positions, the students (mostly twentysomething Brits and Americans) gossip, roll cigarettes, and make plans on their cell phones as they clatter down

Donatello's David, *in the Bargello museum.*

the hall and out into the street. They seem at home here, enjoying the safe, bohemian-lite way of life that has long been part of Florence's allure. It was not so different in Charlie and Gladys's day, when the insider status assumed by foreign residents was founded upon a sentimental view of Florence as an art-lover's protectorate.

It feels like early spring as I walk up the Viale Galileo Galilei. With the help of an old map, I find the Villa Arrighetti, where my grandparents lived from 1922 to 1948. The handsome building, now owned by a religious order, has been renamed Villa Agape and turned into a spiritual retreat. The grounds—an avenue of cypresses, a sloping grass path, olive orchards—are exactly how I imagined they would be.

At the bottom of the garden, I discover the iron gates to the Viale, where in May 1938 Gladys stood and watched Hitler and Mussolini drive by in a convertible on their way to San Miniato. She refused to wave; instead, she turned to her companion, Miss Good, and said, "Darling, if only we had a bomb. Imagine…"

The war, when it came, stranded my grandparents in Switzerland, where they were interned. The Villa

Arrighetti was closed, and their few valuable possessions were taken into safekeeping by their friends the Fioravantis, an unconventional family who enjoyed dancing Highland reels and kept a crocodile as a garden pet. The Fioravantis hid the Maclean candlesticks from the Nazis—just as many villa owners bravely concealed the great art treasures of the city—by burying them in their olive groves on the other side of the Porta Romana.

Looking at art is part of the atelier's curriculum, and with Charles Cecil's help, I make a plan of what to see while I'm here. It is said that one-third of the world's most important works of art are located in Florence. A lifetime isn't long enough—I have a week. Cecil's strategy is based on opening hours: museums in the morning, churches in the afternoon.

First encounters with famous pictures can be awkward. Face to face with Leonardo da Vinci's *Annunciation*, Uccello's *Battle of San Romano I*, Botticelli's magical *Primavera*, I feel an elation tempered by the shock of the familiar, as if reproduction has sucked the life from some images, disconnected their power to astonish. In the flesh, so to speak, Botticelli's women still look to me like English girls of the hippie era, when the poster was king.

Tour groups, ruthless as piranha shoals, boil around the great canvases. While the stars are under siege, I discover lesser-known paintings and enjoy the views from the gallery windows. There's a corner of the Uffizi from which you can look down on one side to the Piazza della Signoria, where the Neptune fountain and the colossal statues of David and Hercules are lined up under the façade of the Palazzo Vecchio, and on the other follow the sludge-green Arno, spanned by five of its bridges, to a vanishing point on the plains of Tuscany.

The intimate scale of Florence makes it easy, if hazardous, to get around on foot. Plagued by noise and traffic, this is a modern working city that stubbornly resists becoming a shrine to the past. Yet the ghosts of the Renaissance shine on. On every street I recognize faces from paintings in the museums. A brush with a scooter at an intersection reveals a proud beauty by Raphael…the Madonna of the Vespa. I glimpse an old man tending a tower of canary cages inside a doorway and recall Ghirlandaio's tender portrait of an old man and his grandson. Even the huge mastiffs that drag their fashionable owners past the dazzling storefronts on Via Tornabuoni could have bounded from a hunting scene by Uccello or Vasari.

The gipsoteca, a repository for sculpture.

*One of the twice-weekly
advanced sculpture classes.*

Thursday is lecture night at the atelier. Cecil's scholarly talk on Masaccio, the first apostle of humanistic realism, attracts a wide audience from Florence's English-speaking community. Afterward, we stand around drinking wine from paper cups and talking earnestly about tradition versus Modernism. My uneasy defense of contemporary art is swept aside by Cecil's magisterial vision of a chain of ateliers extending back to Titian, Velázquez, Van Dyck—and forward to a new renaissance. The discussion continues over roast duck at a restaurant in the Oltrarno, where more-adventurous visitors have always come looking for the "real" Florence.

Next day, after class, I visit Santa Maria del Carmine's Brancacci Chapel and see for myself Masaccio's groundbreaking use of light and shade in the folds of a beggar's cloak. At San Marco, which was my grandmother's favorite church, I detect pencil-work behind Fra Angelico's pious frescoes—the drawing under the skin. My apprenticeship is opening my eyes, learning about line and form is helping me to unlock the secrets of the early masters.

I get "fresco neck" from constantly looking up. In the black and white marbled baptistery, where the visual miracle of Florence began, I notice a pew full of French nuns comfortably studying the ceiling mosaics in vanity mirrors, which gleam from their laps like gold plates.

Back in the studio, Cecil's assistants make regular rounds of the students' easels. I overhear phrases: "building up the values" and "getting the contouring right," and "might need to re-plumb…this leg, that arm…don't shade in too quickly."

There are 14 of us in the life class, 35 in the whole school (the atelier method discourages big numbers). Some are here short-term, to do a year's foundation course for art college or university; others, like Danielle DeVine, a willowy Bostonian, and the wonderfully named Ardis de Fries, from Portland, Oregon, are committed to becoming painters. The training is rigorous and intensive, and, looking around at the easels during break, I can only envy the promise on display.

"We always get a few who don't work out," a teacher explains tactfully. "You can tell by their attitude more than anything. They miss classes or they're not driven, they lack that passionate fury in their eye when they draw."

The moment I enter the studio and get settled at my easel, I become instantly and wholly absorbed. Time stands still, the universe contracts—I even forget a nagging toothache. Fred Hohler, a high-flying executive who attended Cecil Studios' summer school a few years ago, told me that the experience of learning to draw changed his life. I can see what he meant now. I think I may have got the "passionate fury" in my eye.

On Cecil's designated two days for teaching, the master stalks the studio floor using his charisma to breathe fire into our amateur souls. By the time he gets to me, I am eager to hear a critique, which, if you buy his continuity theory, carries an authority invested in him by, well, Michelangelo. He stands back, strokes his jaw (another Charlton Heston moment), and frowns alarmingly at my drawing.

"Lots of good things happening here. Contour is good…that is a likeness. Ideally you would have had more demarcation between light and shadow, then put your *sfumato*—the smoky transition from light to shadow—on afterward. You have a very fine outline. If you'd had another week, there's no telling what you would have done."

His enthusiasm is contagious, but I am under no illusions. I joined the atelier to learn an endangered craft, much as if I'd apprenticed myself to an artisan turning out faux antiques in an Oltrarno workshop. But I can't say that I haven't been affected by the experience. My days at the studio have taught me to look more intently not just at paintings but also at the world around me, and I want to go on doing this.

The myth of the first drawing, recounted in Pliny the Elder's *Natural History*, tells of a Greek maiden who watches her lover asleep by the fire and longs to preserve his beauty. Taking a charred stick from the embers, she traces his shadow, thrown onto the wall by firelight, and so makes permanent his presence in the world. The result may not have achieved all she hoped it would, but in her instinctive urge to make a mark, to record and so stay the fleeing moment, there lay an antidote to the human condition.

On my last evening, up at the Villa Fioravanti, I try to explain to the owner in halting Italian that during World War II my grandparents' *tesoro* was buried in her garden. When language fails me, I use my new skills to sketch a coffer and an open trench under an olive tree, which causes a bewildered Signorina Fioravanti (distantly related to Charlie and Gladys's friends) to comment brightly, "*Ahhh…il coccodrillo!*" Disappointing, perhaps. But then she asks if I would like to see the crocodile, which I've heard was given an elaborate funeral in the garden many years ago. She takes me upstairs to a room with panoramic views of Florence, and there on the wall above the TV, stuffed and glaring, hangs the once formidable guardian of our family silver.

The Masaccio frescoes in the Brancacci Chapel, in the church of Santa Maria del Carmine.

Travelers' Guide to Drawing in Florence

Charles H. Cecil Studios

Amateurs can sign up for the July session (from $3,270); serious students have to enroll for at least a year ($12,330) and must submit artwork to be considered for one of 12 spots.
68 Borgo San Frediano;
39-055/285-102;
charlescecilstudios.com.

Florence Academy of Art

The school runs an all-year drawing program and, in July, month-long courses taught in English, including "Drawing the Figure in Three Renaissance Techniques."
21R Via delle Casine;
39-055/245-444;
florenceacademyofart.com.

Atelier Rebecca Harp

Based on the traditional Renaissance atelier, Harp's centrally located studio rents workspaces to advanced students, who paint and draw under the guidance of this former pupil of Charles H. Cecil. Novices can take late-afternoon courses. Open every month except August.
3 Piazza della Repubblica;
39-055/291-122;
atelierharp.com;
classes, $410 per month;
studio spaces, $685 per month.

Angel Academy of Art

Painter and portraitist Michael John Angel's school teaches ongoing classes in the 19th-century French painting tradition. Two-week summer workshops introduce students to fresco painting and Caravaggio's oil techniques.
34/r Via Fiesolana;
39-055/246-6737;
angelartschool.com;
classes from $1,918.

Galilei Institute

The drawing and painting classes at this language and culture school focus on the human form and 16th-century techniques. Students learn by copying Renaissance masters before developing their own styles.
68 Via degli Alfani;
39-055/294-680;
galilei.it;
classes from $810.

Charles Cecil (center) surrounded by students and a model at his studio in Florence's Oltrarno district.

Supplies

Cartoleria San Frediano

A fantastic art-supply store that carries thick drawing paper, paintbrushes, and oils.

5R Via San Onofrio;
39-055/295-040.

...AND ELSEWHERE IN ITALY

The International School of Painting, Drawing, and Sculpture

Set in an Umbrian hill town, these intensive studio lessons take advantage of the landscape and architecture that once inspired masters like Poussin and Ingres. Choose between weeklong seminars and semester courses.

Montecastello di Vibio;
866/449-3604 or 39-075/878-0072;
giotto.org;
classes from $2,055.

Verrocchio Art Centre

Faculty from leading London art schools teach two-week courses in painting, drawing, and sculpting to students of all levels, at British artist Nigel Konstam's program in the Sienese countryside. Classes run from May to October.

Casole d'Elsa;
44-208/869-1035;
verrocchio.co.uk;
classes from $1,808, including lodging and some meals.

Geoffrey Humphries

Based in Venice for more than 30 years, this former Londoner is among the city's best-known working artists. He teaches drawing, oil painting, and plein-air technique at his studio on Giudecca Island. Lessons available year-round.

Gallery Holly Snapp;
Calle delle Botteghe, San Marco, Venezia;
39-041/521-0030;
galleryhollysnapp.com;
classes are $70 per hour, with a four-hour-per-day minimum.

WHERE TO STAY

J.K. Place

After settling into one of 20 sleek rooms, head to the bijou roof terrace for drinks and views of Santa Maria Novella church.

7 Piazza Santa Maria Novella;
800/525-4800 or 39-055/264-5181;
jkplace.com;
doubles from $$$.

Casa Howard

This intimate guesthouse has 11 themed rooms, from a black-and-white suite to a library room with wall-to-wall books.

18 Via della Scala;
39-06/6992-4555;
casahoward.com;
doubles from $$.

Relais Santa Croce

Built by Marquis Baldinucci, a treasurer to the Pope during the early 18th century, this converted palace retains many of its original frescoes, fabrics, and furnishings.

87 Via Ghibellina;
39-055/234-2230;
relaisantacroce.com;
doubles from $$.

Hotel Bernini Palace

This central 74-room hotel is equidistant from the Uffizi and Piazza Santa Croce. Book one of the spacious suites on the Tuscan floor overlooking the courtyard.

29 Piazza San Firenze;
39-055/288-621;
baglionihotels.com;
doubles from $$$$.

WHAT TO READ

A Room with a View
By E. M. Forster
A brilliant satire of the Edwardian art tourists who put Florence back on the map after a long period of decline.

The Stones of Florence
By Mary McCarthy
This classic history of Florence's art, culture, and architecture paints a sharp portrait of the Medicis.

SEE ALSO

For sights, restaurants, and more places to stay in Florence, plus a map: **Overnight Sensations pp.108–109**

A bird's-eye view of Florence.

La Scala's refurbished auditorium, built in 1778, has been the site of opera premieres in Milan for more than two centuries.

168

Photographs by Martin Morrell

Viva La Scala!

AFTER AN AMBITIOUS THREE-YEAR RENOVATION, MILAN'S CULTURAL CORNERSTONE CONTINUES TO DAZZLE AUDIENCES WITH A LUMINOUS NEW LOOK AND PITCH-PERFECT ACOUSTICS. BY ANDREW PORTER

Each December 7, on the feast day of Sant'Ambrogio (St. Ambrose), the patron saint of Milan, the Teatro alla Scala raises the curtain on a new season of opera and ballet. During a half-century and more, I've been to several of these Scala opening nights. In my student days it was with cheap admission to the topmost tier, where one could stand to hear Maria Callas for less than the cost of a movie; later, when I became a pampered critic, I enjoyed a *poltroncina*, or "armchair," in the orchestra. I learned to shoulder and shove my way through the crowds that gather

A cavalry of wooden horses, built for La Scala's production of Antonio Salieri's Europa riconosciuta (Europa Revealed), waits in the wings.

Venice's La Fenice may be a prettier house, but La Scala is nobler, grander, with its Neoclassical auditorium and perfect proportions

outside the theater to watch, to cheer—in troubled times maybe to jeer at—the arrival of the great ones: the heads of state, foreign potentates, politicians, czars of industry, film stars, writers, famous couturiers, etc., who always attend opening night. In December 2004 the throng was thicker than ever (Sophia Loren, looking wonderful, attended on the arm of, and dressed by, Giorgio Armani), for it was an extra-special occasion. The company was home again. It had spent nearly three years of exile in a newly built opera house in the suburbs, the Teatro degli Arcimboldi, while La Scala itself was being rebuilt. The opera chosen to celebrate the homecoming was Antonio Salieri's *Europa riconosciuta* (*Europa Revealed*)—commissioned for the opening of La Scala back in 1778, and never heard since.

The city's original opera house, Teatro Regio Ducale, burned down in 1776, and the Milanese lost no time in building a larger, grander one, a Nuovo Teatro Regio Ducale. To clear the site for it, the church of Santa Maria alla Scala was demolished, and the new theater became known as the Teatro alla Scala, or simply, La Scala. Its architect was the Neoclassical master Giuseppe Piermarini (1734–1808), also the designer of the Royal Palace in Milan and the grand Villa Reale di Monza. Piermarini's great building essentially still stands, and for operagoers it offers a wonderful adventure: the performance of works both new and old in a setting that has come to represent a temple to the art for more than two centuries. Bellini's *Norma* was first performed there, in 1831; so were Verdi's first four and last two operas and Puccini's *Edgar*, *Madama Butterfly*, and *Turandot*. The list is long, and international, including premieres by Poulenc, Stockhausen, and Berio.

La Fenice, the theater Giannantonio Selva designed for Venice in 1790, may be a prettier house, but Piermarini's La Scala is nobler, grander, with its Neoclassical auditorium and perfect proportions. There's a moment before each performance that never fails to stir me, when the main lights go down while the six tall tiers glimmer. Since 1778 there have been, of course, many changes. Electricity was introduced in 1883, and electric light makes that magical moment possible. In 1907, Arturo Toscanini modernized the theater, adding the orchestra pit.

Allied bombing in 1943 destroyed much of La Scala and left it roofless, but after the war Milan's "secular temple" was one of the first buildings to be restored. Toscanini reopened it in 1946, with a concert of music by Rossini, Verdi, Boito, and Puccini—composers who had come to fame there. The latest rebuilding, so far as the technical resources, the "working parts," are concerned, is the most radical. Its Swiss architect, Mario Botta (designer of San Francisco's Museum of Modern Art), has, of course, left Piermarini's famous façade unaltered. The lofty auditorium, red, cream, and gold, looks essentially the same, although the *poltroncine*, the individual armchairs, have gone, replaced by rows of modern red plush seats with subtitle screens built into the backs. (The touch of a button offers Italian text or English translation.) A new floor, uncarpeted, provides improved sight lines. The acoustics, always good, are now even better. At *Europa riconosciuta*, from a good seat, I heard perfectly: orchestra and voices in fine balance and astonishing intimacy and directness within the vast theater.

But behind La Scala's proscenium arch all is new. The stage, the stage machinery, the spacious wings, the fly tower, the lighting equipment are state of the art. And behind the old building there is now a production annex containing up-to-date rehearsal halls, workshops, dressing rooms. To the left rises perhaps the most controversial, and certainly the most prominent, feature of Botta's reconstruction: a large elliptical tower housing the manifold administrative workings of a busy modern opera company.

La Scala's famous Museo Teatrale has returned from exile, too. In this city of many great museums it is an attraction second only to Leonardo's *Last Supper* in popular attendance. On performance evenings it is sometimes open to the audience during intermission. Visits by day include a side trip to the theater boxes for a glimpse into the auditorium. The museum may not house sublime works of art, but exhibits are deeply moving: the little spinet on which young Verdi learned his métier, portraits of the great singers in Scala's illustrious history.

La Scala, which is now owned by the Commune of Milan and supported by both public and private

funds, tries to make itself accessible to all. Big-screen relays carried the reopening presentation of *Europa riconosciuta* to crowds in piazzas across the city, to several other Italian opera houses, and even to the prisoners in Milan's principal jail.

The Europa of the title, I should perhaps explain, is not the continent Europe but the beautiful Phoenician princess who was carried off to Crete by Jupiter, disguised as a bull—or, in Salieri's version of the legend, by the king of Crete. The December 2004 revival of *Europa riconosciuta*, conducted by Riccardo Muti, directed by Luca Ronconi, and designed by Pier Luigi Pizzi, was large scale and evidently costly, but not ostentatious. In fact, it was sober, almost austere, performed without big-star international singers amid décor that was basically gray—two red costumes providing just about the only color. A cavalry rode wooden, not live, horses, trundled by stagehands. Yet at the same time the show was devised to reveal the new stage resources.

It was a slightly surprising event; but then the season's planned fare was far from typical. March was to introduce a double bill of Hindemith's *Sancta Susanna* (1922) and Azio Corghi's new *Il dissoluto assolto* (*The Libertine Absolved*), with a libretto by José Saramago. Bold choices! *Sancta Susanna*, which has been called the young Hindemith's first masterpiece, is a one-act opera in which a young nun, erotically stirred by the enchantment of a hot summer night, strips naked and runs to tear the loincloth from a life-sized crucifix. A Rome revival in 1977 incurred Vatican wrath. The highly anticipated program was canceled—the result, partly, of a dispute among administration, music director Riccardo Muti, musicians, and production departments; after 19 years as music director, Muti resigned in spring 2005.

Still, that season brought the reprise of an early Scala triumph, the wonderfully beautiful *Bohème* designed and directed by Franco Zeffirelli. The following season was no less auspicious, dedicated to the 250th anniversary of Mozart's birth and inaugurated with the composer's *Idomeneo*, led by young British conductor Daniel Harding.

And in late 2007, Daniel Barenboim began his tenure as principal guest conductor, leading Wagner's *Tristan and Isolde*, in a new production by visionary director Patrice Chereau—kicking off a season that promises to introduce new work, along with fresh interpretations of established repertoire, to Milanese audiences. As ever, La Scala celebrates equally the best of the opera's glorious (at times tumultuous) past and shining future.

The state-of-the-art back and side stages, part of the production annex, designed by architect Mario Botta, who also oversaw Teatro alla Scala's renovation.

Travelers' Guide to Milan's Top Sights

WHEN TO GO

Milan has a mild climate, although the August heat can be oppressive and January snow is common. Milan's trade fairs (March, April, and October) can make finding hotel rooms and some dinner reservations extremely difficult.

GETTING THERE

Milan is served by two airports: Malpensa (30 miles northwest) and the smaller Linate (5 miles east). There are direct flights to Milan from the major North American cities on most US and Canadian airlines, as well as Italy's Alitalia. Most flights arrive at Malpensa.

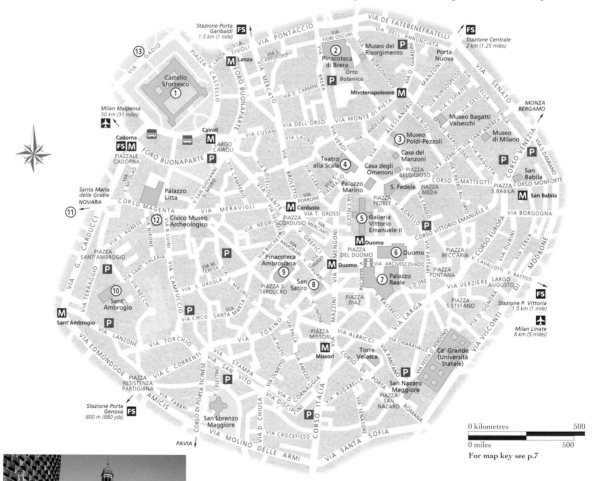

Castello Sforzesco.

TOP SIGHTS IN MILAN

Castello Sforzesco ❶

This sprawling 15th-century castle complex was begun in 1451 for Francesco Sforza, Duke of Milan. Its many collections include art and sculpture from the early Middle Ages to the 18th century, decorative arts, musical instruments, Oriental art, and archaeological artifacts.

Civico Museo Archeologico ⓬

Milan's civic archeology museum's collections range from local, Lombard artifacts of Paleolithic tribes to Italy's last Celtic peoples of the 1st century B.C.

Duomo ❻

The great travel writer H. V. Morton likened Milan's cathedral to a forest within the city, its spires, thickets of columns, and high vaulted ceilings providing the citizens with a spot of welcome shade.

Teatro alla Scala.

Galleria Vittorio Emanuele II ❺
Known as *il Salotto di Milano* ("Milan's drawing room"), this ornate shopping arcade was designed by Giuseppe Mengoni in 1865. With its roof of steel-reinforced glass (the first of its kind in Italy), it spawned copycat *gallerie* in Naples, Genoa, and Rome.

Museo Poldi-Pezzoli ❸
Giacomo Poldi-Pezzoli was a wealthy nobleman who, on his death in 1879, left his magnificent collection of art and precious objects to the state. Its masterpieces all date from the last half of the 15th century.

Palazzo Reale ❼
Milan's Neoclassical Royal Palace was built in the 18th century under Empress Maria Theresa of Austria and extended in 1939–56 with the Arengario, a pair of towering pavilions on Piazza Duomo. The vast ballroom of the Arengario is open for exhibitions. The palace also houses the Museo del Duomo and a contemporary art museum.

Parc Sempione ⓭
This park occupies part of the old Visconti ducal garden. Among the trees are monuments to Napoleon III by Francesco Barzaghi, De Chirico's metaphysical construction, *Mysterious Baths*, the sulphur water fountain, and the Torre del Parco—a tower made of steel tubes in 1932 after a design by Gio Ponti.

San Satiro ❽
This church is one of Milan's most beautiful Renaissance buildings. The interior seems to be in the shape of a Greek cross, but this is an optical illusion created by *trompe l'oeil* effects, since lack of space forced architect Bramante to adopt a T-shaped plan.

Pinacoteca Ambrosiana ❾
Cardinal Federico Borromeo bequeathed his magnificent library and private art collection to Milan in 1618. The gallery includes works by Leonardo, Caravaggio, and Titian, and the original cartoon for Raphael's famed *School of Athens*.

Pinacoteca di Brera ❷
One of Northern Italy's greatest art collections is housed in the imposing 17th-century Palazzo di Brera. On display are first-rate examples of Italian Renaissance and Baroque painting, including works by Piero della Francesca, Mantegna, Canaletti, Raphael, Tintoretto, Bellini, Veronese, and Caravaggio.

Santa Maria delle Grazie ⓫
This beautiful 15th-century convent contains one of the key images of Western civilization: the *Cenacolo* (*Last Supper*) by Leonardo Da Vinci.

Sant'Ambrogio ❿
Second only to the Duomo among Milan's great churches (and to many, rather more beautiful), this 4th-century basilica, with its cloistered entryway,

The Galleria Vittorio Emanuele II.

contains Paleochristian mosaics, medieval carvings, and late Renaissance frescoes.

Teatro alla Scala ❹
Ticket prices at La Scala range from $234 for the best seats to $17 for admission to the top tiers (with discounts for those under 18 or over 65, and for students). *Piazza della Scala; 39-02/7200-3744*; check out *teatroallascala.org* for a schedule of performances.

The imposing façade of Milan's Duomo.

*Interior of the Church of
San Francesco, in Arezzo.*

Photographs by David Cicconi

In the Land of Piero

SET IN A TIMELESS LANDSCAPE, THE TOWNS AND CHURCHES OF TUSCANY'S AREZZO PROVINCE ARE HOME TO A TROVE OF INSPIRING WORKS BY EARLY RENAISSANCE MASTER PIERO DELLA FRANCESCA. BY JONATHAN SANTLOFER

I was balanced on a scaffold staring into King Solomon's face, at cracked plaster and peeling paint, close enough to touch the 15th-century fresco, though I wouldn't have dared. The restorers, who were cleaning and retouching it, were taking a lunch break; the smell of olive oil commingled with those of paint and chemicals. They offered me a sandwich, but I declined, too enthralled by the images to have much of an appetite. I made a promise to myself, that one day I would return to Arezzo and the church of San Francesco, to see if they had succeeded in rescuing Piero della Francesca's *Legend of the True Cross*.

It has taken me a dozen years to keep that promise—and the restorers 15 years to complete their work—but I am back inside San Francesco. The Piero della Francesca trail will take me on a pilgrimage of small daily excursions from my base in Arezzo, in southeastern Tuscany, to Sansepolcro, Anghiari, and Monterchi, nearby towns that played host, or lent inspiration, to the artist's most famous works.

Born in Sansepolcro around 1420, Piero della Francesca was, until the last century, seen as a lesser Italian master, his work minimal and almost primitive when compared with that of other, more boldfaced names such as Botticelli or Leonardo. I zero in on a depiction of the city of Arezzo, rendered in such simple geometry it brings to mind Cézanne and Picasso, and understand why it took a more modern perspective to identify Piero's genius. There is something clean and clear in his formalism that makes a fresco cycle like Michelangelo's Sistine Chapel seem almost too ravishing and extravagant by comparison.

The church is quiet, but I am spinning, trying to take in all 12 frescoed scenes at once. I gaze up at the painted prophets flanking the double-arched windows, which cast a soft, natural light onto the artwork. I work my way down the left side and stop at the *Annunciation*, practically at eye level: the Madonna, framed in an open loggia; Gabriel outside; and God above, his open hands gently directing our attention down into this, a dramatic one-act play in which time has stopped. It takes me a few minutes to realize that the cool church interior has lowered my body temperature and the order and quiet dignity of Piero's paintings has almost calmed me.

Outside, the sky is the same cobalt blue I have just seen in Piero's frescoes, the sun warming the mottled stone of San Francesco's façade, the Piazza

The Duomo, Arezzo's Gothic cathedral.

Piero's Legend of the True Cross *fresco, in the Church of San Francesco, Arezzo.*

barely populated. A young couple walks by; their lips locked, eyes closed, they stumble but remain upright. A group of Italians at a nearby café is savoring cigarettes and coffee, softly nattering away, seemingly oblivious to time.

I realize I'm starting to get it: this is not Florence or Siena, where one races from one art monument to another, masterpieces coming faster than tennis balls from an automatic pitcher, one's responses and reactions a foreshortened blur: Was that a Fra Angelico or a Michelangelo? The Duomo or a trattoria? This is the Arezzo province, Piero country, where life is more tranquil, the art less profuse but equally beautiful, a corner of Italy in which to fully experience one artist's life and work.

Back inside San Francesco, I gaze at Piero's *Dream of Constantine*, at the Emperor deep asleep in his tent while servants and guards stand by. I turn to the *Battle of Heraclius and Chosroes*, in which the artist deftly directs my eye through his densely packed composition with the simple bending of a horse's head, the tilt of a soldier's shield, the calculated angle of a spear. I remember not being surprised to learn that, when he wasn't busy painting, Piero wrote extensively on mathematics and geometry.

On the opposite wall is another battle scene, the *Victory of Constantine over Maxentius*, with a symbolic rendering of the Tiber River dead center — a shimmering blue undulation that takes the viewer for a gentle ride in perspective as it snakes its way into the back of the painting. Everything is fresh and bright, but not colorized-looking.

I linger over the *Death of Adam*, the *Torture of the Jew*, the *Exaltation of the Cross* — scenes of subtle intensity, replete with figures embodying a reverence for the human form that I have rarely seen. Moving out of the choir, I take a seat in the middle of the church, in the middle of a pew; a parishioner in the 15th century could view the cycle only from a distance. Perspectives shift and scenes are foreshortened, but the basic drama remains and is somehow clarified in its aggregate: Piero's sculptural figures and ordered scenes were made for distant viewing.

Outside, the jewelry and antiques shops Arezzo is known for are closed for siesta as I make my way up the hillside to the Duomo. The sun is blazing, but with the streets empty, the square feels slightly ominous. Inside, the church is big, cool, and dark; a hooded monk leads me to a commanding Mary Magdalene beside the altar, her red robe curled

The steeply sloping medieval Piazza Grande is the most picturesque square in Arezzo.

around a green dress that's more sculptural than painterly. Though modest in scale, she fills a painted niche, which makes her appear larger than life.

From Arezzo, it's a 25-minute drive to Cortona, in the southern part of the province. I have dinner there, with friends who exchanged England for Tuscany 34 years ago, at the spectacular Il Falconiere hotel. We dine *en plein air*, talking about art and food as the sun sets over the Val di Chiana. The meal, which turns out to be three courses devoted to mushrooms, is earthy and sublime.

The next day I drive to Sansepolcro, a town characterized, like Piero's paintings, by unadorned elegance. The Museo Civico, for centuries the town hall, contains what Aldous Huxley once referred to as "the best picture in the world" — Piero's *Resurrection* — and it does not disappoint. Hidden for years under a whitewash that had the unintended effect of preserving it almost perfectly, the painting is arresting. A triumphant Christ rises from behind a quartet of sleeping Roman soldiers, leveling a hypnotically powerful gaze at the viewer, one foot

Renaissance scenes against a real landscape, the two dissolving into each other.

The next day, my last, has been saved for one of Piero's best-known, most-studied works: the *Madonna del Parto* (*The Pregnant Madonna*), which was moved 14 years ago from its small graveyard chapel to a modest museum in the center of the quiet town of Monterchi. I saw it years ago; everyone tells me I will be disappointed by its new, sterile home, but I am not. Maybe it's because I am completely alone with the painting, which has been allocated its own room in the museum, or that the painting is so moving it doesn't matter. Mirror-image angels part weighty curtains to reveal a young and beautiful Madonna, eyes downcast, posture timid and somber, her fingertips lightly brushing the swell of her belly. It's as if she has been summoned for a performance she does not want to make, but knows she must. I peruse the beautiful illustrations of various Piero restorations that fill the museum's other rooms, but am drawn back to stand in front of the Madonna again and again.

Leaving Monterchi, I consider making the drive over the Apennines to see some of Piero's later works in Urbino—something to extend the trip, which I don't want to end—but then think again of the *Madonna del Parto* and decide I have, for now, seen enough—that I will follow Piero's lead, and keep it simple.

planted on a painted sarcophagus as though he is about to step out of the picture. I imagine him presiding over the town's civic meetings centuries ago, keeping its officials honest, or at least reminding them that someone important was watching. In an adjacent room is Piero's *Madonna della Misericordia* (*The Madonna of Mercy*), a multi-paneled tempera, the centerpiece a monolithic Madonna towering over a symbolic Arezzo, cape open to protect the townspeople who huddle below her, above her a simple and haunting crucifixion.

I meet a friend for a lunch of truffle salad and porcini pasta just down the street at Da Ventura, a packed and lively restaurant where everyone, except the waiters, is taking his time. As I drive back to my hotel, I see Piero's eye in the trees that line up and vanish in perfect one-point perspective, in the green-and-gold-striped hills. Nearby Anghiari—a hill town I've never set foot in—is somehow familiar, its geometric and orderly battlement architecture a fresco detail vividly come to life; everywhere, the world is imitating art.

I am staying at La Commenda, a beautifully restored 16th-century monastery just outside the town of Arezzo. I eat on my private veranda as the sky goes dark, my mind laying meticulously painted

The gardens of Il Falconiere, in the Arezzo province.

The chapel at Il Falconiere.

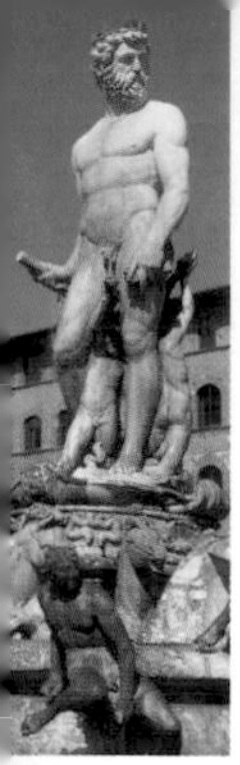

Travelers' Guide to Arezzo

GETTING THERE

United, Alitalia, Lufthansa, and Air France fly from New York to Florence's Amerigo Vespucci airport (also known as Peretola) with one stop; from there, it's a 40-minute drive to Arezzo.

EXPLORING EASTERN TUSCANY

The ancient city of Arezzo and the hilltop town of Cortona, with their steep streets, ladderlike alleys, and ancient houses, will satisfy visitors in search of culture, art, and architecture. The region will also appeal to nature lovers: The woodlands, meadows, and streams are ideal for exploring on foot. There are plenty of well-marked paths and picnic areas, especially within the beautiful ancient forests surrounding the monasteries at Vallombrosa and Camaldoli.

A Sunday antiques market, in Arezzo.

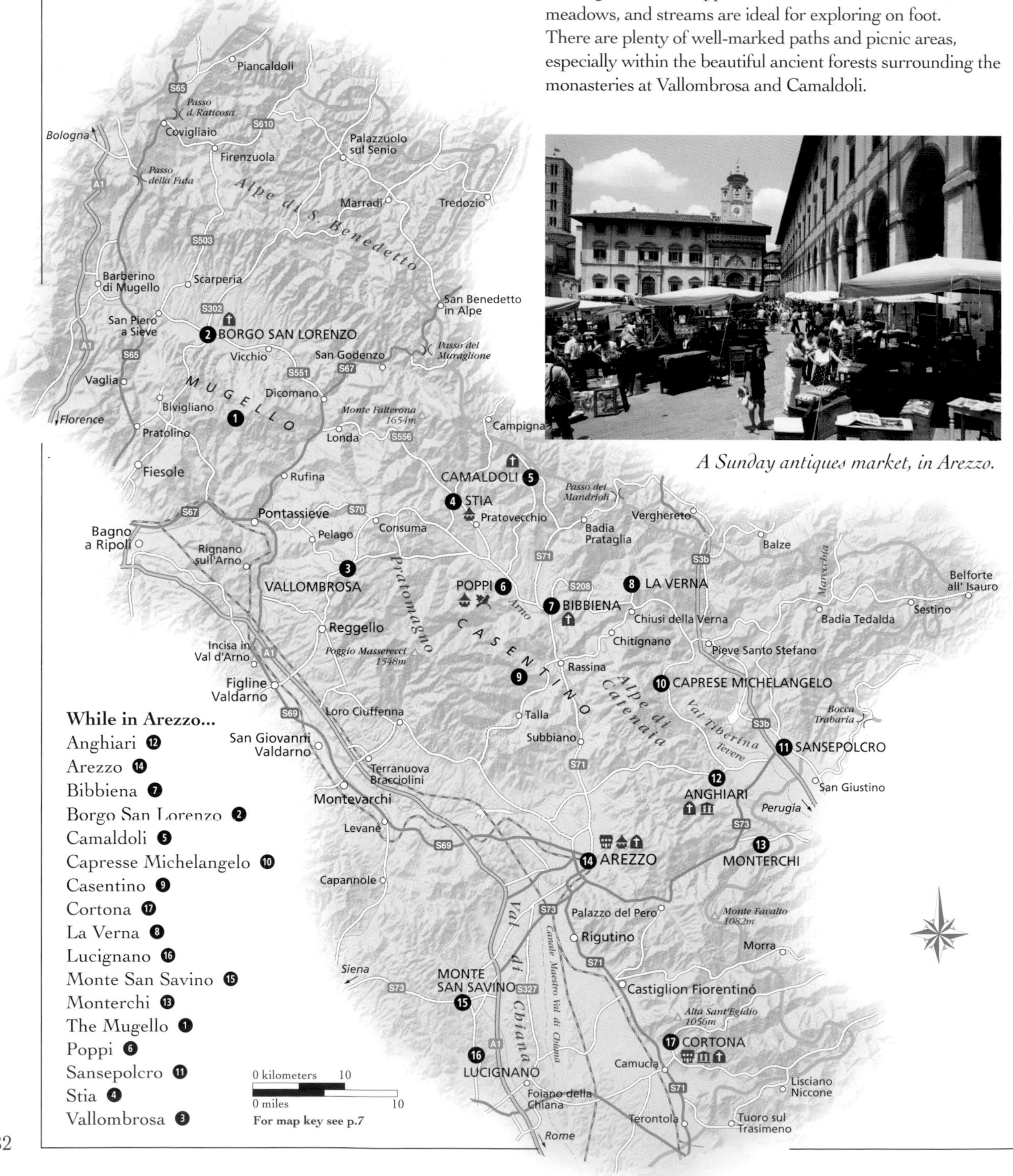

For map key see p.7

While in Arezzo...

- Anghiari 12
- Arezzo 14
- Bibbiena 7
- Borgo San Lorenzo 2
- Camaldoli 5
- Capresse Michelangelo 10
- Casentino 9
- Cortona 17
- La Verna 8
- Lucignano 16
- Monte San Savino 15
- Monterchi 13
- The Mugello 1
- Poppi 6
- Sansepolcro 11
- Stia 4
- Vallombrosa 3

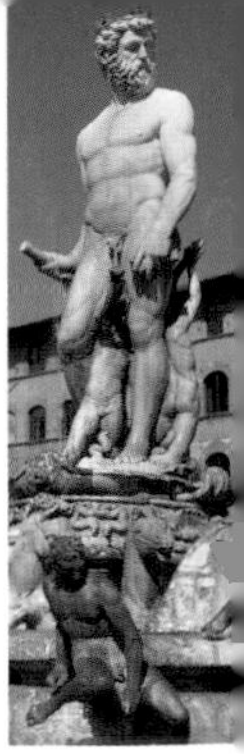

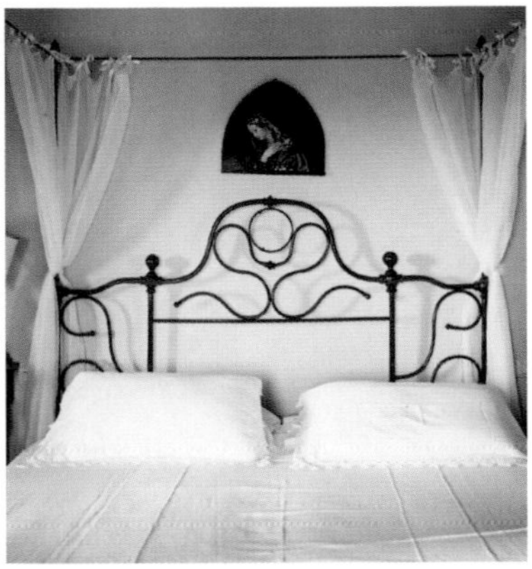

A room at Il Falconiere.

WHERE TO STAY

Relais La Commenda
6 Loc. Commenda,
Tavernelle di Anghiari;
39-0575/723-356;
relaislacommenda.com;
doubles from $$.

Il Falconiere
370 Località S. Martino, Cortona;
39-0575/612-679;
ilfalconiere.com;
doubles from $$$.

WHERE TO EAT

Da Ventura
30 Via Aggiunti, Sansepolcro;
39-0575/742-560;
dinner for two $$$.

WHAT TO SEE

AREZZO

National Museum of Medieval and Modern Art
8 Via San Lorentino, Arezzo;
39-0575/409-050

Church of San Francesco
Book in advance to view the Piero frescoes.
Piazza San Francesco, Arezzo;
39-0575/20630.

Arezzo Cathedral (the Duomo)
Piazza del Duomo;
open daily 7 a.m.–12:30 p.m.,
3 p.m.–6:30 p.m.

SANSEPOLCRO

Museo Civico
65 Via Aggiunti;
39-0575/732-218;
9:30 a.m.–1 p.m., 2:30 p.m.–6 p.m.

MONTERCHI

Museo Madonna del Parto
1 Via Reglia;
39-0575/70713.

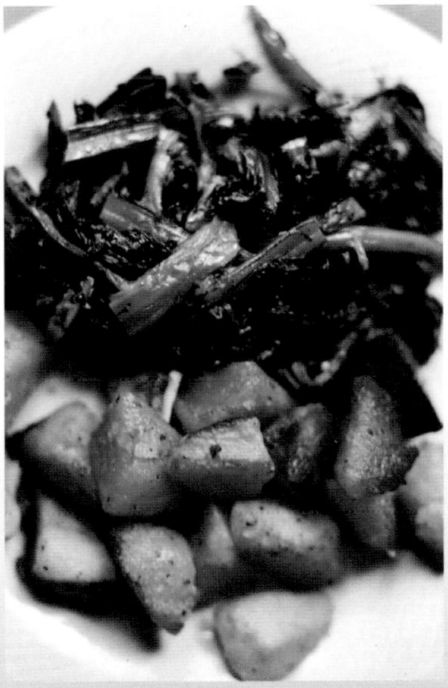

Roasted potatoes and sautéed chicory at Da Ventura, in Sansepolcro.

A view of the town of Anghiari.

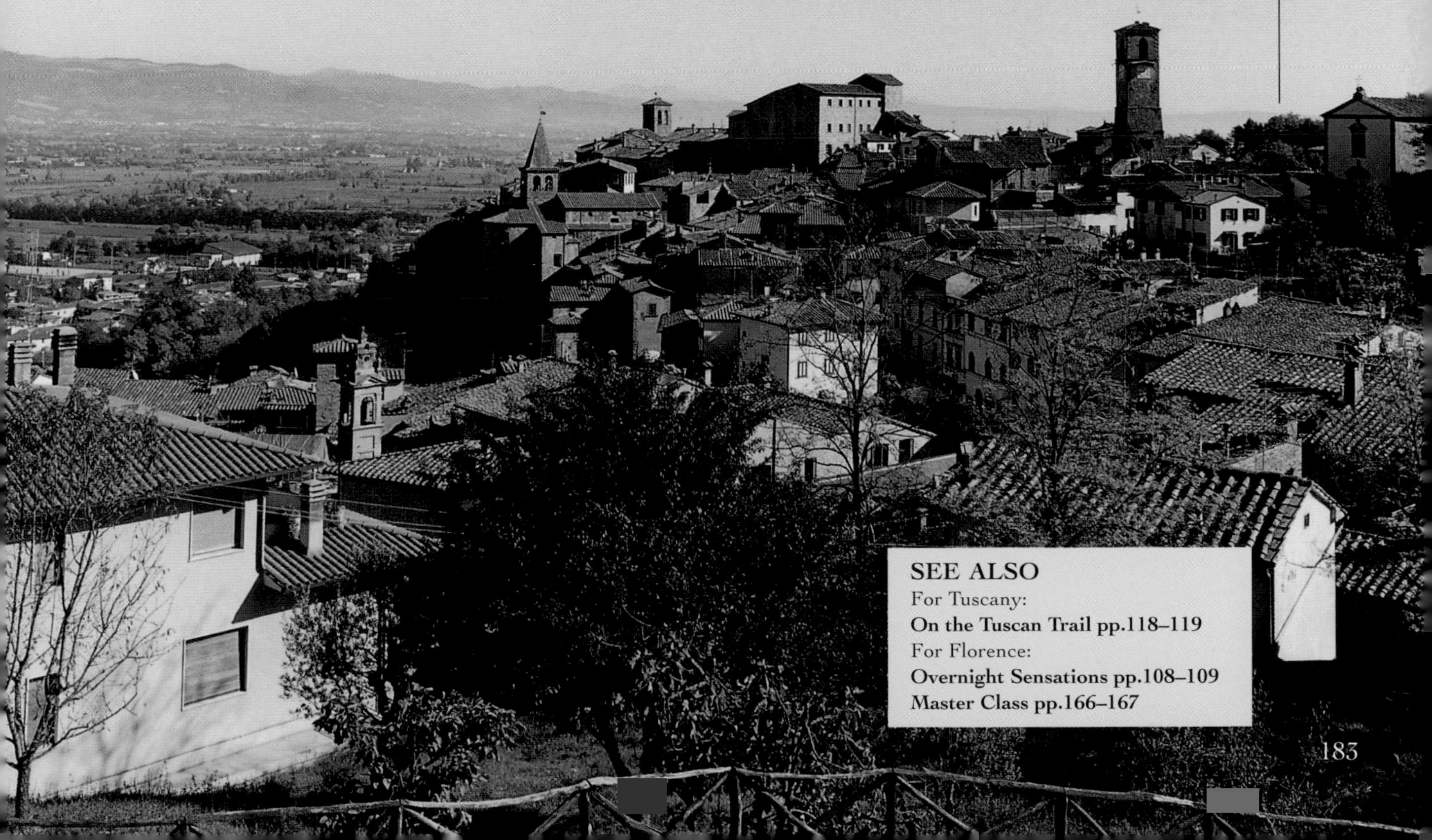

SEE ALSO
For Tuscany:
On the Tuscan Trail pp.118–119
For Florence:
Overnight Sensations pp.108–109
Master Class pp.166–167

Low-Key Classical

CONCERTGOERS AT PIANIST ANGELA HEWITT'S TRASIMENO FESTIVAL IN
UMBRIA DISCOVER THE PLEASURES — AND BURGEONING POPULARITY — OF
THE SMALL, ARTIST-RUN CHAMBER MUSIC EVENT. BY MICHAEL Z. WISE

After an evening performance of works by Beethoven, Stravinsky, Brahms, and Bartók, the audience ambles along a candlelit path outside a medieval castle above Umbria's Lake Trasimeno. As they discuss the music and prepare to return to their hotels, they find themselves face-to-face with the star of the show: pianist Angela Hewitt, among the leading contemporary interpreters of Bach, is thanking concertgoers for attending, dispensing hugs and kisses.

The personal touch is all part of the experience at the weeklong Trasimeno Music Festival, which Hewitt founded two years ago. Chatting with audience members before and after concerts, replying to e-mail inquiries, and generally being a warm and enthusiastic host, Hewitt gives the proceedings the feeling not of a formal event but of a family affair.

For a nomadic performer like Hewitt, the festival is a welcome chance to shed the solitary demands of a soloist and headliner on the international circuit. "We spend so much of our time going from one place to the next," she says. "We're in Korea for eight hours and then we're in Tokyo for forty-eight hours and then we're back in London the next day and then we're off again. When you're always working alone you talk to yourself, but it's something else to discuss a performance with people and to be inspired by others."

She's not the only one who has discovered the pleasures of a smaller scale: Trasimeno is one of a rapidly growing number of musician-led chamber music festivals. In Europe, pianist Leif Ove Andsnes in Risør, Norway; violinist Robert McDuffie in Rome; pianist Lars Vogt in Heimbach, Germany; violinist Julian Rachlin near Dubrovnik; and violinist Janine Jansen in Utrecht, have all launched, or helped to launch, such events. Spanish clarinetist Joan Enric Lluna, who played in three of the six concerts for Hewitt in 2006, is planning to start a festival of his own near Valencia. In the United States, cellist David Finckel of the Emerson String Quartet and his pianist wife, Wu Han, recently founded Music@Menlo, a summer festival of chamber music based in Menlo Park, California, and violinist Curt Thompson created the Mimir Chamber Music Festival in Fort Worth, Texas. These intimate events all stand in contrast to the

Rehearsal at the Trasimeno festival.

Photographs by Christian Kerber   185

A music festival at the Castle of the Knights of Malta, in Magione, Umbria.

Trasimeno is one of a rapidly growing number of musician-led chamber music festivals

Angela Hewitt, founder of the
Trasimeno Music Festival.

the performance itself. "The more concerts you play," says David Finckel of the Emerson String Quartet, "you begin to realize that you're at the mercy of your presenters. You might play your best, but so many things could have been done better, from the acoustics to the lighting to more trivial artist amenities. But even more important is the preparation of the audience—the program notes they read and their general involvement in whatever series you have." Music@Menlo's advance-ticket holders receive specially prepared CD's ahead of the performance that offer in-depth explorations of the music and the historical context of the composers' careers.

Andsnes notes that festivals enable artists to explore a more innovative repertoire than they normally perform at major metropolitan concert halls. While Andsnes plays heavy doses of Brahms and Grieg during the rest of the year, he regularly invites a less-often-heard contemporary composer to be in residence at the Risør festival. Last summer the featured composer was Britain's Mark-Anthony Turnage; an additional focus was the music of Frenchman Henri Dutilleux.

celebrated classical-music extravaganzas held each summer in Salzburg, Edinburgh, Lucerne, and Aix-en-Provence; they are also much smaller than long-established, musician-founded festivals like the Marlboro in Vermont or the Pablo Casals in France. "More and more musicians have done this, and I think it's a healthy thing," says Andsnes. Mimir's associate director, pianist José Feghali, agrees: "It seems every year I hear of a new festival starting up somewhere."

The concept may be the same, but the settings vary a great deal: at Risør, most of the concerts are held in a wood-framed church built in 1647; McDuffie's series is set in the Oratorio del Gonfalone in Rome. Some artists cite as their model two smaller musician-led festivals in Austria that have been quietly attracting connoisseurs for many years: the Musiktage Mondsee, founded by pianist András Schiff and now run by cellist Heinrich Schiff (no relation), and violinist Gidon Kremer's Lockenhaus Kammermusikfest.

Artists hash out their interpretations of sonatas and quintets at Hewitt's festival while rehearsing in her newly built vacation home, which has a panoramic view of the lake, or relaxing over meals at a nearby farmhouse hotel. In Norway, Andsnes deepens the spirit of collegiality by arranging lunches and dinners of freshly caught fish for the participating musicians, some 80 altogether, in the Risør town hall.

On stage at this new breed of smaller festivals, musicians have a chance to take complete control of

View from a loggia in Gubbio.

Musicians and audience members alike refer to the festival-going experience as more intense than a one-off concert during the regular season. "People enjoy listening more at festivals," says Finckel, who, in addition to having founded Music@Menlo, codirects the Chamber Music Society of Lincoln Center. "You don't get off work, rush home and get in your suit, sit down at 8:01 and try to figure out what's going on. A festival is a pure leisure activity rather than a subscription or a social obligation."

Sociability plays an undeniable role, however; by attending several festival concerts in succession, audience members frequently get to know one another. At Trasimeno, concertgoers included lifelong friends of Hewitt's from her native Canada, members of the European diplomatic service, a group of well-heeled Japanese who appeared in Issey Miyake gowns every evening, Israeli academics, and Italian financiers in summer linens.

But in contrast to larger gatherings such as Salzburg, festivals like this one are more about the music itself than a high-octane social scene. Talk among the Trasimeno attendees usually centers on whatever is being heard that evening—how a particular performance compared with one by Murray Perahia or Radu Lupu, or spirited recollections of Vladimir Horowitz's last public concert in New York.

The open-air settings in historic courtyards add charm and, at times, introduce an element of chance to the concerts. At last summer's event, while crickets chirped loudly in the background, evening

breezes obliged the performers to keep a close eye on their sheet music. Rain briefly interrupted one stellar performance, a duo piano recital that Hewitt gave with Akiko Ebi. Tarps were hastily brought in to cover the two ebony concert grands until the showers ceased, and the playing resumed. Downpours the next day caused the festival's final concert to be held in a nearby church rather than the castle's courtyard.

Not surprisingly, many Trasimeno audience members are avid fans of Hewitt herself. Kazunori Shibuya, a former high-tech executive from Japan, attending the festival for the second year running, says he has organized an Angela Hewitt fan club in his homeland. "We call her the prima donna ballerina of the keyboard," he explains.

Of course, Hewitt says, having your own festival can be a good career move—though a financially risky one. "What I'm doing here is really enlarging my audience," she says. "If I'm going to spend money on promotion and publicity, a festival is a good way to do it. Because then people get the right image of you, the right picture of you." By keeping her festival small and very much marked by her own personality, she provides a rich encounter for music lovers. "It's a chance to be a part of something friendly, where people can get to know each other; a chance perhaps for them to feel closer to me."

A balcony at Magione's Castle of the Knights of Malta.

A side room at the Castle of the Knights of Malta.

Travelers' Guide to Umbria

GETTING THERE

The Umbrian Regional Airport of Sant'Egidio is 7 miles from both Perugia and Assisi. Scheduled Alitalia flights arrive here from Milan's Malpensa and the main Italian international airports, as do some charter flights in high season. One option is to fly to Rome or another nearby airport, such as Ancona or Pisa, and take the train or drive from there. Rome to Perugia by car, for example, takes two hours.

EXPLORING UMBRIA

The medieval towns of Assisi and Spoleto are musts, as are the old center of Perugia, the region's capital, and the hilltowns of Gubbio, Spello, Montefalco, and Todi. Umbria's landscapes are equally compelling, from the eerie wastes of the Piano Grande and the mountain splendor of the Monti Sibillini national park (close to Norcia) to the gentler countryside of the Valnerina and Lake Trasimeno's beach-fringed shores.

While in Umbria...

Assisi ❷
Gubbio ❶
Lake Trasimeno ❹
Montefalco ❽
Monti Sibillini ❿
Norcia ⓫
Orvieto ❺
Perugia ❸
Spello ❾
Spoleto ❼
Todi ❻
Valnerina ⓬

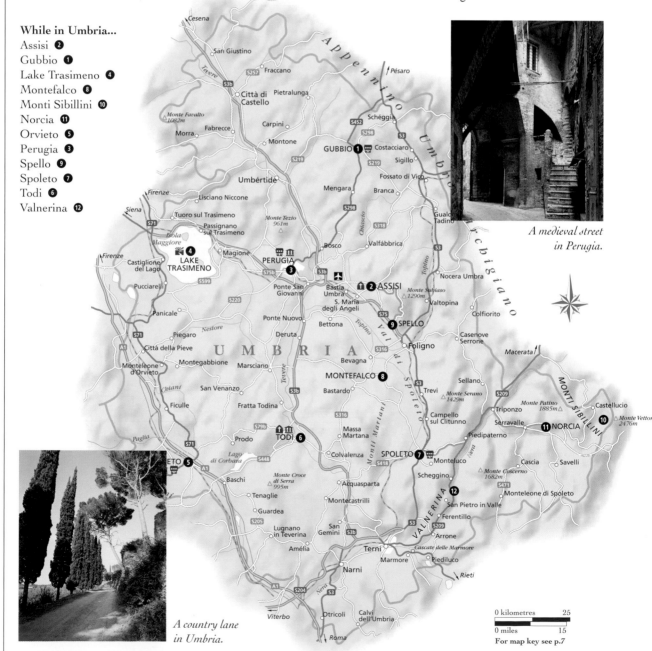

A medieval street in Perugia.

A country lane in Umbria.

0 kilometres 25
0 miles 15
For map key see p.7

LAKE TRASIMENO

The fourth-largest lake in Italy has an area of 48 square miles, and its perimeter is almost 37 miles long. It lies at the fortified heart of medieval Umbria. Wherever you gaze among the low hills that surround the lake, you will catch sight of a castle, a tower, or a fortified village. It was here that the Carthaginians, led by Hannibal, defeated the Romans in 217 B.C.

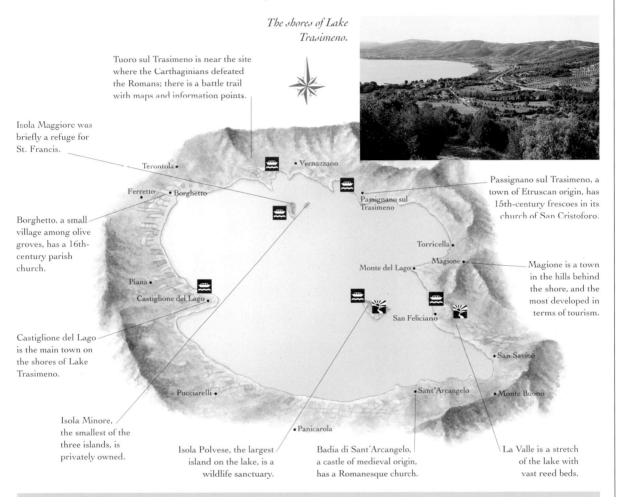

The shores of Lake Trasimeno.

Tuoro sul Trasimeno is near the site where the Carthaginians defeated the Romans; there is a battle trail with maps and information points.

Isola Maggiore was briefly a refuge for St. Francis.

Borghetto, a small village among olive groves, has a 16th-century parish church.

Castiglione del Lago is the main town on the shores of Lake Trasimeno.

Isola Minore, the smallest of the three islands, is privately owned.

Isola Polvese, the largest island on the lake, is a wildlife sanctuary.

Badia di Sant'Arcangelo, a castle of medieval origin, has a Romanesque church.

La Valle is a stretch of the lake with vast reed beds.

Passignano sul Trasimeno, a town of Etruscan origin, has 15th-century frescoes in its church of San Cristoforo.

Magione is a town in the hills behind the shore, and the most developed in terms of tourism.

Map labels: Terontola · Vernazzano · Ferretto · Borghetto · Passignano sul Trasimeno · Torricella · Magione · Monte del Lago · Piana · Castiglione del Lago · San Feliciano · San Savino · Pucciarelli · Sant'Arcangelo · Monte Buono · Panicarola

OTHER MUSIC FESTIVALS

Tuscan Sun Festival

The Teatro Signorelli in Cortona is the backdrop to this annual fête of musicians and singers, including famed Russian cellist Nina Kotova. tuscansunfestival.com; 44-870/040-0161.

Festival dei Due Mondi (Spoleto)

This Umbrian city was nicknamed the Italian Salzburg after it began hosting an annual cultural program of theater, opera and the visual arts in 1958. spoletofestival.it; 39-0743/45028.

Rossini Opera Festival

Each summer, die-hard Rossini fans make haste to Pesaro, on Italy's Adriatic coast, to honor the city's native son and listen to the prolific composer's 39 operas, both famous and obscure. rossinioperafestival.it; 39-0721/38001.

Ravenna Festival

Everyone from Bob Dylan to the Vienna Philharmonic has performed at this festival, where the Byzantine basilicas, cloisters, and piazza venues are as integral to the experience as the music. ravennafestival.org; 39-0544/249-211.

Umbria Jazz

Groove to jazz, soul, samba, and more at this 10-daybash in Umbria's capital city, Perugia, where the likes of Stefano Bollani & Strings, Gilberto Gil, and the Enrico Rava Quintet are regulars. umbriajazz.com; 39-075/573-2432.

Maggio Musicale Fiorentino

Dating back to the 1930's, this May-to-July music festival in Florence draws pilgrims—not to mention big-name conductors like Zubin Mehta—to the historic 2,000-seat Teatro Comunale. maggiofiorentino.com; 39-055/277-9350.

Contributors

Gini Alhadeff *is a* Travel + Leisure *contributing editor and author of* The Sun at Midday: Tales of a Mediterranean Family *(Random House).*

Gael Greene *is a restaurant critic for* New York *magazine and author of* Insatiable: Tales from a Life of Delicious Excess *(Warner Books).*

Michael Gross *is a* Travel + Leisure *contributing editor and author of the best sellers* 740 Park: The Story of the World's Richest Apartment Building *(Broadway) and* Model: The Ugly Business of Beautiful Women *(Morrow).*

Matt Lee and **Ted Lee** *are* Travel + Leisure *contributing editors and authors of* The Lee Brothers Southern Cookbook: Stories and Recipes for Southerners and Would-be Southerners *(W.W. Norton).*

Charles MacLean *is a* Travel + Leisure *contributing editor and author of* Scotch Whisky: A Liquid History *(Cassell Illustrated) and* MacLean's Miscellany of Whisky *(Little Books).*

Niloufar Motamed *is the features editor at* Travel + Leisure *and the host of* Reservations Required *on the Ultra HD network.*

Christopher Petkanas *is a special correspondent for* Travel + Leisure.

Andrew Porter *was a* New Yorker *music critic for 20 years and currently writes for the* Times Literary Supplement.

Jonathan Santlofer *is an artist and mystery writer based in New York.*

Bruce Schoenfeld *is the wine and spirits editor at* Travel + Leisure.

Gary Shteyngart *is a* Travel + Leisure *contributing editor and author of* The Russian Debutante's Handbook *(Riverhead Books) and* Absurdistan *(Random House).*

Guy Trebay *is a reporter at the* New York Times.

Michael Z. Wise *is a* Travel + Leisure *contributing editor.*

Publisher's Acknowledgments

Dorling Kindersley would like to thank Casper Morris and Iorwerth Watkins for their help and advice on the maps, Romaine Werblow in the DK Picture Library for sourcing images, David McDonald for DTP expertise, and Karen Morgan for design assistance.

Original design by Stuart Jackman

Picture Credits